SPECIAL EFFECTS

Also by Ron LaBrecque

Lost Undercover:
An FBI Agent's True Story

SPECIAL EFFECTS

DISASTER AT TWILIGHT ZONE: THE TRAGEDY AND THE TRIAL

RON LaBRECQUE

CHARLES SCRIBNER'S SONS

NEW YORK

Charles Scribner's Sons
Macmillan Publishing Company
866 Third Avenue, New York, NY 10022
Collier Macmillan Canada, Inc.

Library of Congress Cataloging-in-Publication Data
LaBrecque, Ron.
    Special effects: disaster at Twilight zone: the
tragedy and trial / by Ron LaBrecque.
        p. cm.
    Includes index.
    ISBN 0-684-18943-7
    1. Landis, John, 1950– —Trials, litigation,
etc. 2. Spielberg, Steven, 1947– —Trials,
litigation, etc. 3. Trials (Homicide)—California
—Los Angeles. 4. Twilight zone (Motion
picture). 5. Motion pictures—California—
Accidents—Investigation. 6. Cinematography
—Special effects. I. Title.
KF224.L33L33 1988
345.73′02525—dc19
[347.3052525]   88-11334   CIP

Macmillan books are available at special
discounts for bulk purchases for sales
promotions, premiums, fund-raising, or
educational use. For details, contact:
Special Sales Director
Macmillan Publishing Company
866 Third Avenue
New York, NY 10022

10 9 8 7 6 5 4 3 2 1

Printed in the United States of America

This book is dedicated to My-Ca Le and Renee Chen

PREFACE

THE JOURNALISTIC reconstruction of events and conversations in a controversial matter is a demanding task, and it was especially so concerning *Twilight Zone: The Movie.* From the beginning, recollections and opinions clashed in great contradiction.

The story centers on a movie-set tragedy in which three people were killed. The time from the detonation of the first special effects explosion to the instant of death took only nine seconds and was filmed by six movie cameras. Testament to the maxim that film is illusion was that the extensive photographic documentation did not of itself answer the difficult questions posed to a Los Angeles County Superior Court jury, which five years later finally ended the official inquiry into whether anyone bore criminal responsibility for the deaths.

In that time, the values, standards, and actions of the moviemakers—and their Los Angeles County district attorney prosecutors—came under suspicion.

The narrative in this book is based on voluminous investigative records, transcripts, reports, magazine and newspaper articles, television news reports, and, most importantly, my firsthand observations and lengthy conversations with participants.

Important were my interviews with the following: Thomas Budds, the chief investigator in the criminal case; Roger Boren, the trial judge; defense attorney Arnold Klein and his associate Michael Robbins; defendants George Folsey, Jr., Dan Allingham, Paul Stewart, and Dorcey

Wingo; jurors, particularly foreman Lois Rogers, Wilbert Fisher, and Crispen Bernardo; defense attorneys James Neal, James Sanders, Harland Braun, Leonard Levine, and Eugene Trope; Gary Kesselman, the original *Twilight Zone* prosecutor; Lea D'Agostino, the trial prosecutor; and district attorney investigator Gerald Loeb.

Eliza Garrett Simons, a longtime friend of John Landis, was gracious and candid in biographical research. The archives of the American Film Institute in Los Angeles and the library of the Academy of Motion Picture Arts and Sciences in Beverly Hills were tremendously valuable resources.

I wish to thank my editor at Scribners, Edward T. Chase, for the clarity of his guidance; his assistant, Charles Flowers, for his diligence; and my wife, Joan Welles, for her support and review of the manuscript.

I am indebted to two attorneys in the case who gave me unrestricted access to their files, amounting to more than sixteen file boxes of documents, including revelatory material not before made public. Many federal, state, and local investigative documents were obtained from the public record and from various other sources.

John Landis, whose actions as the movie's director became the primary focus of the investigations, through his lawyers declined all requests for an interview. His friend and business attorney, Joel Behr, briefly met with me twice but refused substantial comment on the case. During the second meeting, the lawyer was read a list of approximately twenty-five questions but declined to respond to any. He terminated the meeting when I refused to disclose my source of a transcript of a 1982 meeting between Landis and several of his lawyers regarding his criminal defense. The source, who had ethical use of the document, had asked to remain anonymous.

All events, quotes, and conversations in this book were confirmed with as much assuredness as possible through the investigative record or my interviews and observation. In instances in which a dispute over what is fact could not be adequately resolved, the conflict has been so noted, or the source of the information indicated. Some courtroom testimony has been edited and condensed, with all due care taken to preserve the meaning and context of the speaker's words.

This book attempts to offer an accurate history and fair analysis of the matter. Nonetheless, the intrigue of the *Twilight Zone* case is founded on lingering uncertainty about the true motives of various participants. Even though noble aims are professed by the perpetrators of many questionable actions, some deeds appear to have been the result of baser motivations, including greed, unbridled ambition, and a goal of spectacle.

The *Twilight Zone* case is instructive for its revelations about how key figures in two important institutions—Hollywood and the Los Angeles district attorney's office—dealt with movie-set deaths that were anything but illusion.

No other movie, and its aftermath, could have had such special effect on people's lives, so many of whom are left with little of which to be proud for their participation.

—RON LaBRECQUE

THE MAJOR PARTICIPANTS

*The Twilight Zone:
The Movie*
Production Team

John Landis	director and coproducer
Steven Spielberg	coproducer
Frank Marshall	Spielberg's assistant and executive producer
George Folsey, Jr.	associate producer
Dan Allingham	unit production manager
Paul Stewart	special-effects foreman
Dorcey Wingo	helicopter pilot
James Camomile	special-effects technician
Elie Cohn	first assistant director
Anderson House	second assistant director
Donna Schuman	production secretary

The Victims

Vic Morrow	actor, age fifty-one
My-Ca Le	age seven
Renee Chen	age six

The Investigation and Trial

Daniel and Hoa-Kim Le	parents of My-Ca
Mark and Shyan Huei Chen	parents of Renee
Sergeant Thomas Budds	homicide detective, Los Angeles County Sheriff's Department
Abdon D. Llorente	investigator, National Transportation Safety Board
Harland Braun	Landis's criminal defense attorney, later trial attorney for George Folsey, Jr.
Joel Behr	Landis's business attorney
Ira Reiner	district attorney, Los Angeles County
Gilbert Garcetti	chief deputy district attorney, Los Angeles County
Gary P. Kesselman	prosecutor, deputy district attorney, Los Angeles County
Jack Tice	fire safety officer, Los Angeles County Fire Department
Lea D'Agostino	prosecutor, deputy district attorney, Los Angeles County
James Neal	defense attorney for John Landis
James Sanders	defense attorney for John Landis
Leonard Levine	defense attorney for Dan Allingham
Arnold Klein	defense attorney for Paul Stewart
Eugene Trope	defense attorney for Dorcey Wingo
Roger Boren	trial judge, Los Angeles County Superior Court
Lois Rogers	*Twilight Zone* jury foreman

SPECIAL EFFECTS

ONE

AT THE START of summer in 1982, movie director John Landis's suite of offices at Universal Studios was a place of busy activity in preparation for the filming of *Twilight Zone: The Movie.*

The complex logistics of film production were under way. Actors were being auditioned and a large crew hired. Camera operators, extras, electricians, costumers, makeup artists, special effects technicians, drivers, stuntmen, laborers (grips), administrative assistants, and dozens of others were part of an expensive work force. Hundreds of other details, from building sets to catering meals, had to be considered. And all of this had to be accomplished to meet a precise filming schedule.

The small, single-story building where Landis and his associates worked was inconspicuous amid the giant studio sound stages by which tourist-filled trams continually passed.

Outside the *Twilight Zone* production office, the monologues of cheery young guides drew the attention of visitors to an entertaining display of Hollywood illusion. The Universal back lot ride along European streets and through the Old West, past sights made familiar on television and in the movies, is second only to Disneyland as a Southern California attraction. The movie studio tour is an innocently charming presentation of Hollywood fantasy.

A more vulgar side of Hollywood—the crass manipulations of monied men in Landis's little office building—was hidden from the tourists' view.

Landis was determined that the climactic scene in his film would be a thrilling wartime rescue filmed at night with gigantic fireball explosions

1

punctuating the action. The director was also insistent that only children —not dolls, or adult midgets trained as stuntmen—would provide the realism he demanded.

To accomplish this plan, Landis and his closest colleagues clandestinely conspired to violate California law by illegally hiring two children to work late at night.

The movie project had been offered to Landis the previous March by Steven Spielberg, who, among a new breed of Hollywood wunderkinder, was achieving astonishing success.

A few years before, *New West* magazine had labeled this group of young directors and executives "The Baby Moguls." They were exceptionally bright, hardworking, and ambitious men and women, many with political roots in the student protests of the sixties.

Landis, thirty-one, was a prominent member of this cadre of new Hollywood powers. They were so young in relation to their expanding grasp of influence at the major studios that they were viewed as an industry phenomenon.

Landis was an educational exception among the group. He possessed a keen intellect but nonetheless had been unable or unwilling to adapt to academic structure. After the tenth grade, Landis—in the words of a schoolmate—was "not invited back" to Oakwood, a progressive private school in Los Angeles that he had attended for one year. Without a high school diploma, Landis went to work in the movies.

He told interviewers that he became infatuated with the notion of directing movies after seeing *The Seventh Voyage of Sinbad* when he was eight years old. He went home and asked his mother who had made the movie, to which she answered: "the director."

Landis was willing to start at the bottom. He was eighteen when he got a job as a mail boy at Twentieth Century Fox studios.

With confident persistence he spent years on the fringes of moviemaking. After ten months in the studio mail room, he made his way to Yugoslavia in 1969, where he worked as a low-level assistant during the production of the movie *Kelly's Heroes.* He befriended another young man, Jim O'Rourke, who was working as the stand-in for one of the film's stars, Clint Eastwood. When *Kelly's Heroes* was finished, Landis and O'Rourke stayed in Europe, working as stuntmen in spaghetti Westerns in Spain.

The two eventually returned to Los Angeles, but film production jobs were scarce. Landis, then twenty-one, wrote a script for a satiric, low-budget horror film. He and O'Rourke borrowed $60,000 from family to produce Landis's first movie, *Schlock.* Landis directed and starred—playing a murderous gorilla kind only to children.

Landis did not squander his film-directing opportunities when they were finally presented to him. After *Schlock,* he waited six years, a time filled with odd jobs, before he was offered his first paid directing assignment.

A 1973 appearance on *The Tonight Show* with Johnny Carson, just after *Schlock* was released, had caught the attention of aspiring comedic film producers Jerry and David Zucker and Jim Abrahams.

The three young men collaborated on a project, but it was 1977 before they were able to finance the filming of *Kentucky Fried Movie,* a collection of mostly sophomoric satiric segments that became a cult hit, in its fifth year of continuous showing at a theater in Amsterdam as Landis began work on *Twilight Zone* in 1982.

Even before *Kentucky Fried Movie* had been completed, Landis's fresh approach to directing was being lauded to a rising Universal Studios executive named Sean Daniels, whose girlfriend worked with Landis as a script supervisor on the twenty-one-day filming of *Kentucky Fried Movie.*

Daniels was looking for someone to direct a movie from a script previously rejected by many established comedy directors. Market research conducted for the studio had indicated that a movie about college fraternity life would have little appeal to a mass audience, and the project was dimly viewed by most studio executives. Daniels decided to give Landis a chance.

By applying a deft understanding of the era's comic sensibilities, Landis created *National Lampoon's Animal House,* which, according to a 1987 accounting in the trade publication, *Variety,* has earned over $150 million. The movie's success catapulted Landis, then twenty-eight years old, and his new friend at Universal Studios, Sean Daniels, a year younger, to industry prominence.

Landis and the other fresh-faced powers of Hollywood became the bridge between the studios and the vast spending of the youth market, which they tapped deeply with their popular movies. They were vested with unusual autonomy, even though studios might risk budgets as high as $25 million or more to make one movie.

Landis was unquestionably a financial asset to the studios. He followed *National Lampoon's Animal House* with *The Blues Brothers* and *An American Werewolf in London*—two comedies and a fantasy thriller that in combination generated income totaling hundreds of millions of dollars.

One staple of his films was a demolition derby realism. He calculated that in *The Blues Brothers* there were 300 car crashes that destroyed 60 of the 120 stunt cars used in the film.

The movies mirrored facets of Landis's personal style: fast-paced, exuberant, and spontaneous. He was a man who could display childishness at times but who also showed great responsibility to the studio executives who employed him. In contrast to some of his cruder and more obvious comic film sequences, Landis possessed a knowledge of film history of remarkable breadth, as well as a keen insight into its social impact.

Steven Spielberg was on a plateau high above the other young filmmakers, firmly established with hits including *Jaws, Close Encounters of the Third Kind,* and *Raiders of the Lost Ark.* Two years before, his first attempt at comedy, *1941,* was considered a flop. That would soon be forgotten with the release later in 1982 of *E.T.,* his magical and touching story of the loving bond between a group of children and a vulnerable extraterrestrial. *E.T.* would earn more money than any other movie in history, and with that film Spielberg would rise to Hollywood legend. (According to show business newspaper *Variety,* by 1987 *E.T.* had earned $228,379,346 —just in rentals to U.S. movie theaters.)

Landis and Spielberg had shared a mutual respect for some time, reaching back to their prefame days, according to a Landis friend. Landis had a minor role in the 1979 production of *1941,* as a bicycle messenger boy. Whatever success Landis had had, though, it did not match that of Spielberg, whose acclaim and respect were much broader-based.

Now, over dinner in the spring of 1982, Spielberg was offering Landis a serious collaboration.

Of several projects suggested, Landis was most intrigued by a feature film based on Rod Serling's hit television series *The Twilight Zone.* He was a Serling fan, and he must have relished the opportunity to do a noncomedic film. A few months before, in a speech to some students at the American Film Institute (AFI) in Los Angeles, Landis had said: "I'm offered every goddamn comedy script in town." Referring to Robert Redford's sensitive, Oscar-winning film about complex family relationships, he had added: "I want to be offered *Ordinary People.*"

Landis's work thus far raised doubt about whether he possessed the subtlety to orchestrate scenes of delicate intimacy. Film critics often credited Landis for a certain craftsmanship, but more often than not his films were rejected as overly broad comic fluff lacking intellectual substance.

Landis's distaste for the American press was rooted early in his career. (He differentiated American from European critics, particularly the French, who praised him highly.) He expressed the view that both he and his movies were vilified in the United States simply because the writers didn't understand what he was trying to do.

Such hard-baked opinions represented Landis's intolerant attitude toward much of the world around him. For all of the illuminating perspective he could dispense regarding film history, he displayed only an elementary understanding of other societal institutions, which he quickly dismissed with disdain. ("I don't trust any reporter or politician," he said to me and several others at his trial one day.)

Landis described himself as a "classic Jewish liberal" who claimed that his films had a political core. Landis did make genuine efforts to integrate his cast and crew (he was proud that *The Times* of London noted that there seemed to be more black bobbies in his film *An American Werewolf in London* than actually worked in England), but it was difficult to find strong political messages in the body of the films.

For example, Landis believed that an oblique epilogue reference to the off-screen death of a dislikable *Animal House* fraternity brother (the movie was set in the early 1960s, and the victim would be killed by his own troops in Vietnam) qualified the movie as "an extremely political film." In *The Blues Brothers,* two buffoonish American neo-Nazis plunge off a bridge in a slapstick chase scene. Earlier in the year Landis had told the AFI film students that when he saw foreign audiences applaud the chase scene he concluded: "That [in itself] is worth twenty-seven million dollars" [the film's production cost]."

Landis, using his opportunity to make a socio-political statement in *Twilight Zone,* decided to use the fantasy element central to a Serling-styled story to explore the destructiveness of racism.

Twilight Zone was to be a relatively quick project, requiring only about three weeks of actual filming for Landis to direct.

He and Spielberg had decided the movie would be a four-segment anthology plus a short prologue. Landis would write and direct only the prologue and the first segment. Spielberg would direct the second, and Joe Dante and George Miller would handle the third and fourth segments. Spielberg and Landis were also coproducers. Warner Brothers would finance the picture.

Although he was working for Warner Brothers on *Twilight Zone,* Landis persuaded studio executives to allow him to maintain his offices at Universal Studios rather than move the few miles away to The Burbank Studios jointly operated by Warner Brothers and Columbia Pictures.

The year 1982 was promising to be busy for Landis. Later that summer he was scheduled to direct a comedy murder mystery in Manhattan, followed by a major film for Paramount Studios based on the comic strip detective Dick Tracy. Landis had joked to the AFI students about the growing catalog of work he and his partner, George Folsey, Jr., were creating: "It's going to be Metro-Folsey-Landis."

Folsey was forty-three, a decade older than Landis. Many people believed he was a steadying influence on the young director. Folsey's sensitivity and maturity were personality traits Landis did not often exhibit. Folsey had grown up among Hollywood's biggest movie personalities. Folsey's father, George Folsey, Sr., then retired, is one of Hollywood's most respected cinematographers. He was nominated for Academy Awards fourteen times during his career, which had begun in 1919 and spanned much of modern filmmaking. The Metro-Goldwyn-Mayer studio where the elder Folsey worked had its impact on the younger Folsey. For example, the family didn't buy its first television set until well into the 1950s because studio executives didn't want employees supporting the competing new medium.

George Folsey, Jr., and Landis had begun a business relationship in 1971, when Folsey did the film editing on Landis's satiric gorilla movie, *Schlock.* Landis once said that *Schlock* is "seriously the most self-indulgent movie ever made" and that Folsey, who was "the best film editor in the world," had taught him a great deal about moviemaking.

Folsey joined Landis again in 1977 as the film editor for *Kentucky Fried Movie* and *National Lampoon's Animal House.* They remained a team, with Folsey getting greater shares of power as the two did more films.

John Landis was the only employee of Levitsky Productions, Inc., a company he had formed to "loan out" his services to the studios. Under the agreement between Warner Brothers and Levitsky, Inc., negotiated by Landis's agent, Michael Marcus of the Creative Artists Agency, one of the most influential agencies in Los Angeles, Landis would receive a salary of $150,000 for his few months of work on *Twilight Zone: The Movie.* Of that, $30,000 were for writing the script, $30,000 for producing a prologue sequence and his segment, and, finally, $90,000 for directing services.

In addition, as coproducers, Landis and Spielberg also would receive a percentage of gross receipts, a sum that, depending on the success of the film, could amount to millions of dollars.

An important element of Landis's contract gave him "final cut," the right—providing he finished the film on schedule—to do the final editing of his segment, which would then be contractually unalterable by the studio. This was a much-sought-after creative perquisite in Hollywood and was granted to a limited number of directors.

By mid-April, Landis had finished the first draft of his *Twilight Zone* script, whose main character he named Bill Connor.

There was no subtlety in Connor, a fifty-five-year-old salesman rejected for promotion and, in the opening scene, nursing his bitterness in a San Fernando Valley bar.

"They passed me up for that Jew son of a bitch," Connor angrily tells two buddies over a drink. The depth of his bigotry is further affirmed as he goes on to say: "Arabs are just niggers wrapped in sheets. It's the kikes and the niggers and the kooks, it's all of them."

Venting his rage and venomously dissatisfied with the inequities he perceives have been levied against him, Connor leaves the bar and, once outside, finds himself transported back thirty years in time and place to Nazi-occupied France, where French and German officers accost him as a Jew.

William Connor has entered the Twilight Zone, according to the script by John Landis.

Connor is buffeted from place to place, next finding himself in the rural South, where a harassing lynch mob of Ku Klux Klansmen perceive him as a black man. Then, as he emerges from a Vietnamese swamp, a patrol of American soldiers views him as a Viet Cong soldier.

Landis would later testify that he saw in Connor's plight the lesson that he "lives the results of his own ignorance. He's forced to confront, he's forced to use the language and walk in the shoes of the people he has been castigating."

There was, though, an emptiness to any moral, because of the unremitting harshness of Connor's personality. That was a storytelling flaw not immediately recognized by Landis.

Copies of the first draft of the script, dated April 15, 1982, were sent to Warner Brothers production executives Lucy Fisher and Terry Semel; Steven Spielberg and his top assistant, Frank Marshall; and Landis's partner, George Folsey, Jr., who was the associate producer of the film.

In a second draft, dated May 24, 1982, Landis made slight revisions to the script. Warner Brothers approved a budget for the Landis segment with "some criticism" of the writing. Then, in early June, Landis met with Fisher and Semel to discuss their reservations about Connor's one-dimensional personality.

"They were concerned that I painted Bill so harsh," Landis later said. "His character was so ugly. They said, 'He is so unsympathetic. Why watch the episode? What are you trying to prove?' And I thought, they were right. We discussed if there was a way of literally having [Connor] redeemed. Not just learn an object lesson, more or less, but act upon it. And it was out of that meeting we came up with the idea of an additional scene to try to soften the character."

On Sunday, June 13, the day after his second meeting with Fisher and Semel, Landis revised the script, which was then twenty pages long and in its third draft.

Landis's new notion was to have Connor brought back to Vietnam as before, but this time he would meet two Vietnamese children stranded in an otherwise deserted village. "Through dialogue with these children, he comes not to just an intellectual but an emotional realization that these children are in the same position he's in, that they are victims, too, and he understands that," Landis later explained.

The instance of redemption in Landis's view, however, would not arrive in a tender moment, such as when Connor first meets the children, a boy and girl, and offers a touching and simple expression of empathy for their suffering. When the little girl hands him a broken Barbie doll, the script called for Connor to respond: "I won't hurt you, baby. I'm just as lost and scared as you are."

Landis envisioned a more daring and physical trial to demonstrate a shift in the inner spirit of the character he had created. True to his penchant for spectacular action, Landis wrote that a combat helicopter would then appear above the village. Connor, assuming rescue by the American military craft, would run to the shore of the river that passed by the village. The children would cling to Connor as he yelled up to the hovering helicopter, "Help us! I've got children down here!" As he called out, he would become the target of machine gun and rocket fire, because he is in the *Twilight Zone* and perceived by the Americans as a Viet Cong.

The script further stated: "The helicopter makes another pass over the village and then one of the huts EXPLODES in a spectacular fireball. One after another [of] the buildings blow up in flames as the helicopter systematically destroys the village in its search for Bill. Finally Bill, holding a child in each arm, makes a herculean effort and runs for the shallow river. With the village burning behind them Bill runs as best he can across the river."

On film, the escape was to be Connor's salvation from the conflagration.

On the opposite shore Connor would place the children in the safety of a shed. Then the reformed bigot would be transported instantaneously back to the rural South, occupied France, and finally outside the suburban bar where his journey had begun. In Landis's scripted finish to the segment, Bill is struck by a car in front of the bar. Lying hurt on the ground, he stares in wonderment at the broken Barbie doll the little Vietnamese girl had given him.

The script revision was sent to Warner Brothers executives for approval, because more money would be needed for construction of a Vietnamese village and the many other costs of at least one more day's filming necessitated by the additional scene. Equipment and crew alone could cost as much as $50,000 a day.

Cast and crew are a costly labor force in moviemaking. Each of the different specialties of craftsperson, from cameraman to truck driver, is usually hired project by project, primarily from the memberships of industry unions and guilds. In the movie business there are two categories of employees: "above the line" and "below the line." Actors, producers, and directors are "above the line." The bulk of the support staff—makeup artists, cameramen, stuntmen, special effects technicians, electricians, carpenters, greensmen, and those in a myriad of other trades—are "below the line."

As unit production manager, Dan Allingham was largely responsible for below-the-line procurement, including the preparation of a budget for building and maintaining location sets, props, and other physical equipment required. He was the third-ranking member of the Landis production team, having been brought to the office the year before by Folsey, with whom he had worked in the 1970s.

Allingham, thirty-seven years old, had once been an actor but had turned to administration of television and movie production because he wanted to make more money. He was also serving as first assistant director on *Twilight Zone,* a duality then allowed under union rules.

While Allingham took care of his responsibilities, Landis and Folsey set out to assemble a cast. On Wednesday, June 16, they met in their production office at Universal Studios with the *Twilight Zone* casting agents, Michael Fenton and Marci Liroff, of Fenton-Feinberg Casting. It was one of a dozen or so audition sessions held for the movie.

The casting session had begun about noon, and it was after 5:00 P.M. when the discussion turned to the recently written Vietnamese village scene that Landis had completed only three days earlier. The director vividly described the additional scene, including his plan to film it at night with special-effects explosions, a helicopter, and child actors.

Landis would later dispute their accounts, but both Liroff and Fenton said that he requested of them that they hire two Asian children to work in the village scene. On the bottom of her appointment sheet for that day, Liroff wrote:

> 2 Vietnamese kids Boy/Girl
> (Chinese or Korean Thai 2 nights)

California state law did not permit children of the age Landis wanted, six to eight years old, to work late hours. In addition, the state mandated that whenever any child, up to age eighteen, worked on a television or film set, a state-certified teacher-welfare worker had to be present. The teachers had the authority to have production stopped if they discerned any activity or influences, physical or moral, injurious to the child.

Liroff later testified that she mentioned those rules to Landis and Folsey and also told them that the rescue scene sounded "kind of dangerous." When Landis told Fenton that the children did not have speaking parts, the casting agent said that that classified them as extras, positions not hired by his theatrical agency. According to Liroff, Fenton's response was a diplomatic way to avoid involvement in what appeared to be a questionable venture.

Landis, Liroff later said, reacted angrily to the response of the casting agents: "He was a little gruff, I believe, because we wouldn't be involved in this and he said, 'The hell with you guys. We don't need you. We'll get them off the streets ourselves.' "

A few days after that casting session, Liroff later recalled, she mentioned the incident to Frank Marshall, Steven Spielberg's executive producer, and advised him that it was illegal to hire children for night work. "He said he would take care of it," Liroff said.

Marci Liroff was not the only person working on the film who expressed concern about the illegal use of children in the Vietnamese village scene. Anderson House, hired in mid-June to serve as second assistant director, talked to Allingham about the script shortly after he had begun work. House's duties included communicating the first assistant director's scheduling to the cast and crew, writing the call sheets (a list of which actors and crew are needed on the set each day), daily production reports, and supervising the crew at the end of work each night.

House knew it was against the law to work children after hours. He also questioned the wisdom of using children in a scene with a helicopter overhead and special-effects explosions.

There are alternatives to filming a potentially risky scene that do not involve placing actors in proximity to special effects. For example, even though a script calls for a scene to take place at night, filming can be done during the day in a studio where night is simulated ("day for night" in movie jargon) and no explosions are detonated. Film of explosions can then be inserted when the movie is edited. House wanted to confirm which procedure would be used and called Allingham. The unit production manager confirmed that the scene would be filmed "night for night."

House made a second call to Allingham a few days later and asked if consideration had been given to substituting the children with dummies or adult midgets trained as stuntmen. That proposal had been considered and rejected by Landis, Allingham said.

In a third call to Allingham, House urged the production manager to try to convince Landis to consider names of some adult midgets he had located. Allingham firmly resisted and emphatically stated that the issue was closed to further discussion.

Among the actors considered for the role of Bill Connor were Peter Coyote and Glen Campbell. Landis chose fifty-one-year-old Vic Morrow, who was seeking a good feature film role to revitalize his career. Morrow was a talented actor whose first movie role, the 1955 production of *Blackboard Jungle,* had earned him acclaim. His starring role as Sergeant Chip Saunders in the 1960s television series *Combat* resulted in theatrical overexposure, however, and afterward he was offered few movie parts.

The role of Bill Connor required a tough physicality as well as the ability to portray sensitivity. Morrow could turn his rough good looks into a cynical sneer, but he could also show the emotional nuance necessary to demonstrate Connor's spiritual transition from bigot to victim of discrimination.

Morrow was still inclined to do stunts that many actors would gladly allow their "doubles" to do. He had been doing so since his days on *Combat,* when each episode included special-effects explosions simulating battles of war. Gary McLarty was to be Morrow's *Twilight Zone* double as well as stunt coordinator for the movie. Prior to filming, McLarty, Landis, and Allingham visited Morrow, who announced that he wanted to do all but the most obviously dangerous scenes.

Hired to supervise the extensive special effects, including rain, gunfire, grenade explosions, and billowing fireballs for the climactic scene, was forty-five-year-old Paul Stewart.

He was a skilled, blue-collar tradesman whose first job had been in a muffler shop in Burbank, where he had grown up and gone to high school. After two stints in the Army, the first in Germany and the second on standby in Texas during the 1961 Berlin crisis, he started in the movie business as a welder at Metro-Goldwyn-Mayer. Stewart completed a long apprenticeship, beginning in the studio's gun room, where he learned the use of weapons for movie work and how to handle explosives. In time he became recognized as one of the top special-effects foremen in the industry. Coincidentally, Stewart had worked with Morrow on *Combat.*

Stewart was unflappable, a man who could shut out the frenzy of a movie set to get his job done, someone who preferred quietly working with his labor-weathered hands to sparring verbally with the bosses.

When Allingham recommended Stewart for the job, Landis went to a

Hollywood Boulevard movie theater to see a film called *The Exterminator.* One striking action scene involving a helicopter and special-effects explosions, which Stewart had helped coordinate, was particularly impressive to the director. In addition, the movie had been filmed at the same location that Landis had selected for his Vietnamese village scenes.

In a 1980 article in *On Location* magazine, Stewart had told the article's author that special effects required "a state and federal license, a fire company standing by, a permit, and a whole bunch of experience." Describing the production of *The Exterminator,* Stewart said, "We had a helicopter fly down into the canyon and we had [gasoline] explosions around it. One explosion surrounded the whole tail of the helicopter, so it looked like it was engulfed in flames. We put an explosion near the Viet Cong camp with two actors and three Vietnamese men; it scared them so bad they went running down the creek, and as they ran, the explosions by the creek went off. They were very real. One gas explosion was only twenty feet away from them. The main thing is to know the timing and where to put the explosions."

A particular special effect in the movie—shown to the audience as a character's flashback memory of combat in Vietnam—was cheered for its realism by the *On Location* writer. To accomplish the effect, a life-size dummy of a soldier had been used to simulate a battlefield decapitation.

Filming of the Landis segment of *Twilight Zone* began on July 1, 1982, on the back lot at Universal Studios, where an all-purpose European street created by building facades provided the backdrop for Connor's escape from Nazi soldiers.

Elie Cohn, who had been hired as first assistant director when Allingham's work load became too heavy, approached Allingham on the set and expressed the same reservations about the illegal use of children that House had previously offered. Allingham told Cohn that he had already suggested the use of dummies to Landis, and the director had rejected the proposal.

Special-effects foreman Paul Stewart said he found it necessary to guide Landis away from risky practices that the director apparently suggested unwittingly. "You got to slow him down," Stewart later told me. "He's so hyper, he'll run down to the corner before he thinks he wants to do it."

According to Stewart, Landis's lack of foresight on the *Twilight Zone* set was exemplified by his direction of a scene in which Morrow is being shot at. Squibs, or small explosive charges, were imbedded in the walls near

Morrow to simulate bullet hits. The holes were then covered with a material that exploded out. Landis wanted Morrow to be surrounded by bullet hits. Stewart then explained that it would be safer to wait until Morrow passed the squibs to ensure that none of the packing material injured his eyes. Landis, Stewart said, readily accepted his suggestions.

Stewart had experience with close calls. His closest had been while filming a scene on a barge off the Texas coast when a stuntman driving a car forty miles an hour missed his mark and nearly killed Stewart, who was wedged into a confined area in order to detonate his special effects. "I don't do that usually, I always got a place to run," Stewart said.

Although he liked to perform some of his own stunts, Morrow was anything but foolhardy, and he easily acquiesced to some dangerous scenes being performed by Gary McLarty. One involved a chase along a narrow ledge three stories above the street after Connor has been detected by Nazi soldiers trying to hide in the apartment of a Parisian family. Close-up shots did show Morrow balancing precariously on a ledge, but those were filmed while the actor stood on the first-floor ledge, with mattresses spread out on the ground below him. The more dramatic shots of Connor high above the street, in which his face is not discernible, were played by McLarty.

The scene in which Connor flees from the soldiers and bursts into the apartment of the family, a mother and two children, was filmed during the day on a sound stage. Both children had been hired legally through the Screen Extras' Guild, and a teacher-welfare worker was present.

After Warner Brothers executives officially approved the addition of the village rescue scene, a search for two child actors was begun in earnest by the Landis production team in early July, without the cooperation of casting agents Fenton and Liroff.

According to Landis and Folsey, Frank Marshall confirmed then that the producers would not be able to obtain a nighttime waiver for the children. Marshall's associate (and girlfriend), Kathleen Kennedy, had purportedly made an anonymous telephone call to state officials to obtain the information.

The task of finding two Asian children for the roles fell upon George Folsey, Jr.

Folsey asked a number of people in and out of the office if they knew of Oriental children. "We have to be careful," he told production assistant Carolyn Epstein.

Folsey was given the most help in his search by Dr. Harold Schuman, a psychiatrist whose wife, Donna, was working temporarily as a secretary in the *Twilight Zone* production office. The Folseys and the Schumans were old friends. Both Donna Schuman and George Folsey had worked for George Schlatter when he was producing the seminal late-1960's television comedy show *Rowan & Martin's Laugh-In.* Folsey had been one of the show's film editors, and was seen in a recurrent film skit playing a man in a raincoat who falls off a tricycle.

Donna Schuman first learned about the village scene and the children when she began receiving requests from others on the production staff for copies of Landis's third draft of the script. She did not have any, so she went to Landis's secretary, Alpha Campbell, who had typed the original draft from Landis's longhand.

"You can't have one," Campbell told Schuman.

"Why not?" Schuman asked.

"Because they are under lock and key," Campbell replied. She said that Landis "told me to lock the third and fourth drafts in the drawer, and not give them out to anybody." Folsey then explained to Schuman that he and Landis didn't want "the word getting out" about children working illegally.

Folsey told me later that he had always assumed that he and his colleagues would be caught and pay a monetary fine for their violation of the state labor code, which he said was committed with the knowledge of other high-level production team members: "We wouldn't have hired the kids on a Spielberg picture unless either Spielberg or his people knew it. I mean, that would have been a terrible thing to do, put them in that position. The fact that Frank [Marshall] agreed to do it made me feel that it was okay, that it was really his responsibility, too."

After encountering difficulty in finding suitable Asian children, Folsey called Harold Schuman, who worked for the Los Angeles County Department of Health and for many years had run a neighborhood mental health clinic with a large Asian staff and Asian clientele. On July 12, on Folsey's behalf, Schuman called Peter Chen, a county social worker, to ask whether he knew of some children who could work in the movie. Chen was told that the parents would have to accompany the children and that they would be on the location from about 7:00 P.M. to 1:00 A.M. (Afterward, the two men would disagree on whether Schuman had advised Chen that the children would be working without a state permit.)

Schuman had been told by Folsey that the scene would include special-effects explosions and a helicopter, neither of which would be used near the children. The pay for each child would be $500 for the evening's filming, considerably higher than the going rate of $90 a day for child extras hired routinely—and legally—through the Screen Extras' Guild.

Chen's first thought was of his niece Renee, who had just turned six on April 1 and was the only child of his brother Mark, an accountant at a Los Angeles tool company. Mark Chen liked the proposal and presented it to his wife, Shyan Huei. "We feel it would be a very fine experience for her. When she grow up, she would have a lot of memories," Mark Chen later recalled.

In the meantime, Peter Chen had called a colleague, Dr. Daniel Le, a clinical psychologist and director of the County Indo-Chinese Mental Health Clinic.

When Peter Chen asked Le if he knew of any parents who might allow their children to be in the movie, Le immediately thought of his two sons, seven-year-old My-Ca and four-year-old Christopher. My-Ca, especially, loved television and the movies, and Le knew that his son would be excited about being in the film. "I think it might be fun for him to be there," Le later said about his interest in the movie. My-Ca had been born in Saigon in January 1975, just before his parents joined the exodus from war-weary South Vietnam to escape the Viet Cong takeover of their city.

Le was eager to get home that evening and talk about the exciting movie offer to his wife, Hoa-Kim. His only concern was whether the actor would be strong enough to carry the children across the river safely. That fear was later alleviated when they met Morrow, who seemed adequately strong for the task.

"Daddy, I want to be in the movie. It's fun," My-Ca told his father.

Folsey was soon notified that the Le and Chen families accepted the offer. That, however, did not conclude the deal; John Landis still had to approve.

Dr. Le would later say that he did not pay attention when Folsey discussed the issue of permits with him: "I don't know the law. We are the new immigrants into this country. I trust Dr. Schuman and Mr. Chen, what they are doing. I do not question them."

By now, the production company had moved to the reservoir in Franklin Canyon in Los Angeles, where scenes of Connor's encounter with the Ku Klux Klan were being filmed.

Anderson House, who knew the production company was searching for children, still had his reservations about the illegal hiring. Walking back from an on-set dinner one night with Elie Cohn, he decided to make his feelings known again. John Landis was walking not far ahead of the two. House later testified: "I had mentioned to Elie that not only—because we were using children—not only could John Landis lose his ability to work with children in the future, but in fact, Warner Brothers, the entire studio, could have its license revoked to work with any children at all. John Landis turned around and he asked me what I said. And at that point—

I was speechless for a moment—Elie repeated what I had said to John Landis."

Landis did not respond, and House had no further discussions with the director about the illegal hiring of the children.

Several other children located by Folsey were brought to the Franklin Canyon set for Landis to look at during the week.

Julie Hua was a parent who came to the set with her children on Thursday night for an interview with Landis and Folsey after learning about the movie from the principal at a neighborhood school. Later she was told that Landis had found her children acceptable for the roles. Hua had been particularly excited about meeting Vic Morrow. He had been famous in South Vietnam in the 1960s because *Combat* was shown on television there.

Mark, Shyan Huei, and Renee Chen, and Hoa-Kim and My-Ca Le were picked up by a studio driver on Friday, July 16, and driven to the set. Daniel Le attended a church meeting that night.

The Chen and Le families watched the moviemaking for a while, and the children were invited to the catering area for some food. They met Folsey; his wife, Belinda; and Landis's mother. Vic Morrow came by to say hello. After Folsey explained the story of the village scene, Landis came over to greet the families and take a look at the children. Folsey had once said that Landis wanted "adorable" kids, and My-Ca Le and Renee Chen were certainly that. After a few minutes, Landis told Folsey that he preferred these two. One reason was that My-Ca and Renee were smaller than the Hua children.

The families were driven home after being told that the filming would be done one night the following week.

TWO

DAN ALLINGHAM needed a military model UH-1B helicopter, commonly called a Huey. The sounds of the aircraft, ominously familiar to most adult Americans, had punctuated a decade of nightly television news reports from Vietnam. The UH-1B would be the central prop in the Vietnamese village scene, and the threat Bill Connor needed to face in order to achieve redemption—according to Landis's script.

On July 15 Allingham drove to Rialto, fifty miles east of Los Angeles, to negotiate a contract with Western Helicopters, a small subsidiary of Rocky Mountain Helicopters and owners of a Huey, an aircraft still in wide civilian use. Western's UH-1B, initially owned by the U.S. Army, had also been owned by the federal Department of Health, Education, and Welfare and the Maryland State Police.

Allingham had spoken twice on the telephone with Dorcey Wingo, Western's director of operations and a Vietnam veteran, who was interested in the job. Wingo was thirty-five, a native of Duncan, Oklahoma, who grew up in several western states as his schoolteacher parents followed work. Wingo had a pilot's sensibility: reserved and precise, confident in both himself and his aircraft. In flight, he was a man of bravery but not daring.

When Allingham arrived at the Rialto airport he went into the wood-paneled office of Western's president, Clair Merryweather. Western had contracted its helicopters to movie companies before, but not always with good results. The company president was firm: He required assurance that Allingham would carefully guard against damage to the aircraft from the special-effects explosions.

"Safety first" was Allingham's response—then and later—whenever doubts were raised about the risk entailed in the moviemaking.

Movie and television work was attractive to companies like Western, which could charge rates higher than for routine industrial jobs. The entertainment industry's constant appetite for spectacular action scenes was supplied by pilots who found the work, if sometimes riskier, also more exciting than the mundane ferrying of heavy equipment, crop control, or the simple transportation of people from one place to another. Wingo found the *Twilight Zone* job particularly appealing because it did not call for stunt flying, only routine maneuvers of hovering and turning.

Merryweather's warning was not the first time that Allingham had been cautioned about potential safety problems in the Vietnamese scene planned by the *Twilight Zone* production company.

John Gamble, a veteran stunt pilot with extensive experience in television and movie work, had told Allingham a few days previous that he disapproved of the plan for the village destruction scene. "What about all this wood and debris?" Gamble had asked, assuming from Allingham's description that the Vietnamese huts would be exploded during the scene while a helicopter hovered nearby. "I doubt if you will crash the helicopter, but you're certainly going to do some severe damage to it," Gamble told Allingham. The pilot explained that a hovering helicopter is far more vulnerable to damage from debris than is a moving aircraft. It is also less maneuverable in the event of problems.

Allingham did not mention to Gamble that the script also called for children to be in the scene.

When Gamble described a recent incident in which a piece of splintering wood from a special-effects explosion had damaged his helicopter's rotor system—and hesitated about taking the *Twilight Zone* job—Allingham interrupted the conversation to consult with Landis, but he was unsuccessful in reaching the director by telephone. Negotiations with Gamble ended after the pilot said that the one-day job was "not financially interesting" because he would have to transport a helicopter from a distant location.

Clayton Wright of Wright Airlift International in Long Beach, who believed that his bid had been accepted by Allingham, was surprised when it was later rejected in favor of Western Helicopters, which had bid a lower price.

At Western Helicopters, Allingham did not mention to Merryweather his dealings with Gamble or Wright. Wingo walked into the room as

Merryweather was talking about Western's bad experience during the filming of the movie *Blue Thunder* the year before. A Hughes 500D helicopter had sustained $10,000 worth of rotor damage when it was struck by debris launched in a mistimed special-effects explosion during a war scene. "It could have been a worse accident," Merryweather told Allingham.

Allingham mollified Merryweather and Wingo when he called special-effects foreman Paul Stewart "the best in the industry" and assured them that the scene would be done safely. Later that day, after he had signed the contract, Wingo checked with a friend, a respected and skilled pilot named Art Scholl, who spoke highly of Stewart's expertise. Scholl, who had flown in many movies, had been the inspiration for Wingo to seek film work and the year before had helped Wingo join the Screen Actors' Guild.

(Scholl was killed in 1985 at age fifty-two while flying a propeller-driven stunt plane on which a camera had been mounted to film a pilot's-eye view of aerial maneuvers for the movie *Top Gun.* He had been flying five miles off the California coast when he radioed to shore to report that he was close to the ocean's surface. In a calm voice he said: "I've got a real problem." The cause of the crash was not determined. The plane and Scholl's body were never found.)

The same day, Stewart called Wingo to discuss the proposed scenes. Stewart has a puckish sense of humor and asked Wingo if he would have any problems flying three feet above a riverbed as thirty to forty special-effects explosions detonated, knowing full well that the script did not call for any such maneuvers.

"That depends on a lot of things," Wingo said, not perceiving Stewart's jesting. "Did you have anything to do with the *Blue Thunder* movie?"

"No," Stewart said.

"Well, we're off to a good start," Wingo replied.

Although Wingo's flying record and skill were especially noteworthy, including nine hundred hours of flight time in Vietnam and two thousand hours fighting forest fires throughout the West, he had never flown in a feature film before, nor had he worked with special-effects explosions.

Stewart was disappointed that Wingo did not accept his offer to visit the movie location to discuss the placement of special effects. Other pilots Stewart had worked with, including Gamble, had always expressed more concern about such details.

Wingo, though, placed his trust in Stewart and accepted that the special-effects foreman would have all the details in order on the day of filming the following week. Western Helicopters was a small and busy company, and Wingo didn't believe he had the time to spare for the trip.

The Vietnamese scenes would be filmed at Indian Dunes, six hundred acres of varying landscape that were wonderfully diverse for movie-makers. The land was privately owned and located in the Santa Clarita Valley, about twenty miles northeast of Universal Studios in the town of Saugus. The owners promoted its use by the studios, and the area served as the backdrop for many television shows and films. Indian Dunes had been recommended to Landis by his production designer, Richard Sawyer.

A particular spot on the south bank of the Santa Clarita River seemed ideal for the Vietnamese scenes. The shore area, where the village would be built, was overshadowed by a cliff rising one hundred feet to a grass-covered mesa.

Sawyer constructed an eleven-hut village of bamboo, grass thatching, cardboard, and eucalyptus tree branches. The structures were held to-gether with baling wire intertwined with hemp and rope for an authentic look. Six huts in a row at the base of the cliff wall had corrugated metal roofs, and five huts along the shore had roofs of thatching. A sampan floated in the river next to a flimsy, twenty-eight-foot-long pier.

One of the buildings along the shore was unlike the others, a re-creation of a food-drying shack with no walls. A platform floor of bamboo poles was sturdily attached to the four corner posts about three feet off the ground.

In early July, Sawyer accompanied Landis, Allingham, Stewart, location manager Richard Vane, and others on one of several scouting trips to Indian Dunes.

One of Vane's assignments was to gather the information required by the Los Angeles County Fire Department to issue a permit for pyrotech-nics and other special effects. Once the permit was authorized, fire safety officers—retired firemen whose presence was required on all movie sets using flammable special effects—would be assigned. They were not re-quired to provide detailed inspection and approval of each special-effect sequence beforehand, and in actuality, little beyond basic fire control was expected—or demanded—of the retired firemen. Their $17.50-an-hour movie salaries were viewed as easily earned retirement bonuses.

On the morning of July 7, Dewitt Morgan, the Los Angeles County fire official who issued motion picture "special-event permits," received a call from Richard Vane. A permit, authorizing the use of a helicopter, special-effects gasoline explosions, gunfire, squibs, and smoke effects was granted in routine fashion.

*   *   *

The entire production company arrived at Indian Dunes on Monday, July 19, to film the Vietnamese sequences, the last to be done for the Landis segment of the movie. The call sheets indicate that more than 110 cast and crew members were present for work.

Elie Cohn, Landis, and Allingham decided to bring the children on the set for the shortest time possible on the last day of filming, then scheduled to be two days later, on Wednesday.

At Landis's Universal Studios office, an effort was under way to conceal the illegal hiring of My-Ca and Renee, who had been approved by the director the previous Friday night. Donna Schuman complied with Allingham's request to delay transfer of revealing documents to Warner Brothers executives. Anderson House, whose job it was to prepare a number of production reports, was told by Allingham not to list the children on the call sheets, the production report, or the actors' time report.

If Landis, Folsey, and Allingham were concerned about the potential of any real risk to the children's safety, they apparently were not openly expressing it to others. They were, however, anticipating the spectacle of the village scenes, and there were joking comments about the illegal hiring.

"I want it big, I want it big," was the way Landis described his wishes for the rescue scene backdrop of special-effects explosions.

Cynthia Nigh, engaged to marry Allingham at the time, was a *Twilight Zone* production assistant who answered phones, coordinated messenger service, watched over the petty cash and payroll, and acted as a liaison between the crew and the office. She recalled that following a closed-door meeting Folsey jokingly said to Landis: "We'll probably be thrown in jail after this, just because of the kids." Nigh later testified that she also once saw Landis walk down the hallway and throw his arms in the air and say: "Arrrgghhh, we are all going to jail."

Both Schuman and Nigh overheard Folsey talking on the telephone to people they assumed were parents of My-Ca and Renee. "It is going to be like watching fireworks," Folsey was heard to say, also explaining that the helicopter and explosions would not be dangerous to the children.

Schuman asked Folsey why he bothered to mention the explosives to the parents if they would not affect the children. "It is the right thing to do," she quoted him as saying. "When we are going to have explosions on the set, you ought to tell everybody up front. I mean, you know, God forbid anything goes wrong, and then if you tell everybody then you are covered."

On Tuesday, Allingham and Folsey were in the office discussing how they would obtain the cash to pay the parents of the children. Cynthia Nigh was asked if there was enough money in the petty cash supply, but before she answered, Allingham interjected and said, "We'll get it elsewhere." Folsey then sent a request for $2,000 to Warner Brothers, using a Spielberg production worker as an intermediary.

Although the sum was modest in terms of the flow of money during filming, the request did arouse some suspicions in a Warner Brothers accounting executive, who, on the advice of a superior, signed a check and sent it to the Spielberg office. Frank Marshall cosigned the check and gave it to an associate, Bonnie Radford, who cashed it. Twenty bills of $100 each were sealed in an envelope. Carolyn Epstein, an assistant in the Landis office, drove to Spielberg's office at The Burbank Studios, picked up the envelope, and returned to Universal Studios, where she gave the money to Folsey.

County fire safety officers George Hull and Jack Tice arrived at Indian Dunes at about 6:00 P.M. on Tuesday to meet with Paul Stewart. The special-effects foreman explained that on Wednesday night he planned to shoot fireballs rising 150 feet into the air, and he showed the county officials where the mortars had been placed. The three men decided that six fire safety officers and three trucks carrying a total of ten thousand gallons of water would be needed to control any resulting fires.

One of the first scenes filmed at Indian Dunes was of Connor's arrival in Vietnam, as he emerges from a swamp and encounters a group of American soldiers.

(In contrast to the underlying seriousness and morality of his *Twilight Zone* segment, Landis's depiction of the soldiers was less than respectful. They were shown talking inanely and noisily, high on marijuana, and playing a Jimi Hendrix song loudly, even though they were supposedly trying to avoid detection by the Viet Cong as they marched in camouflage on night patrol through the jungle. Although the quick remark of one of the soldiers may have been missed by many who eventually saw *Twilight Zone: The Movie*, Landis also made murderers of the soldiers by his reference to the platoon members having killed their lieutenant—whose name was Neidermeyer, the obnoxious fraternity brother from *Animal House*.)

Before encountering the Americans, Connor sees a patrol of Viet Cong approaching, and he hides neck deep in the water, hidden by plants, as the patrol, and a large water snake floating a few feet from him, pass by.

When the group of American soldiers soon follows, Connor rises and eagerly makes his way toward them with a smile and a yell: "I'm an American! I'm an American!" Seeing Connor as the enemy, the soldiers aim thunderous blasts of gunfire at him.

"Is it gonna be big?" Landis asked Paul Stewart about the special effects he planned to simulate the gunfire directed at Connor.

Three witnesses—cameraman Steve Lydecker, photographer Morgan Renard, and makeup artist Melanie Leavitt—later testified to essentially the same sequence of events. All remembered that Landis was displeased with Stewart's initial effort to portray bullets shredding some nearby banana plants by utilizing an air-powered gun shooting marbles. Lydecker, who was filming the scene, said the marbles just bounced off the leaves.

Stewart then suggested putting squibs (small explosive devices, approximately one inch long, which simulate bullet hits) on the leaves, but according to the witnesses Landis objected to the fifteen minutes that procedure required. Stewart then brought three Remington shotguns from the special-effects truck after telling Landis that he could give him the effect he wanted by shooting live ammunition at the leaves.

Just before the scene was to begin, though, Morrow angrily confronted Landis about the use of live ammunition, and several times the two walked the path Morrow would take. Rarely, if at all, was live ammunition shot in such close proximity to an actor so soon after he left the range of fire.

When the scene was filmed, Morrow stood in the water in front of a wall of banana plants. Reacting as though he were being fired upon, he dove underwater, swam away, and was pulled up onshore about twenty feet from the three special-effects men, including Stewart, who were holding the shotguns skyward. When Morrow was out of the line of fire, Stewart and his crew members lowered the weapons and fired blasts of pellets that violently tore into the plants, cutting them down as though they had been scythed. In the edited film version, Connor appeared to have missed being shot by a fraction of a second.

"Yeah, it was my decision," Stewart later told me of the idea to fire live ammunition. He referred to the scene as "the slaughter of the banana plants." He had used live ammunition with an actor once before—with John Wayne, who had fired an Israeli-made Uzi submachine gun in the detective movie *McQ*.

Gary McLarty served as a double for Morrow in one scene also filmed on Tuesday night, a sequence in which Connor is literally blown out of the water—and off-camera—by a supposed grenade explosion. To produce the effect, McLarty stood on a high-powered hydraulic lift placed underwater. The lift catapulted McLarty just as squibs detonated to simulate the grenade effect. Use of the lift was dangerous because it could easily break the leg of an actor unaccustomed to its power and unskilled in the proper body position to absorb the force safely.

Even though he deferred on such scenes, Morrow was still working hard and enduring discomfort, particularly in the scenes in which he spent a great deal of time in the Santa Clarita River. Still, he was happy to have a good role in a feature film.

Although he had been successful in winning a few good television parts after *Combat*, Morrow's feature film work had been extremely limited. Job offers were no longer as prolific as they had been when he had first moved to Hollywood in the 1950s. Before *Combat* and after his critically acclaimed screen debut in *The Blackboard Jungle*, Morrow's movies had included *King Creole*, with Elvis Presley; *God's Little Acre; Cimarron;* and *Portrait of a Mobster*, in which he portrayed Dutch Schultz. Since *Combat* Morrow's most notable movie role had been as a Little League coach in *The Bad News Bears*. He had not had a leading part in a feature film in twenty years.

Morrow, born in 1931, grew up in the Bronx, New York, and was a man with a strong sense of the street. When he was seventeen, he joined the Navy, later earning his high school diploma at night school. He attended Mexico City College and Roosevelt College in Florida before joining the Actors' Workshop in New York City. A summer stock performance in the Tennessee Williams play *A Streetcar Named Desire* won him critical notice.

The Metro-Goldwyn-Mayer studio brought him to Hollywood in 1954. Years later he told a reporter for the *Los Angeles Herald Examiner:* "I knew I was in the big time when I found myself amid these huge sets on the MGM lot, which looked just like New York streets. And then Richard Brooks, the director, backed into a wall when looking through his viewfinder. Waving his arms and shouting without taking his eye off the potential shot, he said, 'Move it,' and a bunch of men immediately relocated the wall."

Morrow was serious about his acting, saying in the same interview: "At one point, they offered me a job as the voice of a dog. I said 'no' and went through the whole trip about being a professional actor and a human being and so on. But then when I went home I thought about it, and it seemed rather an interesting challenge."

Morrow kept a small circle of friends and socialized little. Divorced twice, he had been devoted to his mother prior to her death in 1978. His attorney, Al Green, thought that Morrow was a frustrated lawyer. Frequently Morrow would spend time in Green's law library and later argue cases with Green. For all of his onscreen toughness, Green thought that Morrow was a man of vulnerability who had erected an impenetrable shell between himself and all but his most intimate friends and family.

He did not limit his show business work to acting, having written screenplays and directed and produced films.

One of his favorite roles had been in a 1972 television movie called *The Glass House*, filmed on location at the Utah State Prison, in which he played a manipulative inmate leader named Hugo Slocum. His performance was gritty and realistic. A homosexual seduction and rape scene, in which Slocum terrifies a young, recently jailed prisoner, was especially chilling. Morrow's portrayal of Slocum showed the character's evil through telling nuance. A television critic wrote: "If Morrow ever gave a performance superior to this one, we've never seen it."

On Wednesday, July 21, 1982, there was excitement in the homes of My-Ca Le and Renee Chen as the time for their departure to Indian Dunes approached.

Daniel Le had decided that he would accompany his son, because his wife was tired from work. That plan changed, however, when Hoa-Kim Le came home and asked her son, "My-Ca, would you like Mom to go with you?"

"I really, really want you to go, but you are tired, you can stay at home, Mom," he replied. Touched by My-Ca's generosity, Mrs. Le decided to be with her son that evening.

In late afternoon, Folsey and studio driver Jeff Powell left in a van to pick up the families. Their first stop, though, was at the home of Julie Hua, to whom Folsey paid $600 in cash, $200 for each of the three children who had originally auditioned for the roles. The money was for remaining on standby throughout the evening in case it was later determined that My-Ca and Renee could not perform for some reason. Coincidentally, Julie Hua knew Mrs. Le, who had been the Hua family social worker when they first arrived in the United States.

Daniel, Hoa-Kim, My-Ca, and Christopher Le were picked up at their home in Pasadena. Folsey had said that the four-year-old Christopher could be in the movie if My-Ca got tired. After picking up Mark, Shyan Huei, and Renee Chen in Cerritos, Powell began the hour-long drive to Indian Dunes.

Folsey chatted with the parents during the trip. Daniel Le did not join in, though. He enjoyed the scenery and talked with his son, My-Ca, imagining how he would look in the movie.

The film set was off California Highway 126 and was reached by a bumpy, two-mile-long dirt road. When the van was on the Indian Dunes property, Folsey turned to the parents and thanked them for participating with the production company, particularly because the producers had not been able to get the children work permits. He said that if anyone on the set inquired, the parents should just say they were friends of his and not mention that the children were working as actors.

Dorcey Wingo had arrived at about 4:00 P.M. Wednesday after flying the Huey from Rialto in San Bernardino County. He had been accompanied by his mechanic, Harry Ferguson. It was the pilot's first view of Indian Dunes.

The helicopter had already been colored olive drab with easily removable strip paint. When Wingo arrived, a studio artist painted a large logo on the front of the helicopter, to lend military authenticity. The design was of a large eagle, with outstretched wings, on a background of red, white, and blue. In white letters was written, "Fly By Night," a joking tribute to Steven Spielberg, who had called his own production company by that nickname.

Wingo was greeted by Richard Sawyer, who asked the pilot if he wanted to cross the river and inspect the village. Since Wingo didn't have boots to wear he declined, not wanting to get wet or remove his flight suit.

Earlier in the week an earthen dam had been constructed downriver by bulldozer, backing up the Santa Clarita beginning about two hundred feet west of the village. The dam allowed the moviemakers to keep the water level about knee high during Morrow's crossing scene and provided a broader shoreline in front of the village.

The village, on the south shore, was located on a sandy strip of land measuring about fifty feet wide from the cliff wall to the river.

When Wingo was asked again whether he wanted to inspect mortars in the village, this time by Paul Stewart, he declined once more. Wingo told Stewart that he would visit the area later. Stewart replied: "When we get to the shot, that's when it really counts, because we'll know the position of the helicopter and where the explosions are gonna be."

Earlier in the week, Stewart and his crew had used a backhoe to dig holes for two dozen special-effects mortars—large, heavy pots—placed variously throughout the village. Which mortars would be armed with bombs would be decided later in the evening, after consultation with Landis.

The mortars were of standard, steel construction, each weighing fifty to one hundred pounds, with walls three-eighths inch thick. They were of two shapes. The base of square mortars was smaller than the opening at the top. This forced the explosion to diffuse and spread to the sides as the fireball left the slant-walled container. Round mortars, cylindrical like a gun barrel, created a more powerful and concentrated blast. The mortars were of three sizes: thirty-two inches high by thirty inches wide, eighteen inches by eighteen inches, and twelve inches by twelve inches.

A special-effects crewman arms a mortar by first placing a plastic-wrapped black powder bomb, containing from six to twelve ounces of powder, at the base of the container. An electrical wire, leading up to forty feet away from the mortar, is attached to the bomb. The container is then filled with sawdust soaked to a mushy consistency with four to ten gallons of gasoline. A second, cellophane-wrapped "igniter" bomb, containing only one or two ounces of black powder and also connected to the electrical wire, is rested on the rim of the mortar.

The electrical wires lead to a "firing board," a two-foot-long plank of wood held by a special-effects technician. A series of three-inch-long brass plates is mounted on the firing board. Each wire leading to a mortar is connected to one brass plate. One end of another wire is attached to a metal nail held by the technician, while the other end of the wire is connected to a battery just before filming. A bomb is detonated when the "man on the board" touches the nail to a brass plate, completing the electrical circuit among firing board, battery, and bomb.

When the bomb at the base of the mortar explodes, it forcefully lifts the sawdust and vaporizes the gasoline, which is set ablaze in a roaring fireball, 2,600 degrees Fahrenheit at its core, by the igniter bomb on the mortar's rim. The sawdust is used in night explosions to give the fireball its brilliant orange hue, creating a stunning film effect.

The black powder bombs used for *Twilight Zone* had been handpacked by a San Fernando Valley woman who had been supplying special-effects crews with explosives for many years.

Water mortars are open-ended cylindrical mortars placed just below the river's surface and contain black powder bombs without the gasoline. They shoot massive columns of water into the air.

The safety of the special effects was the responsibility of Paul Stewart and his crew. Dewitt Morgan, the man who had issued the fire department permit, later admitted that he was so inexperienced with special effects that he had come to the set Wednesday night so he could learn more

more about them. Morgan had never before seen gasoline explosions of the size Stewart and Landis had planned.

Before darkness, Dorcey Wingo made several reconnaissance flights above the set, accompanied by Allingham, Ferguson, and the man whose company had supplied a powerful spotlight mounted on the nose of the helicopter. Allingham would operate the spotlight during filming, shining its beam on Morrow and the children.

Wingo wanted to locate all the trees and power lines in the area during daylight because the terrain could be deceiving viewed from the air at night. During these afternoon sorties he also flew by the village at a low altitude so those on the ground—Landis, cameramen, and others—could sense the scale of the helicopter against the village.

After completing his aerial survey at about 6:00 P.M., Wingo and his mechanic located a landing site near the dam, a two-minute walk along the sandy river shore to the village. Wingo's boss, Clair Merryweather, had flown to Indian Dunes in a small airplane and was readying to leave for Sacramento as Wingo landed. He said good-bye to Wingo and added, "I know you'll be safe. Have a good time."

At the landing site a gun rental company put a mounting on each side of the helicopter for .50-caliber machine guns that would be operated by stuntmen firing blanks. Checking afterward, Wingo noticed that one mounting was so loose that had the stuntman leaned against it during flight, he could have fallen out of the aircraft. Wingo ordered the fixture to be secured, put on his costume—a Vietnam-era military flight suit with captain's bars—and waited for instructions to take off.

Landis was not often sensitive to how others on the set reacted to his blunt behavior. Fire safety officer George Hull, for one, was not impressed with the director's demeanor. Hull asked Elie Cohn if Landis always acted so demonstratively.

"Yes, he's an artist," Cohn replied.

"Bullshit, he's crazy," Hull said.

Camera assistant Lee Redmond was another person who reacted poorly to Landis's bursts of temper. He later told of an incident involving cameraman John Connor, who was asking Paul Stewart if his camera placement was safe in relation to the upcoming mortar explosions. According to Redmond, before Stewart could answer, Landis testily interrupted and said, "It will be safe and if you don't want to operate the camera you can go home and I will do it for you."

Neither was Landis's curt manner appreciated by cameraman Steve Lydecker, who would film the wide-angle master shot of the rescue scene.

Lydecker had worked previously as a special effects technician in over two hundred films. He later testified that he expressed concern to Landis that the concussive effect of bombs detonated in front of the cliff could be reflected back over the village.

Lydecker was shocked by Landis's intemperate response: "Well, we may lose the helicopter." The cameraman recalled that he stood silently, too intimidated to reply to the joke he did not find funny, as Landis walked away.

Wingo's first impression of Landis, however, was a good one. The director greeted the pilot warmly. Wingo himself was an exceedingly polite and courteous man, who worked at not offending others. Deferential to movie set authority, he asked Allingham what the "pecking order" was on the production team. Allingham, as unit production manager, normally would not be part of the on-set hierarchy during filming. His work was largely administrative. But because he had decided to be in the helicopter to operate the spotlight, he told Wingo that he would be the pilot's liaison with Landis.

Wingo's introduction to Landis's impatience came during the filming of the helicopter's arrival over the village. This was a scene shot without actors, depicting what Connor would see as he looked up at the aircraft as it first appeared over the top of the cliff.

Landis had in mind a specific angle of flight that could be accomplished if Wingo flew over a particular tree on the mesa at the top of the cliff. It was dark on the mesa, one hundred feet above the set. Wingo had difficulty finding the tree that Landis had pointed out to him.

Wingo had been flying about ten minutes when Landis shouted into the radio, "What the fuck are you doing up there?"

"Tell him to keep his shirt on," Wingo said to Allingham, choosing not to confront the director himself.

"Give us a chance. It isn't like positioning a Volkswagen up here," Allingham radioed back to Landis. Then he said to Wingo, "Don't let that bother you. John gets a little excited and talks like that."

Throughout filming, several people said, Landis talked so loudly into the radio that he was often unintelligible. Wingo later told investigators, "There's no mistaking John when he talked. He was pretty abrasive at that point. And I was a little surprised to hear that kind of language over the radio because the FCC [Federal Communications Commission] does monitor radios. And it's a good way to lose your ability to use radios."

The evening hours were consumed by a technically complicated shot of Morrow's first entry into the village. The crew had built a long, two-camera dolly track, supported above the riverbed by a wood structure that had taken much longer than expected to erect.

The children and their families grew impatient as the hours passed. For much of the time, they waited in a comfortable dressing room trailer, which crew members called a "honey wagon." Provided for their comfort, the trailers also hid the children from the view of the fire safety officers, the only outside authorities on the set who could discover that My-Ca and Renee were working illegally after hours.

The families had been escorted to the trailers by Hilary Leach, a Directors' Guild of America trainee and one of several crew members who knew the details of the illegal hiring. A few days before, Anderson House had told her about his unsuccessful attempts to convince Allingham to use dummies or adult midgets instead of the children, and also told her that he was worried about the children's safety during the river crossing scene.

As midnight approached, the parents pressed the production team for information about when their children would be filmed. Mrs. Le frequently talked to Folsey, who kept reassuring her: "Any minute. Anytime now. Just wait until we are done with Vic Morrow, your son will be in."

Mark Chen grew concerned as the children tired. "How come they haven't started for their part yet?" he asked Folsey, who urged him to be patient, that he would come to the trailer for the children when they were needed.

By contract with the various unions of the cast and crew, staples of any movie set are a catering area and established mealtimes. At about midnight, My-Ca, Renee, and their families had some food and then returned to the trailer, where they met Belinda Folsey and her children. Afterward the children and some of the parents took naps.

At about 2:00 A.M., first assistant director Elie Cohn advised Folsey that it would be impossible to complete everything that had been planned for that night. They decided that no scenes with explosives should be filmed until the following night. The proposal was brought to Landis, who readily agreed.

Paul Stewart had also realized that there was too much work to complete that night. "I knew by one o'clock that we would never finish," he told me later. "When you do a motion picture you know the assistant director is gonna say, 'Oh, yeah, we're gonna finish.' But you walk away knowing he's full of it. I know what I gotta do and it's not humanly possible."

The children, though, would remain for one of the four scenes in which they were scheduled to appear. This one depicted Connor's first encounter with the children, a scene in which there would be no explosions or helicopter overhead.

Because they would not be needed for the upcoming scene, the special-effects workers finished their work at about 2:00 A.M. George Hull of the fire department noticed that the crew members then began drinking liquor out of plastic cups. Hull thought that Paul Stewart appeared unaffected by the alcohol, but some others seemed to get more boisterous and obnoxious.

Meanwhile, others on the production team were readying for the final scene of the night. Folsey went to the trailer and said, "Let's go, children."

"Wait a minute," Mrs. Le said. "I'm coming with My-Ca."

Renee and My-Ca were taken to the makeup trailer, where some dirtlike powder was applied to their faces and they were changed into scruffy clothes.

The children were driven from the makeup trailer to the village accompanied by all the parents except Daniel Le, who remained on the north shore holding his son Christopher in his arms.

In the chronology of the movie, the scene takes place as Connor, weary from the chase by Nazis in which he was wounded, awakens to find the Vietnamese children standing near him. He asks them where their parents are and if they have any food or water.

As Landis rehearsed the children's movements several times with them, My-Ca and Renee were asked to pretend that an attacking helicopter was flying overhead, and to run and hide behind Morrow. There were several false starts because the children couldn't control their giggling. Finally, after Landis comfortingly asked them to be serious, the scene was completed.

Folsey waited until the dialogue scene had been completed before he told the parents that the remaining scenes with the children could not be finished that night. He apologized and asked the parents if they would allow their children to work again the following evening, by now only about twelve hours away. "It will be very simple. We will try and finish as soon as possible," he promised and offered a second five hundred dollars for each child.

Both Mark Chen and Hoa-Kim Le later said that when they hesitated, because they were exhausted and had to go to work during the day, Folsey said that the parents did not have to return with the children.

"I will treat your children like my own children," Folsey said.

The parents, who had neither seen the helicopter fly overhead nor observed any special-effects explosions, agreed to let their children come back, but also decided that at least one parent of each child would also return.

Before the parents were driven home, Folsey handed each an envelope containing five $100 bills. Folsey asked the parents to keep secret that he had paid them in cash. Daniel Le later said he did not question the secrecy because Folsey "appeared to be very honest, nice person and I trust him. And I thought in my mind, because I am ignorant about the movie industry in this country, I thought this may be the way the movie industry working at dealings in this country."

As second assistant director Anderson House was completing his paperwork at about 3:30 A.M., one of the fire safety officers approached him.

"Hello, we've worked together before," he said, but House didn't recognize him at first.

"I'm also a studio teacher. My name is Jack Tice."

House then remembered the man, and as they exchanged pleasantries, a realization came to House. Tice, whom he knew as a man of responsibility, would probably notify the labor department and have production stopped if he learned that My-Ca and Renee were working illegally after hours. Apparently Tice had not yet seen the two children on the set. Or if he had seen them, he didn't realize that they were there as paid actors. There had been an unusually large crowd of spectators, including children, invited to watch the special-effects scenes and attend the traditional "wrap" party at the close of filming, now postponed for one more night.

After Tice left, House wrote a note to Allingham warning that Tice was also a credentialed teacher-welfare worker. House put the note in an envelope, along with the day's production reports, which were then taken to Universal Studios by messenger for Allingham, who would go there after getting some sleep.

Jack Tice, who had closed movie sets in the past when he believed children were endangered, would be a problem for the production team to deal with Thursday night when filming resumed.

THREE

"Vic, I've got no problem, I can pull you off right now. It won't be a violation of your contract," lawyer Al Green said to Vic Morrow during a telephone conversation several hours after the actor had left the Indian Dunes set early Thursday morning.

"Nahhh, I've got one more day to go and it will be behind me," Morrow said with resignation about returning to the set in the evening.

During the three weeks of filming, Morrow had complained angrily about drinking and drug use on the *Twilight Zone* set, worrying about safety. But he had not been specific about who was using the drugs. Still, Green was eager to help his client—and friend of twenty years—whom he was trying to convince not to return to the set that night.

Whether Morrow's concerns were grounded in something specific that he had witnessed during the previous three weeks of filming, or if his uneasiness was the product of instinct, will never be known with certainty. Morrow was, of course, accustomed to working near special effects and helicopters, although not always comfortably.

A year before *Twilight Zone* Morrow had expressed apprehensions about a helicopter scene—fears founded only in his imagination. Working in a television movie in which he was scheduled to fly in a helicopter, Morrow had demanded that an attorney (not Green) obtain a $5-million life insurance policy for him before the scene was filmed. Morrow told the attorney that he had had a premonition that the helicopter would crash and he would be killed. The policy was secured and Morrow did the scene without incident.

Green had been hearing complaints from Morrow since shortly after he began work on *Twilight Zone.* The actor had talked about the banana plant scene with the live ammunition, but now he was ambiguous about the reasons for his uneasiness. Green thought that Morrow had a legal foundation for leaving the job without being vulnerable to a breach-of-contract lawsuit.

"It will take me thirty seconds to take care of this with a telephone call," Green said.

"Leave it alone," Morrow finally decided. Implicit in his decision, and understood by Green, was Morrow's frustrating recognition that his career was not strong enough to risk a reputation for being a petulant quitter. *Twilight Zone,* after all, was his first feature film leading role in almost two decades.

When Anderson House awoke late Thursday morning, he called Allingham to talk about Jack Tice and the possibility that the fire safety officer could have the set closed down if he saw the children—the same concern House had already written in a memo to Allingham.

"When he sees the children on the set he'll shut the set down," House warned.

"Maybe he won't," Allingham said.

Meanwhile, at the Landis production office, secretary Donna Schuman inadvertently opened House's memorandum as she was sorting through the production documents that had been brought in by messenger from Indian Dunes. She read the message and then put it back with other material Allingham was to be given when he came into the office in late afternoon.

In midafternoon, Folsey called the Les and the Chens to confirm that My-Ca and Renee would be needed for work that evening. My-Ca had slept until noon and then called his grandmother, whom he told, "We had a wonderful time, grandmom. Renee and I were laughing. We tried to hold it but we couldn't do it."

At about 4:00 P.M., Warner Brothers vice president Edward Morey, one of the studio's liaisons to the production office, called Allingham at the Universal Studios office to discuss a discrepancy he had just noticed in his paperwork.

Morey, who had recently returned from two weeks' vacation, wasn't able to reconcile earlier documents that indicated children were to be used in the Vietnamese scenes with more recent reports that didn't mention children at all.

"I was checking the schedule and I noticed that there were no children or welfare worker listed, and that the description indicated that children should be working," Morey said.

"Well, I have been up in a helicopter all night and I really wasn't taking care of that end," Allingham replied, explaining that an assistant director was handling the reports.

"Will you please check it out for me?" Morey requested.

"Yes, I will," said Allingham, who went to tell George Folsey about the call as soon as he hung up the telephone. Donna Schuman later recalled that the two decided they would have to "be careful."

Daniel and My-Ca Le and Shyan and Renee Chen were picked up by the studio driver at about 5:00 P.M. My-Ca's mother, Hoa-Kim Le, tired from being up most of the night before and then working all day, stayed at home. Mark Chen had a meeting to attend.

At Indian Dunes in late afternoon, House told first assistant director Elie Cohn about Tice's background as a teacher-welfare worker, and Cohn relayed the information to John Landis. Cohn later said that Landis replied, "You know we must be careful and try not to get caught."

Throughout the evening, efforts were made to keep the children out of Tice's view. As a fire safety officer, Tice was free to roam where he wished, but he would remain in one location some distance from the huts, primarily to watch for fires on the mesa, when the children's scenes were filmed.

By House's instruction, location manager Richard Vane several times asked Tice, "Where are you going to be?" Tice had not been pressed so vigorously for such information on other sets, and he wondered why he was being asked now.

Hilary Leach, the Directors' Guild of America trainee, whose job included escorting the children on the set, was told by House to refer to My-Ca and Renee on her walkie-talkie only as "the Vietnamese," just in case any of the fire safety officers overhead the radio transmissions.

The six fire safety officers had divided into two groups for the night's work. George Hull, Willard Major, Francis Groat, and Richard Ebentheuer would be on the mesa, which was covered with acres of dry grass and which was the area most susceptible to fire from burning embers sent adrift by the special-effects fireballs.

One fireman warned cameraman Michael Scott, who would also be on the mesa, not to move uphill if a fire started, because the flames could move faster than he could. Those working on the mesa used hoses from the water trucks to put a light spray of water on the grass. They were careful not to wet it too much, fearful that the ground would be so slippery that the camera crew might accidentally slide off the edge of the cliff.

Jack Rimmer and Jack Tice would remain at river level.

The bulldozer that had been used to build the earthen dam was put into operation to grade the riverbed along the path Morrow would later follow during the rescue scene.

The first scene to be shot was of Morrow picking up the children as they huddled, frightened, in a hut. The helicopter above would supposedly attack the village with rocket fire as Morrow ran.

Landis planned this scene as a close-up shot to show everyone's faces. There had been no consideration of using Morrow's stunt double for this or either of the other two scenes still to be filmed.

Instead, Gary McLarty would fly in the helicopter and fire one of the machine guns. Later, the moviemakers would say that they did not consider the scenes stunts, which would have given McLarty, as the stunt coordinator, more authority in the planning.

Once the two cameras that would film the scene were in place, Stewart explained to everyone working nearby where the bombs had been placed. Two explosions to the sides of the hut would set the building ablaze seconds after Morrow and the children left the structure.

The technician operating the firing board was James Camomile, a Navy veteran, and a longtime friend and hunting companion of Stewart's. Of the four men on the special effects team, only Stewart and Camomile held "number one powder cards," California's highest-ranking pyrotechnic licenses of the three grades issued by the state.

Morrow arrived on the set and rehearsed his movements several times. Timing was particularly important for Camomile, who would fire the mortars when Morrow passed a marker about fifteen feet from the hut.

Neither Stewart nor Camomile knew that the children were working illegally. "I figured that everything was legal," Stewart later told me. "I thought that everybody had permission because I had my permits, [the producers] had their permits for the location, and I saw the parents there."

At the makeup trailer someone took a Polaroid photograph of My-Ca and Renee wearing their movie clothes. Renee's hair had been braided, and both looked into the camera with big, expectant eyes. They were unquestionably attractive children.

Renee Chen was anxious and asked Hilary Leach, "What if we get sick?"

"You'll be fine, don't worry," Leach said. Nearby she heard Landis explaining to My-Ca that he would hear a loud bang and not to be afraid.

After the special-effects electrical circuit was completed by attaching the detonating wires to a large battery, the children were left alone in the hut for perhaps a minute or so, their bodies about three feet from the armed mortars.

When everything had been set, Elie Cohn radioed the takeoff order to the helicopter, which then came into position about sixty feet above the hut, creating noise and a strong wind (rotor wash) from its swirling rotor blades, which swept dust and small bits of debris through the village.

"Scene thirty-one! Take one! Three cameras! Mark!" a crew member yelled as the cameras began to roll.

Allingham was having trouble keeping the spotlight focused on Morrow and the hut, and the beam bounced from place to place.

"Be ready, you guys!" someone yelled to the children.

Landis called, "Action!" and Morrow moved into camera range toward the hut, limping as he went—because Bill Connor had suffered gunshot wounds in the previous scenes.

Renee was the first of the two children to be picked up. Morrow held her around her waist, pressing her tightly against his body under his left arm. Then he bent over to pick up My-Ca. With a muscular thrust of his legs, Morrow straightened himself up, turned, and ran away from the hut, toward the river.

He had taken about five steps when he reached the stick that was Camomile's cue to fire the mortars. The larger of the two explosions was behind the hut, and the fireball erupted in brilliance, creating a curtain of flame in the background. The second mortar, called a "push" mortar, was smaller, and knocked over a ladder leaning against the side of the bamboo structure. In combination, the two mortars gave the appearance of the hut being destroyed by rocket fire.

Only a second or two after the mortars had been fired, Morrow passed beyond the camera's range, and Landis yelled, "Cut!"

Renee's mother had watched the fireball rise quickly up the cliff from a spot close to where her daughter had just been. "Is it dangerous?" she asked Folsey.

The producer patted her on the shoulder and said, "It isn't dangerous. It's just a very loud sound."

Soon afterward, the woman saw Landis carrying Renee in his arms and trying to comfort her, because she was crying.

"Are you scared?" Shyan Chen asked her daughter.

"A little bit," Renee said. "I have sand in my eye and the actor hold me so tight I am a little bit hurt from that."

Also, both children had gotten their feet wet when Morrow ran into the shallow river just beyond the camera.

Folsey accompanied the parents and children back to the trailer, where he asked them to remain for the time being.

The second shot of the night was known as the "rage scene," in which Bill Connor, assuming that the American helicopter above is about to rescue him, becomes angry when he is fired upon. In the chronological order of the movie after editing, this scene would be placed just prior to the scene that had been filmed at nine-thirty.

Dorcey Wingo, who had never before witnessed a special-effects explosion of the size to be used at eleven-thirty, asked Stewart what it would be like. The special-effects foreman explained that fireballs from three mortars placed at the base of the cliff, to the rear of the village, would sweep up the cliff wall, dissipating as they traveled, finally disappearing about 150 feet in the air. The cliff itself rose variously ninety to one hundred feet to the mesa.

When Wingo asked about the water mortars in the river, he was told that they would produce a "grenade effect," which the pilot assumed meant only that they would generate a loud noise.

Wingo then told Landis that he didn't want anyone directly underneath any part of his fifty-two-foot-long helicopter, including the "tip path plane," that area below the entire sweep of the forty-four-foot-long main rotor blades.

Although Landis had asked the pilot to fly even closer in, Wingo determined that the tip of his rotors could be no closer than ten feet from the cliff wall. Because the river had been widened by the construction of the dam, the village area was only about fifty feet from cliff wall to the water's edge.

For this shot, Wingo would descend lower than he had at 9:30 P.M., this time hovering about thirty-five feet above the river. The main camera would film the village, Morrow yelling up to the helicopter, and the soldiers firing machine guns in the aircraft back down at Morrow. The three mortars on the ground were supposedly to simulate rocket fire from the helicopter.

Before Wingo returned to the landing area, Morrow asked him if he recalled any particular invectives soldiers had yelled at pilots in Vietnam. The actor wanted to add some historical authenticity to his lines. Wingo told him that he didn't recall soldiers being angry with helicopter pilots. Then he gave Morrow his standard preflight briefing, the one he gave to work crews and others who would be on the ground below him while he hovered.

The pilot told Morrow to keep alert for any changes in the motor noise that would indicate engine failure, always a possibility while hovering. If so, Morrow was to run while Wingo attempted an emergency landing. "Be like a chameleon," Wingo said, telling Morrow always to keep one eye on the helicopter, no matter what else he was doing on the ground.

A constant reminder of the special effects was a thick odor of gasoline permeating the area. Cynthia Nigh, the production assistant, was standing nearby to watch the filming and had trouble breathing because of the heavy fumes.

The children were not in this scene, so they and their parents remained in the trailer, about a quarter of a mile away from the village in an area separated from the set by a grove of trees and bushes.

As Morrow saw the helicopter approach, he poured water from a styrofoam cup over his head, because in the chronology of the script, Connor had just emerged from the river. The actor then threw the white cup into the bushes behind him and used his hand to shield his eyes from the bright lights and the rotor wash, enabling him to see Landis's cue.

Morrow peered through the windwhipped, dusty air, his suit jacket pressed tight against his body by the force of the rotor wash. Bushes in the village were bent over, almost touching the ground, and a string of bare light bulbs hanging between the huts bounced wildly.

The fuselage of the helicopter, which Wingo was maintaining in a steady hover, was directly above the river's shore parallel to the cliff. The tips of the aircraft's rotor blades were about twelve feet from the cliff wall.

Camerman Roger Smith, secured around his waist by a nylon safety strap attached to a harness clipped securely to a metal hook inside the helicopter, stepped outside onto the skid on the left side of the aircraft. Morrow was standing almost directly below him. Smith was using a wide-angle lens on a hand-held camera, which he had propped on his shoulder.

Cued by Landis, Morrow walked out into the river, waving joyously at the helicopter and yelling, "Come on down!" Morrow's words, radioed by a transmitter taped to his back under his suit jacket, were picked up clearly on a Nagra tape recorder operated by a soundman across the river.

When the blank shells in the helicopter machine guns were fired, eighteen-inch-long muzzle flashes spit out. Squibs exploding in the river thrust water sprays a foot high to simulate bullet hits near the actor.

The first water mortar exploded about ten feet behind Morrow and powerfully propelled a column of water upward, obliterating Wingo's view through the windshield. The water also covered Roger Smith's camera lens, and he decided to jump back into the aircraft. As Wingo leaned toward the side window to his right, to make sure his rotortips did not graze the cliff wall, a second water mortar exploded and sent water washing against the front and left side of the aircraft.

Wingo was looking out of the right-side window when one of the cliff mortars detonated and sent a large fireball soaring straight up and past the helicopter. The heat was so intense that Wingo's cheek turned pink.

"Chickenshit!" Wingo yelled several times.

Smith thought the heat felt just as though someone had opened an oven door. McLarty, who had been at the open side door firing one of the machine guns, rolled back into the helicopter to avoid getting burned. The fireball was quickly followed by two more. Wingo was so stunned that he jostled the controls and the helicopter wavered.

"That's too much! Let's get out of here!" Allingham yelled.

From his vantage point several hundred yards away, mechanic Harry Ferguson had watched the fireball pass the helicopter's rotors as it moved up the cliff, but then he saw globs of flame being sucked back into the rotor system by the downdraft suction of the blades.

"This is bullshit!" Wingo yelled at Allingham as he pulled the helicopter up and away from the village. He kept repeating angrily, "They didn't tell me about that!"

Even as Wingo hastily left his hovering position, Western Helicopter's mechanic, Ferguson, may have been the only person on the ground who recognized that the helicopter had encountered trouble. Morrow continued his performance, yelling at the helicopter, his face showing the anger and confusion he had rehearsed. He turned his body in circles to see the explosions around him, then ran back into the village, as called for in the script.

With the helicopter off in the distance and Morrow back in the village, Landis yelled "Cut!" The director, wearing roomy rubber waders that rose above his waist, crossed the river toward Morrow. Halfway, Landis was called by one of the cameramen, who still needed Landis to clap his hands, signifying the end of the scene for the sound editor. Landis raised his hands over his head, clapped, and then continued sloshing his way across the river, excitedly greeting Morrow in the village. There was applause from the crew and spectators.

From around the set, people were yelling "Great!" and "It couldn't have been better!"

Nigh had stood near George Folsey. The size of the explosions amazed her. She later said that Folsey, who also seemed surprised at the magnitude of the explosions, turned to her and said he was glad that his wife and children had not come to the set that night.

The Chens and the Les, secluded in the dressing-room trailer, saw or heard none of this activity.

Wingo fumed with anger as he flew his helicopter back to the landing site west of the dam. He told Allingham, who had also been surprised by the explosions, that he would just not tolerate such close calls. Wingo wanted to be assured that all precautions were taken to prevent a recurrence when the next scene was filmed. Then he calmed down, and apologized for leaving the scene early.

"You're right, Dorcey, safety first," Allingham responded. "I've got a vacation to start this weekend. Safety first."

The firemen on the mesa extinguished three grass fires and a fallen tree trunk that had been set ablaze.

As soon as Wingo landed, Ferguson began checking the helicopter for damage. First, he cleaned dirty water droplets from the windshield. Concerned that the fireballs could have damaged the rotor blades, he took a coin and carefully tapped the entire surface of each, to see whether the aluminum alloy skin, only $^{25}/_{1000}$ inch thick, had separated from the inside support material to which it was glued.

Wingo didn't even realize that the heat had affected him until Ferguson noticed the pilot's flame-generated ruddiness. Then the pilot told Allingham that he wanted to attend the planning session for the next shot, so that he could make his feelings known to Landis.

"Let me handle it, Dorcey," Allingham said, and the pilot agreed. The pilot's anger was again showing, and he later speculated that Allingham wanted to prevent a confrontation between him and Landis.

Landis knew that the fireballs would be close to the helicopter, but from his vantage point on the ground he was unaware that those in the helicopter had been troubled by the experience. Neither Wingo nor Allingham radioed their complaints to him from the air. Unaware of how close to disaster the shot had taken everyone, Landis called for the meal break, primarily on the suggestion of Elie Cohn, who advised him that the special-effects crew needed the time to set up the mortars for the next shot, scheduled to begin at about 2:00 A.M.

Some who had been in the helicopter talked among themselves during the meal, going over the experience, and were overheard by others. Jack Tice, for example, radioed George Hull, who was up on the mesa, and said that he had been told that Wingo's face had been singed during the flight.

But there was no single meeting involving everyone concerned in which the explosions—and the distances necessary for safety—were discussed with specificity, even though the next shot, with the children, called for additional special effects.

* * *

Forty miles away, in a onetime criminal courtroom converted to an office for homicide detectives, Sergeant Thomas Budds of the Los Angeles County Sheriff's Department arrived for duty. This shift was known as being "in the barrel," a lonely, usually quiet night watch spent waiting for industrial accidents, suicides, and murders. Budds, thirty-six years old, carried a paperback copy of Irving Stone's *The Agony and the Ecstasy* with him.

"What are you trying to do, bring culture to this unit?" a colleague joked with him as he left Budds alone for the night.

The detective scanned the previous shift's log entries, watched Johnny Carson on television for a while, and read his book. He took his shoes off and put his feet up on the desk. The relaxation was owed him. As did other detectives, Budds put in a healthy share of uncompensated overtime each month. Plus he had already worked a full shift earlier in the day, pursuing the investigation of a murder.

The children were awakened from their naps at about midnight, and Hilary Leach brought them some hot soup. The next scene, in which the children were to be filmed, was the most important to Landis at Indian Dunes. This was the climactic rescue scene, in which Morrow carried the children to safety across the river while the helicopter chased them from above and fireballs exploded all around.

Because there was still the possibility that Jack Tice, or another fire safety officer, could question the propriety of children working in the scene, Folsey went to the trailer at about midnight to make a request of the parents. He was also unaware of the problems caused by the eleven-thirty explosions, and his primary concern was ensuring that no authorities stopped the next shot.

Folsey asked the parents: "If the firemen approach you, please do not tell them that you are working for me. Tell them you are my friends. You are here to help me. Don't tell them anything about the money, nothing about the children working."

Folsey knew that Shyan Chen was not proficient in English, so he asked Daniel Le to repeat his request to her. Le did, but in English, because he was Vietnamese, Shyan Chen was Chinese, and neither spoke the other's native language.

After the meal, Wingo walked to where the camera crews were adjusting their equipment. Landis was about twenty feet up in the air, on a crane checking a shot. (According to Landis's later testimony, he had already been advised by Allingham about the problems encountered in the helicopter.) As Wingo stood below, the director asked the pilot what he thought of the eleven-thirty scene. Wingo answered by saying the next shot would be fine—as long as the explosions didn't come close to the helicopter again.

"You ain't seen nothing yet!" Landis yelled at him in his cheeky, joking manner.

"How would you like a fireball under you?" Wingo said back jestingly.

"Don't be squeamish, now," Landis replied.

Then, more seriously, Wingo said that he must be given advance warning of exactly what is to occur.

Katherine Wooten, the script supervisor whose job it was to ensure that the action on film matched the chronology of previous events, asked Landis why rocket explosions were being set off on the ground when only machine guns were being fired from the helicopter.

"Don't worry, it works. It will work for the logic of the movie," he said.

If Morrow was deeply concerned by what was going on around him on the set, he apparently did not take decisive action to change the course of events. After the eleven-thirty shot he joked to the movie's still photographer Morgan Renard, "What else can they do but kill me?" Virginia Kearns, the hair stylist, would later tell investigators that Morrow did wonder about the physical and mental conditions of Wingo and Landis, and said to her, in an apparent reference to his suspicions about drug use by the director: "Look at the son of a bitch, look at his pupils." Morrow, however, did not elaborate, nor did he take any further action.

In a concession that took into account only the cliffside mortars—and not the additional mortars placed farther out along the shoreline for the two-thirty shot—Wingo told Landis and others that he would move the helicopter twelve feet away from the cliff for the next shot. He calculated that that would give him a safe margin to avoid the cliffside fireballs from again being sucked back down through the rotor system.

Wingo knew that more explosions were being added along the shoreline, but he later would testify that he had assumed that they would not be detonated while the helicopter was near them.

James Camomile again operated the firing board. As was routine for special-effects men, he was under the assumption that the bombs were to be detonated so that the fireballs came as close to the helicopter as safely possible. From past experience and his perspective of the eleven-thirty shot, Camomile presumed that he could safely send a fireball soaring a few feet to the side of the aircraft.

No one had told James Camomile that the aircraft's occupants had been angered—or endangered—by the explosions at eleven-thirty.

Camomile's primary cue for detonating the mortars was when Morrow, carrying the children in his arms, passed a stick imbedded in the river mud about fifty feet from the village.

Neither had other special-effects technicians been told about the eleven-thirty problems. Harry Stewart, who was assigned to fire two large mortars at the dam, later said about the eleven-thirty filming: "I thought people were just tickled to death with it. It was a good shot and it went off very clean."

The special-effects crew had been isolated in the village during the meal break as they prepared their equipment and had not heard the complaints of the helicopter's occupants.

Jerry Williams, the fourth special-effects crew member, had overheard part of a conversation among Allingham, Landis, and Wingo, but it did not indicate to him that there had been trouble with the bombs. Williams had heard Allingham say that something would have to be done "if it got any heavier," but the special-effects crewman didn't know to what Allingham referred. Williams later testified: "As far as I was concerned, if there had been a problem they would have stated so at that time. And they were talking as though it had been a neat ride at Disneyland."

Sometime after the meal break, Landis asked Stewart to destroy the sampan with a bomb during the two-thirty scene. Stewart said he couldn't, because of the danger of debris, and he told the director that he could provide the same visual effect, without the danger of debris, by merely placing a mortar nearby in an open area. The special-effects foreman had already told Landis previously that he would not put bombs inside the huts along the cliff's base because of the danger that the roofs would be shot into the air.

No one heard Landis, at any time, disagree with Stewart's assessment of the danger of debris.

Several people did, however, overhear a discussion between Landis and Stewart about the placement of an additional mortar in a hut along the shoreline prior to the 2:20 A.M. filming. Several people understood the conversation to be in reference to the food-drying shack with the raised bamboo platform floor.

Camomile said that he heard Landis tell Stewart that he wanted to "see something happen in the shack." When Jerry Williams returned from lunch, he saw Landis and Stewart talking but could not hear what they were saying. Yet, within a few minutes of the conversation between the director and the special-effects foreman, and as Landis stood nearby, Stewart directed Williams to place an eighteen-inch square mortar under the shack. Then Stewart directed Camomile to arm it with a six-ounce black powder bomb and the gasoline-sawdust mixture. (It was customary for the man who would detonate the bombs to arm the mortars as well.)

The structure straddled the river shore, and Williams had to struggle to place the mortar in the mud. After Camomile had finished arming that mortar, he placed and armed a cylindrical mortar just west of the drying shack and south of the sampan. The mortar under the shack would be the fourth in his succession of detonations during the next shot, and the round mortar the fifth. The first three would be near huts at the base of the cliff.

Set designer Richard Sawyer was in the village to supervise the re-arrangement of foliage that the rotor wash had knocked over during the eleven-thirty shot.

Earlier, he and Stewart had discussed that bombs placed under any of the structures could dangerously propel debris into the air—the same warning Stewart had given to Landis previously. When Sawyer saw the recently installed square mortar, he said to Stewart: "I thought we talked about not having anything underneath any of the huts?"

"Everything's okay with it. I've directed the mortar toward the cliff, and this is an open [no walls] hut," Stewart said.

Sawyer, satisfied with Stewart's explanation, went about his work.

To achieve the film effect of destruction while allowing the structure to remain intact, the huts were painted with a highly volatile fire fuel, similar to rubber cement. The flame of mortars near the huts ignited the fuel, which erupted as if an explosion had occurred inside the structure. Thus far, none of the huts had actually been demolished from explosions inside the structures. That made the placement of a bomb under the food-drying shack even more unusual.

Stewart later told me that even though the square mortar had been placed directly under the food-drying shack, he assumed that because it was a slant-walled mortar, canted toward the cliff, the only effect would be to ignite the fire fuel. He did not expect that the explosion would be strong enough to break off pieces of bamboo from the hut and then hurtle them into the helicopter's rotors.

Curiously, though, when Wingo walked through the village sometime after 1:30 A.M., Stewart did not reveal that a mortar had already been placed under the shack but only said that it was being considered: "They're thinking about setting off something in one of these huts."

The pilot reacted angrily, reminding Stewart that the issue had been discussed before. Wingo insisted that no fireball or debris could occupy the same airspace as his helicopter. To illustrate his point, he grabbed a piece of muslin hanging on one of the shacks and warned that even such a small strip of cloth, if it were blown into the air, was enough to interfere dangerously with the rotor system. Then he stuffed the muslin into his pocket and walked away. Still, Stewart did not move the mortar.

Wingo also had to caution Morrow about the danger of debris. The actor, carrying a piece of bamboo more than a foot long, approached the pilot and said he thought it would add flavor to his character if he threw the object in frustration up at the helicopter when it was hovering over-head at the beginning of the scene. Wingo replied, "Well, Vic, you know if you were to hit the rotor system of this aircraft it could work its way into the tail rotor, or if you hit the tail rotor it could bring the helicopter right down on your head."

"Well, what if I miss the helicopter?" Morrow asked. Wingo, attempt-ing diplomacy, suggested the risk was too great and wondered whether a lighter piece of material, such as balsa wood, could be substituted for the thick, heavy bamboo. The discussion ended, Wingo later said, when Landis interjected, "Fuck it! Fuck it! Forget it. We won't do it."

Wingo, as he returned to his helicopter, was under the mistaken as-sumption that Paul Stewart would be operating the firing board. The pilot had not talked to James Camomile—and Stewart did not relate to Camomile the conversation he had had with Wingo about the danger of debris.

When cameraman Roger Smith returned to the helicopter for a 2:00 A.M. rehearsal flight, he asked Allingham what corrections had been discussed during the meal break to ensure that the helicopter would not endure a repeat of the eleven-thirty buffeting.

Allingham told him not to worry, because the plan now called for the helicopter to be well away from the village when the shoreline explosions went off. Smith was told that the helicopter would head across the river and hover as a camera platform above the opposite shore so that Smith could film the village "being blown up." Allingham told Smith that he had discussed that plan with Landis.

Smith accepted the report, later recalling, "I've known Dan a long time, worked with him, and I knew he wouldn't jeopardize himself any more than I would."

To lighten the helicopter's load, Wingo asked the stuntmen to remove some boxes that contained blank ammunition for the machine guns.

At about 1:30 A.M. My-Ca and Renee were picked up at the trailer and taken to the makeup area one more time.

Landis and others repeatedly walked the path Morrow would follow across the river as the helicopter chased him and the children. The director instructed Morgan Renard, whose photographs would be used in publicity for the movie, to be sure to get in his shots the combination of the helicopter, the explosions, the village, and the actors.

"This is it, let's get it," Renard remembered Landis telling him.

At about 2:00 A.M. Wingo flew upriver, east toward the village, for a rehearsal flight in which Landis would tell him where he wanted the helicopter to be positioned for the final shot.

As he approached, the pilot could hear Landis, both on his bullhorn and over the radio.

"Do you see me? If you see me, hit me with the light."

Allingham complied and shined the spotlight on the director. When they were finished, Wingo had been positioned about thirty-five feet above the sampan, approximately twelve feet farther out over the river than he had been during the eleven-thirty shot. Wingo returned to the landing site without practicing any hovering stops above the opposite shore.

Landis was ready to begin filming shortly after the rehearsal, but when Jack Tice saw that the director was about to start, he asked Landis to wait. George Hull, Tice explained, had not yet returned from the catering area to his position on the cliff.

"When the fuck can we start?" Landis yelled at Tice, who was already accustomed to hearing the director scream at others. In just a few minutes, Hull radioed Tice that he had returned to his fire watch on the mesa. Then Tice informed Landis that all of the fire safety officers were now in place.

"Thank you very much," Landis said to Tice with condescending politeness.

Tice's position for the shot was about one hundred yards west of the village. As he walked past the huts, he could see Morrow standing on the shore, but he did not see any children.

"It's probably just going to get warm," Tice heard Landis say to Morrow in reference to the upcoming special-effects explosions that would be detonated less than a few dozen yards behind the actor as he carried the children across the river, fulfilling Landis's vision of a spectacular, climactic rescue scene.

FOUR

AT ABOUT 2:15 A.M., Landis turned to more than one hundred crew members and guests, raised a white, battery-powered bullhorn, and instructed everyone to stand. Cynthia Nigh, relaxing against a pile of boards, heard him say, "Be ready to move in case anything goes wrong."

Some crew members were already taking precautions. Jerry Williams, whose firing board was connected to six mortars at the rear of the village and in the water, covered himself with a furniture pad for protection against heat, wind, and debris that might break his concentration during the scene. Katherine Wooten, the script supervisor, had pulled a knitted cap over her ears and put on a pair of safety goggles.

At the helicopter landing site, the six men who would be flying were seated inside the aircraft and waiting for the order to take off. Assistant cameraman Randy Robinson, still upset about the eleven-thirty experience, asked if anything had been done to ensure that he and the other aircraft occupants would not encounter similar problems.

Robinson did not receive a response. He later testified: "The longer I thought about it, the more concerned I was that I never had an answer. I said [to Allingham], 'Don't you think we ought to get on the horn and say something about the intensity of those blasts?' "

Even though Allingham did not answer, Robinson was hesitant to force the issue, because he feared that he would be perceived as a coward: "Then I spoke to Dorcey and I said, 'Don't you have any qualms about flying through blasts like this?' And he turned around to me and he said, 'No, I'm more worried about the kids running underneath us.' "

Robinson had not known that children would be in the scene. "I had seen one of the kids and patted one of them," he said later, "but it never really dawned on me what the situation was."

After a few minutes, Allingham turned to Robinson and the others and repeated what he had already told Roger Smith: "Don't worry about the blasts, because we are not going to be there when they go off."

That explanation satisfied Robinson, who thought that, finally, someone in authority was dealing with the issue.

My-Ca and Renee were brought to the village by Hilary Leach, who left the children with Morrow and Landis, then walked upstream along the south shore of the river.

During the shot, Landis would stand on a peninsula that jutted into the middle of the river just east of the village. One of the six cameras, directly in front of which Morrow would pass as he crossed the river, was also on the peninsula. The second camera was a bit farther south, toward the village. The third was on the mesa aimed downward over the edge of the cliff. The fourth was across the river and about twenty-five feet in the air on a camera crane (Morrow's path would take him straight toward the crane, with the village behind him). The fifth was on a tripod in the river at the base of the crane. The sixth camera was in the helicopter.

After finishing his last-minute instructions to Morrow and the children, Landis, bullhorn in hand, splashed through the ankle-deep water fifty feet to the peninsula.

The night was clear, with only high-scattered clouds. The air was calm and the temperature a comfortable seventy-five degrees. Wingo flew upriver, approaching his position above the sampan at the edge of the village. Morrow stood at the river's edge, holding the children under his arms in about the same position as when he completed the nine-thirty shot. He jostled each child a bit, apparently to move his arms for a more secure grip. The combined weight of the children was close to one hundred pounds. Morrow would have to carry them much farther than he had at nine-thirty, when he had to move only about fifteen feet over solid ground. Now he would have to travel about one hundred feet through knee-high water to the opposite shore of the dam-widened Santa Clarita River.

The camera operators and sound crew received their mark—the sharp crack of the striped-board clapper denoting that filming for scene thirty-one was beginning.

When Wingo stopped and hovered the helicopter about thirty-five feet above the ground, Jack Tice, from his vantage point one hundred yards to the east, thought that the aircraft was closer to the cliff than the position that had been established at the rehearsal twenty minutes earlier.

"Lower! Lower! Lower!" Landis yelled, and Cohn, standing next to him, transmitted the order to the helicopter via the VHF radio transmitter.

This direction from Landis to descend was unexpected by Wingo, who thought that the helicopter's height had been firmly established at thirty-five feet during the rehearsal flight.

Without questioning the instruction, though, the pilot methodically lowered the aircraft until the skids were twenty-four feet above the ground. The helicopter's nose pointed at Morrow and the children, who were below and just a few feet beyond the area under the helicopter's swirling rotor blades.

Landis waved his megaphone over his head, the prearranged signal for Morrow, standing about fifty feet away, to begin crossing the river.

The helicopter had been hovering only briefly when Dan Allingham instructed Roger Smith to take his position on the skid. Wingo, sensitive to changes within his aircraft, could feel the movement of Smith's body and a thump when the cameraman's foot landed on the skid. Smith was on the left side of the helicopter, away from the cliff, and could not see the village, which was off to the lower right of the aircraft. He was surprised to see that Morrow was already several feet past the river's shore when he looked through his camera's viewfinder. He had expected more time to establish his framing.

With the scene under way, Landis yelled, "Fire! Fire! Fire!," the cue for the helicopter machine guns to begin their bursts, and the cue for Camomile and Jerry Williams to begin firing the mortars against the cliff.

Camera assistant Randy Robinson in the helicopter, who could hear the cue on his radio headset, tapped stuntmen Gary McLarty and Kenneth Endoso, their cue to begin firing the machine guns.

Before the shot, James Camomile had put on a heavy, metal welder's hood with a clear, plastic eyepiece, because the wind and dust from the rotor wash had bothered him in earlier shots.

Paul Stewart, whose job it was to radio Harry Stewart (no relation) at the dam when it was time to fire his mortars, stood a foot behind Camomile. They were about thirty-five feet west of the village, their view of Morrow and the village enhanced by their position up on a sandy berm. Camomile was resting on his haunches with the firing board in his lap.

Camomile, waiting for the machine-gun cue, glanced up at the helicopter off to his left and saw the muzzle flash from the weapon being fired by Endoso. McLarty's gun had jammed and would not fire.

The helicopter, Camomile believed, was exactly where it was supposed to be. He did not expect that the aircraft would move until all of the mortars were fired.

After seeing the gunfire, Camomile then turned his attention groundward, to his firing board and to Morrow and the children, who were moving across the river to his left. He was readying to fire his six mortars —at the planned beat of about one second apart.

At first Morrow moved at a fairly quick pace, the water at ankle depth. The helicopter was above and behind him to the left, and because of the low altitude, its rotor wash was more powerful than ever. The water splashed up by his feet was swept away in a fine spray by the strong wind. The noise of the helicopter's engines was loud, and the rotor wash created its own storm of wind, dust, and water spray.

Just when Morrow passed the bow of the sampan, Camomile fired the first of three mortars located at the base of the cliff. The brilliant explosions illuminated the valley floor of Indian Dunes. Morrow kept moving, the water now at about knee level. He must have felt the heat from gasoline fireballs behind him. Hilary Leach, who had moved only seventy feet away from the village, felt the fireballs' warmth on her back through her jacket.

Squibs exploded in the water near Morrow. Machine-gun fire was also being simulated by another method during this shot. Mike Bedrow, a water truck driver, who had previously worked with special effects, had been enlisted to fire an air-powered marble gun from the peninsula, aiming to hit the water near Morrow and the children.

The first three mortars had been fired on schedule—about one second apart. The third rushed up the cliff directly at the camera operated by Michael Scott, who was thrust backward by its concussive force. Because he had been afraid the cliff edge might give way, Scott had tied two ropes around his waist and secured the other ends to trees farther back on the mesa. As the fireball soared past him, he scrambled up the hill, away from the cliff, leaving his camera to tilt upward on its tripod, filming only burning embers floating against a black sky.

Dorcey Wingo could feel the concussion of the first three explosions, for which he had been prepared, and he continued to hold the helicopter in a steady hover. Allingham's job was to keep the spotlight on Morrow as the actor moved across the river.

"Turn, turn," Allingham directed. Wingo looked to his right and saw that the third fireball, which he believed was the last to be fired for the time being, had already risen above the cliff. He began to execute a simple left turn, the helicopter rotating on its axis.

Paul Stewart could see Morrow pass the stick that had been imbedded in the river's mud, and that meant that the actors were in range of the peninsula camera aimed downriver. Stewart turned away from the three people in the river, looked west toward the dam, and over the radio yelled, "Harry! Fire!"

Harry Stewart detonated two mortars in succession, each containing twenty-four ounces of black powder and ten gallons of gasoline. A wall of flame rose above the dam, forming a radiant backdrop to Morrow and the children from the perspective of the peninsula camera.

The children appeared to become more difficult for Morrow to manage; their feet were now being dragged in the river. The rotor wash sent across the river's surface a continuous stream of waves that struck Morrow on the back of his legs.

Three seconds had passed since Camomile had fired his third mortar, and he touched the nail in his hand to the fourth brass plate on his firing board, exploding the bomb underneath the food-drying shack. One-tenth second later he detonated the fifth mortar. The fireball from the fourth rose as it should, but as the gasoline burst from the fifth mortar, it remained unignited for a fraction of a second, although a volatile cloud of gasoline mist and vapors continued upward.

By now, the tail of the helicopter was over land, the helicopter's nose facing away from the cliff. The gasoline from the fifth mortar combined with the fire of the fourth and burst as one explosion in the air well above the ground, instantly engulfing the helicopter's tail.

Onlookers could see thick, black smoke being sucked back down through the helicopter's rotor system, and the aircraft became wobbly.

During the explosions, the Indian Dunes set became an inferno, the fireballs sending off flashes of red, yellow, and white flame. Wind from the explosions and the rotor wash forcefully scattered dirt and embers all around. John Landis stood on the peninsula, his feet implanted slightly apart for balance, his body bent forward, seemingly to protect himself.

The parents watched in growing terror at the sight before them. Daniel Le felt the pressure of the wind throwing dirt and moisture all over his body.

Something terribly wrong was happening to the tail rotor, which was engulfed by the combined fireballs. The damage occurred in fractions of seconds, as the blades churned at the powerful rate of 1,655 revolutions a minute, or more than 27 revolutions a second.

Just as the tail emerged from the flames, cameraman Roger Smith, exposed to the dangerous forces as he stood on the skid, could feel the concussion of the explosions, the heat of the flames, and the aircraft vibrating. When he felt the helicopter begin to spin out of control, he jumped back inside. Randy Robinson thought it was "like flying through hell."

Wingo heard a clinking sound from the rear of the aircraft. He assumed a fragment of debris had blown into the rotor system because he had lost antitorque control, the ability to use the tail rotor to keep the helicopter from spinning wildly on its axis. Under normal conditions the pilot controls the tail rotor blade with a foot pedal, but as Wingo moved the pedal the aircraft did not respond properly and the entire fuselage began a clockwise spin.

The aircraft's occupants began to scream as Wingo tried to control the aircraft's flight.

"Get out of here! It's too much!" Allingham yelled.

"We finally bought it! We're going in!" McLarty said.

Endoso heard someone yell, "Oh, shit!" and then he, too, yelled, "We're going in!"

Steve Lydecker, operating the camera on the crane, was focused on Morrow and could tell something was wrong only because the spotlight's beam began to move wildly over the water's surface. He moved his head away from the camera eyepiece and saw the helicopter spinning as pieces of metal flew off. In its uncontrolled flight the tail passed twelve feet above his head during one spin.

Fire safety officer Jack Rimmer could only see a firestorm obliterating his view of the aircraft.

George Hull, who had been watching from above at the edge of the cliff, had turned away after the third explosion to begin extinguishing fires on the mesa. (There were fifteen grass fires and two trees ablaze.) Hull had lost sight of the helicopter in all the smoke and flame. When he heard the engine noise change he knew that everyone down below was in jeopardy.

The helicopter spun in the air above the river, descending like an autumn leaf floating to the ground.

When special-effects crewman Jerry Williams on the peninsula watched the tail pass eighteen feet over his head, he ripped his firing board wires from the battery and ran.

Not everyone realized what was happening. Cameraman John Connor, on the peninsula, was focused on a close-up shot of Morrow and the children and had no notion of what was happening to the helicopter above him. His assistant, Lee Redmond, did, though. Redmond screamed at Connor and then grabbed him as they both ran off, leaving the camera running, still filming Morrow just a few feet away.

George Folsey, standing farther back on the peninsula with Daniel Le and Shyan Chen, was amazed when he saw the fireball engulf the helicopter's tail. After he saw pieces of metal flying from the tail of the aircraft he spun on his heels, grabbed each of the parents by an arm and dragged them along as he ran toward a clump of bushes. He pushed them on the ground in front of him, then fell on top of the two in an act of protection.

Le was horrified as people ran for their lives, pushing and yelling. Shyan Chen was struck with the fear of her daughter being in danger and screamed out for Renee.

Wingo saw alternating fireballs and blackness as the helicopter spun out of his control. As the seconds passed, he tried a variety of maneuvers to see if some combination of hand controls and foot pedal movements would help. He couldn't figure out what was wrong. He could see that the nose of the helicopter was dangerously low, but he could do nothing to level the aircraft.

From his spot on the berm, Camomile heard the strange noises of the helicopter and stood up just in time to see it dropping.

Morrow was struggling in hip-deep water when, in a horrendous-looking movement, he stumbled. His body dropped forward and sank into the water to chest level, but he continued to hold the children tightly. Renee was dunked to her neck, and as Morrow struggled to stand upright, a spray of water flew off her arm when she moved quickly to grab onto Morrow's shoulder.

For an instant, Renee appeared to slip from Morrow's grasp. He tightened his grip and pressed her more closely to his chest, continuing to keep a tight hold on My-Ca.

Kevin Quibell was surprised at seeing Morrow stumble and stopped firing squibs, to avoid exploding any close to the actor.

Then the helicopter hit the ground almost upright, landing between Morrow in the river and Landis on the peninsula, its nose facing the camera crane, its tail to the village.

Upon striking the ground, the helicopter turned on its left side in an easy, almost gentle motion.

The still-spinning main rotor blades, though, were filled with an immense power yet to be unleashed. They cut through the water with a great splash, sending up a massive spray of water that hid from everyone's view the terrible moment when one blade transformed into a killing scythe and decapitated Vic Morrow and My-Ca Le. At the same time, Renee Chen was crushed by some portion of the aircraft which now bore the full weight of the fuselage.

From the time Camomile detonated the first mortar to this result, less than ten seconds had elapsed.

When Paul Stewart turned his gaze back from the dam, he heard Camomile yell, "My God, the helicopter crashed!"

John Landis was stunned. He had been concentrating on Morrow's movements and was not watching the helicopter. For a few seconds, the director could not understand what had happened just feet in front of him. "What the fuck is this helicopter doing in my shot?" he said. In an instant, though, he perceived the horror.

He ran in desperation around the helicopter, to where he had last seen Morrow and the children.

David Lawson, the movie company medic, ran into the water and yelled for someone to telephone for an ambulance.

Folsey held Shyan Chen, who was trying to run toward the helicopter, now at the place where she had last seen her daughter.

As dozens of people scrambled to help the survivors, the aircraft emitted a high-pitched whine, which provided a terrible background noise to the chaos on the set.

Wingo, strapped to his seat and hanging sideways in the air, was panicked. He heard people outside yelling for him to get out. He made motions at switches in front of him, trying to shut off the engine. He undid his seat belt and slipped, landing on Allingham. As he stretched his hands through an opening in the windshield, which was now above him, he could feel someone grab and pull. He and the others were helped out one by one.

Wingo was dazed when he walked to the riverbank and encountered Steve Lydecker.

"What the hell happened?" the pilot asked.

"Don't worry, Dorcey, I've got everything on film," the cameraman said.

Wingo looked down on the ground and saw the tail rotor gearbox lying completely separated from the aircraft.

Randy Robinson was trapped under a machine gun that had tipped over on him. One of the ground crew members reached in to help free him. Then Robinson was handed a knife so he could cut Roger Smith loose from his harness in which he had become entangled.

No one inside the helicopter had suffered more than cuts and bruises.

Paul Stewart was making his way to the aircraft when he stumbled on something just below the surface of the river. To his horror, he saw the lifeless torso of Vic Morrow. Stewart had never before seen a dead body. He bent over and held on to it, to prevent the remains from floating away while others ran to help.

Someone yelled to Lawson, "You better come here. It's Vic."

"There's nothing I can do," he said at the sight of the body.

Jack Tice was the first person to see Renee's body. Someone attempted mouth-to-mouth resuscitation, but Lawson knew the efforts were hopeless and told everyone so.

Across the river, the village huts burned, sending up pillars of black smoke.

Jack Rimmer helped Stewart drag Morrow's body to the peninsula, where they covered it with a blanket. In an act of decency, Rimmer and Tice in their shock hid the two severed heads in a plastic wrap.

Seconds after the crash, Richard Vane had run to his car, speeding along the bumpy dirt road to Highway 126 to call for help from the nearest phone, almost two miles from the set. When he got there, he found that a studio driver had already made the call, which soon brought ambulances and sheriff's cars to Indian Dunes.

Near the helicopter, Wingo saw people picking up papers and manuals that had fallen out of the helicopter and were floating in the water.

Having regained his composure, Wingo asked with concern, "Where's Vic?"

His fuel truck driver, Craig Wooten, looked at the pilot sadly.

"Dorcey, the main rotor got Vic and the kids."

Wingo became faint and slumped into a nearby chair.

In the clear, night air, when the frantic commotion had turned to quiet shock for everyone, one sound continued to travel a great distance. Up on the mesa, fire safety officer Willard Major shivered with fright at what he heard rising from the valley floor near the now-silent helicopter: It was the uncontrollable wailing of Shyan Chen, in utter grief at what she had just witnessed.

FIVE

WHEN THE telephone rang in the sheriff's homicide squad room just before 3:00 A.M., Tom Budds was stretched out on a thin mattress he had laid out over two desks, after pushing in-baskets and other office items aside. He had thought he was about to get a well-deserved rest.

A deputy at the Santa Clarita Valley substation told Budds only that three actors had been killed in a helicopter crash during the filming of a movie at Indian Dunes.

Even though Budds didn't yet know whether the dead had been famous or not, he was aware—just because the case involved Hollywood—that whatever had happened would attract a great deal of publicity. And that, Budds understood, put extra pressure on him to make no mistakes of judgment or procedure. He was sensitive to the bad press the Los Angeles Police Department was receiving because of its much-criticized investigations into two celebrity deaths, one of which was decades old but still controversial.

The more recent death had occurred just four months before, on March 5. John Belushi had been found in his cottage at the Château Marmont on Sunset Boulevard, dead of an injected drug overdose. (That Budds thought about the Belushi death on his way to Indian Dunes was coincidence. He had not yet learned that the deaths he would investigate had happened on a movie set supervised by Belushi's friend John Landis.) A lackluster LAPD investigation looked even more inefficient with the recent announcement that a Los Angeles County grand jury would investigate the published claims of a Canadian woman—who had previously been questioned and released by the LAPD—that she had administered the fatal injection of a cocaine and heroin mixture to the comic actor at Belushi's request, neither of them aware that it would kill him.

Another lingering controversy in the news again was the LAPD's 1962 investigation into the death of Marilyn Monroe. The city police continued to refuse to release classified documents concerning the apparent suicide and were accused by various parties of a cover-up.

All of this controversy ran through Budds's thoughts as he called his lieutenant and suggested that 4 detectives be sent to the scene to begin the interviews of the 6 injured and the estimated 150 witnesses.

"Handle it like an industrial accident," the lieutenant said, which meant that Budds would be the only detective to go to Indian Dunes that morning.

Before leaving the office at the county's Hall of Justice in downtown Los Angeles, Budds directed that a bomb expert, a crime scene photographer and a graphics artist also be dispatched.

As he made the forty-five-minute drive along the Hollywood Freeway north to the Golden State Freeway, Budds determined that he would follow a precise crime scene procedure until he was absolutely sure that the tragedy was just an unprosecutable industrial accident. He didn't know yet that two of the victims were children who had been working illegally.

Budds is a good investigator, named one of the top ten detectives in 1979 by the International Association of Chiefs of Police for crushing a Mafia-connected home repair fraud. He was a star high school runner and basketball player. Afterward he went to junior college. While working as a policeman, he completed a masters program in management at the University of Southern California.

He comes from a hardworking family of Polish ethnicity. His older brother is also a policeman. Budds has a gentle, friendly manner, devoid of the cynical edge found in many of his law-enforcement colleagues. His agreeable laugh hides an investigative tenacity and strong sense of justice.

While the detective was still on the highway, word of the crash was already spreading in a ripple effect of shock.

Donna Schuman was awakened by the telephone at about 3:30 A.M.

"Donna, this is Folsey. There has been an accident. Actually, the worst possible thing has happened: Vic and the kids have been killed."

Schuman listened in stunned silence as Folsey continued his narration.

"A helicopter fell on them."

"What were they doing underneath a helicopter?" she was finally able to ask.

Folsey said that for inexplicable reasons the helicopter pilot had lost control and the aircraft careened through the air before crashing. He asked his longtime family friend if she would accompany him as he took Daniel Le home. My-Ca's father, so distraught that his body was trembling with grief, still had the burden of telling his wife about what had happened to their son. Schuman was not up to complying with the request, so Folsey went alone.

Le couldn't muster the courage to go into the house and tell his wife about their son's death. So he and Folsey first stopped at the home of a Le family friend, a social worker, until Le had regained the emotional strength to break the news to his wife.

At Indian Dunes, a dejected Paul Stewart walked past Hilary Leach. "I'm going to get drunk," he told her. And he did, starting with vodka from the special-effects truck and continuing with his own liquor at home. The next day, he left with Jerry Williams for two days of mind-numbing drinking and fishing on Williams's boat off the central California coast, near the Channel Islands.

It was dark when Budds arrived at Indian Dunes at 4:00 A.M., and he was surprised that there were so few people there—he counted about a dozen—because he had been told there had been 150 witnesses to the crash.

His first action was to speak to uniformed deputies Robert Sinclair and William Strait, who had been the first law-enforcement personnel to arrive. The detective wanted to ensure that the area was secure from tampering. As far as he was concerned, the area was technically a crime scene. When Budds found Jerry Williams walking through the now-charred village, he ordered the special-effects technician out until the sheriff's arson investigators had made their study.

Budds received a curious, if small, demonstration of the special effects that had been employed when one of the blank cartridges in a machine gun belt lying in the dirt on the peninsula detonated spontaneously.

Confident that the set was secure and ready for inspection by the other investigators on the way, Budds began his own survey of the area.

First, he crossed the Santa Clarita River into the village and noted that two huge, fresh, black scorch marks, one rising sixty feet and the other eighty feet, marred the face of the cliff.

There was debris scattered throughout the village, including five-gallon cans of fire fuel, burned leather and rubber boots, and blackened palm fronds and bamboo poles. Budds knew little about special effects, but he noted that the mortars were variously round and square, and he particularly noted that under the food-drying shack, which had no roof and was tilting eastward, there was a square mortar.

Returning across the river, Budds tripped in an indentation on the sandy bottom—in just the spot, he would later learn, where Morrow had stumbled. Later that day a police graphics artist would tell Budds that he, too, noticed a dip in the riverbed at that location.

In the quiet, Budds circled the crashed helicopter, which was six thousand pounds of inert metal lying on its left side with its nose facing north. The fuselage just crossed the tip of the peninsula. A few feet from the helicopter, Budds found a white megaphone lying on the ground, and a radio headset next to it.

A few feet farther east were several director's chairs; the one bearing the name of Vic Morrow was lying on its back, apparently knocked over by a rotor blade fragment Budds found in the dirt at the base of the chair.

Morrow's torso was nearby, the clothing still wet. About seventy feet north of the peninsula, under a canopy of trees, were the bodies of the two children, covered with blankets. In his small notebook, Budds methodically wrote that the two decapitated heads had been placed in a plastic bag.

After inspecting the corpses, Budds ordered that the dam be knocked down to drain the area of water and allow a deputy coroner to locate missing body parts in the mud near the helicopter.

At the same time, Budds found several still-cold cans of Budweiser beer, some open and partially filled, and several empty vodka bottles. He later learned that they were from the area reserved for guests.

By 6:00 A.M. the Indian Dunes location was under scrutiny by investigators from a number of agencies: Abdon ("Don") Llorente of the National Transportation Safety Board, J. E. Knoebber of the Federal Aviation Administration, and Leonard Kamp and Charles Hughes of California Labor Standards Enforcement.

At about this time, two deputy coroners removed the bodies for autopsies, which would be performed on Saturday.

Of the investigators at Indian Dunes Friday morning, Llorente and Budds would prove to be the two most important to the *Twilight Zone* case. They decided that Llorente would take custody of aircraft evidence. Eventually, the interviews and other investigative material collected by the NTSB would be shared with Budds.

As dawn arrived, Budds was growing anxious about the lack of witnesses available for him to question.

He was satisfied that the set was being surveyed properly; police photographers and graphics artists would work for several more hours. But now the detective wanted some witnesses to the crash. He needed those firsthand accounts to determine how he would proceed in the matter.

"I want to find out what the hell happened here," he said to one of the uniformed deputies. "You have people laying around here dead all over the place, and I don't know what caused it. I'd like to talk to somebody."

Budds's method of investigation was to compare the statements of witnesses with what he observed himself, and look for inconsistencies between the physical evidence and the witnesses' statements. He knew that even in occurrences that are labeled industrial accidents—as this incident was initially being classified—there was still usually some recklessness involved. His job was to determine if any recklessness rose to the level of criminal behavior. Sometimes the investigators were lucky and someone came forward to demonstrate that blatant warnings of danger had gone unheeded.

Such testimony would not be so easily obtained in this case.

Budds was told that many of the witnesses, including the survivors in the helicopter, had gone to the Henry Mayo Newhall Hospital in Valencia. In fact, one of those who had provided ad hoc ambulance service was Spielberg executive producer Frank Marshall, a man for whom Budds would eventually develop an abiding disdain.

For the survivors, it was soon evident that the physical injuries were of little consequence, but the emotional wounds were deep and, no doubt, would linger painfully forever in some of those who witnessed the tragedy.

Elie Cohn and production assistant Barry Pener saw the effect on Shyan Chen, whom they drove to the hospital. In her frenzy of sorrow, she pounded on their chests, crying, "You murdered my baby!"

John Landis was seen slumped over in a chair, his head buried in his hands, looking pitifully disconsolate. The sincerity and depth of his remorse, however, would be questioned by others later.

When Budds learned that Dorcey Wingo had sustained only minor injuries, he asked the pilot to return to the set for questioning. Wingo arrived shortly after daybreak, wearing a neck brace but in a cooperative mood.

The set looked much grimmer in daylight than it had under the cover of night following the crash. The burned frames of the huts gave the village a truly shoddy appearance. The helicopter was a hulking, listless carcass of green metal. The bright red and orange hues of the fireballs had given way to the only color of the day: long strips of shiny yellow police tape marking the area.

The investigators now knew that the children had been working illegally. Ironically, Jack Tice was the first official to happen upon that information. When the uniformed sheriff's deputies first arrived they were gathering basic information from production crew members about the two dead children.

"How do you know their names?" Tice had asked, as he heard that and other detailed information about My-Ca and Renee being readily offered by crew members.

At about 9:00 A.M., Wingo was formally interviewed by Llorente and Budds. The pilot's responses—seemingly honest, Budds thought—gave the detective his first inclination that undue carelessness may have played a role in the crash. Unfortunately for Wingo, Budds also concluded that at least some of the responsibility for any recklessness was borne by the pilot.

Budds and Llorente first learned from Wingo about Landis's last-minute "Lower! Lower! Lower!" order. As Wingo talked, Budds wondered about the pilot's standard of professional care. "I knew there was gonna be explosions," Wingo said, but added, "of course, I knew nothing about the location of the explosions other than what had happened previously."

Budds thought it should have been elementary for the pilot to determine before the flight exactly where all of the explosions were to take place.

The investigators confirmed that Wingo had recognized before the crash that potential danger existed and had talked to others in responsibility on the set about his worries.

"All the blasts were close—uh, close enough to concern me that it was a risky thing to film," the pilot said. "I told Paul Stewart I was concerned about debris."

When Wingo described the final scene to the investigators, he did so succinctly, and in a manner far more incriminating than he realized at the time: "It was only said we're going to blow the village, and indeed they did. And right out from under me."

After just a few hours, Budds was convinced that, at the very least, he possessed the foundation of a child-endangerment case. Nothing dissuaded him from that belief as the investigation wore on.

In the morning, Alpha Campbell, the secretary at the Landis production office, was the only one to come to the Universal Studios office. She began a list of the many phone calls that were coming in from reporters, investigators, lawyers, and friends.

George Folsey called and instructed Campbell to pack up all the *Twilight Zone* documents in preparation for a messenger who would deliver them to lawyer Joel Behr's office. That afternoon Folsey and Behr went to Landis's house where, Folsey told me later, they found the director "inconsolable. He was absolutely distraught."

Little investigative work was done over the weekend. Dr. Joan Shipley, a deputy medical examiner, performed autopsies on the three victims and, for the official record, concluded the obvious about the causes of death. Toxicology tests performed on Morrow's remains—seeking indications of drug or alcohol use—were negative.

On the Sunday following Morrow's death, two hundred people attended the actor's funeral at Hillside Memorial Park, just off the San Diego Freeway near Los Angeles International Airport. The cemetery is a pretty oasis of green in a highly commercialized area. Viewed from the freeway, a large fountain dominates the property. A tall, white-columned memorial, with open sides and a rounded dome, marks the grave of Al Jolson.

George Folsey, who was a friend of Morrow's ex-wife, delivered a eulogy at the request of Morrow's daughters, Carrie Morrow and Jennifer Jason Leigh. Folsey had met Morrow for the first time only two weeks before, when *Twilight Zone* shooting began, but they had become friendly, discussing their common interest in stock market investments each day.

In his eulogy, Folsey commended Morrow's acting skills: "It would have been easy to get someone to play a one-dimensional racist, but to play a bigot whose feelings and motives can be understood and even sympathized with requires a true actor. The part was very demanding, both emotionally and physically. Vic did many of his own stunts and it was only a couple of nights into the shoot that Vic had earned the complete admiration and respect of our crew."

Folsey concluded, "If there is any consolation in this terrible situation, it is that the film is finished. There is nothing more to be shot to make the film work. Thank God, because his performance must not be lost. It represented for him something seldom attained—the culmination of all his idealistic dreams when he was first starting out in acting school in New York. It was Vic's last gift to us."

Of his children, Morrow was closest to Carrie, and had been estranged from Jennifer for several years. The mourners listened to a song written by Carrie called "Time Together":

You were here
I was there
We were happy when we were together
You are here
I am somewhere
We are laughing because
We'll always remember our time together

Dominating the television news coverage of the funeral, though, and embittering some who listened, was a brief but highly charged eulogy by John Landis. Landis looked haggard with hair almost shoulder-length and his beard bushy. He wore a dark sport shirt and tie with a sport coat, which seemed an artistically casual look in contrast to the more formal suits and white shirts of other men there.

In a halting, choking voice, as he tightly gripped the edge of the lectern, Landis read what had been written on a piece of his personal stationery. He seemed to struggle to maintain his focus. He was hunched over, and his long hair fell to cover much of his face from view.

"I met Vic for the first time in my office one month ago. Having always admired his acting, I was delighted to learn that Vic's performances were the result of a keen intelligence and deep emotions. Vic was a professional, and his role as the lead in our story was brilliantly realized. There is no way to express my feelings at this overwhelming time."

Landis's voice cracked and, as he held back tears, he gave his head a quick shake, apologized, and continued: "Just before the last take, Vic took me aside to thank me for this opportunity. He knew how wonderful his performance was and he wanted me to know how happy he was with the work."

The director then appeared to summon a final burst of resolve as he neared the end of his comments. His conclusion was later widely criticized as inappropriately shallow and maudlin:

"Tragedy strikes in an instant, but film is immortal. Perhaps we can take some solace in the knowledge that through his work in stage, television, and film, Vic lives forever."

With his head bowed, Landis walked back to his seat with a lumbering, sorrowful gait and took his place next to his wife, Deborah.

One of those who found Landis's comments disingenuous was Al Green, Morrow's lawyer who had been numb with grief since early Friday morning, when the police called to tell him about the death, less than twenty-four hours after he had tried to convince Morrow to leave the production. He had spent the weekend helping prepare the funeral arrangements, and he was one of the pallbearers. Green later told me that he thought Landis's funeral comments were "as phony as a three-dollar bill."

In deference to the mourning, ABC television canceled an episode of *Fantasy Island* starring Morrow that had been scheduled to air the following Friday night.

The misery of an innocent child's death was painfully obvious in the Le and Chen homes, where relatives told reporters that the parents were in grief-filled shock. At the Chen home, the reporters could hear the wails of the mother of the dead girl from inside the house. Neighbors had placed pots of flowers on the porch—near the little girl's red wagon and tricycle.

John and Deborah Landis, and George and Belinda Folsey attended the children's funerals, both of which were held on Tuesday. Reporters covering the events later wrote that Landis, looking distraught, appeared to be propped up by his wife and an unidentified man, as he slowly walked into one of the churches.

Renee Chen's funeral was in the morning held in the Church of the Recessional at Forest Lawn Memorial Park in Glendale, where her body was later buried in the Everlasting Love section of the sprawling, sculpture-filled cemetery. Some of her classmates from Webster Elementary School in Pasadena attended the service, conducted primarily in Chinese, which was filled with the sobs of mourners.

Afterward, Renee's father, Mark, said to reporters: "She was only child I have—now she is gone."

My-Ca Le was buried in the afternoon at Forest Lawn Memorial Park in Cypress. At his funeral service, the boy's classmates sang "Jesus Loves All the Children of the World" and "Jesus Loves Me" in tribute to the religious little boy who sang in the choir and had played an angel in his church school's Easter pageant a few months before.

Four-year-old Christopher Le carried a picture of his brother, framed in gold, throughout the service and to the burial.

My-Ca's name was a Vietnamese combination of the words for the United States and Canada, a tribute by his parents to the people who had helped the family flee Southeast Asia.

SIX

ON MONDAY, July 26, the day after Morrow's funeral and three days after the crash, four members of the *Twilight Zone* camera crew, including director of photography Steve Larner, held a press conference and offered the first detailed, public eyewitness accounts of the fatal incident. The most startling comments concerned John Landis and his unplanned, last-minute orders at 2:20 A.M. that the helicopter fly lower —viewed by many as ill-advised instructions that may have contributed significantly to the crash.

The camera crew's statements did not draw a portrait of a mere accident, but of a movie set out of control. There were some relatively minor inaccuracies in the recollections. For example, Randy Robinson said the voice on the radio ordering "Lower! Lower! Lower!" had been Landis's, an understandable error on Robinson's part, given the turmoil of the event. Standing on the peninsula at the river's edge and watching the helicopter fly overhead, Landis had yelled the order for the aircraft to lower, but it had been first assistant director Elie Cohn who had then relayed the director's instruction to Wingo and Allingham by radio.

Steve Lydecker raised the issue of inadequate planning and on-set communication. The plan for the 2:20 A.M. scene, as he understood it, was for the helicopter to be clear of the village when the bombs were detonated.

Also made public was the confrontation between Landis and Wingo after the 11:30 P.M. shot, when the director had initially dismissed the pilot's concern with the joke, "You ain't seen nothing yet."

Larner told reporters that he and the others were not assigning blame for the deaths, but only wanted to ensure safety on other movie sets in the future. Nonetheless, the harsh comments of the cameramen provided the confirmation reporters needed to bolster their stories, which, as more details became known, were increasingly and decidedly unfavorable to Landis.

A week after the deaths, the first government actions against the movie-makers were taken: in this instance by the California Department of Industrial Relations, Division of Labor Standards Enforcement. On July 30, John Landis, George Folsey, Jr., Dan Allingham, and Warner Brothers as a corporation were cited for violating state codes and fined civil penalties of $5,000 each. The three men and the studio backing the movie were accused of taking actions injurious to the health of a minor and for having children work after hours.

In early August, Donna Schuman met for lunch with George Folsey, Jr., at Hampton's restaurant in Toluca Lake. She was not pleased with the answers she received to her questions about the fatal night. In time, the deteriorating friendship between the two would play an important role in the prosecution of the *Twilight Zone* case.

"I would like to know why three people are dead," she said challengingly.

"It was an accident," Folsey said.

"I don't understand how you can have that kind of an accident."

"It's just the same as if you have two cars running down the street, and they get in an accident."

"It's not the same at all. That analogy just doesn't work."

"We rehearsed it at least thirty times," Folsey said—quite inaccurately. "Everybody knew exactly what they were doing. There was no question about what was going on. At the time of the accident the helicopter was far away from the children. No one could have predicted it. It was an act of God. No one ever knew."

Folsey was obviously wrong in his assessment because not everyone at Indian Dunes had been in accord before the helicopter was damaged by the fireballs. As I would observe in my later conversations with Folsey, he was a man of gentle spirit who had been greatly disturbed by the deaths—in conversations with his priest in the days following the deaths he had discussed the morality of his involvement in the matter—but also resisted suggestions that the crash was anything but an innocent happenstance of unavoidable fate. He told me, "I feel terrible about the fact that children got killed. I don't feel guilty about the fact that the children got killed. That may sound like a hard thing to say. I don't feel that we did something that caused their deaths."

The distance which was growing between Folsey and his old friend, Donna Schuman, would not serve him well as the case progressed. Tension had begun to develop right after the deaths. On the day of the children's funerals, the Schumans told Folsey that they would like to talk to Landis about what had happened. Folsey initially agreed to set up a meeting. He changed his mind, however, when the Schumans made comments critical of the moviemakers after the funerals. "Donna and I had a fight about it," Folsey told me. "Then John [Landis] and I realized that talking to the Schumans at this point wouldn't have done any good."

In the weeks following the deaths, the parents of My-Ca and Renee not only underwent extensive questioning from a number of investigators, including Budds, the NTSB, and state agencies, but also took their own legal action that accused the moviemakers, and others associated with the production, of "outrageous conduct beyond the bounds of human decency."

The Chens were first to file a civil lawsuit. Less than two weeks after the crash, lawyers for the parents of Renee filed a wrongful-death lawsuit that sought $200 million from nine individuals and five corporations, including members of the production team, Warner Brothers, Steven Spielberg, the company that owns and leases Indian Dunes, and Western Helicopters.

Later, the Les also filed a lawsuit, and eventually both actions were combined.

Because the actions sought an astounding amount of money, the civil lawsuits moved at a slow pace and became secondary to the investigations. No one expected that the civil suits would be resolved until all the criminal actions had run their course.

Particularly in civil cases, there are standard legal responses from the defendants' lawyers to explain why their clients bear no liability. Eventually, the *Twilight Zone* civil case papers would fill box after box in a county courthouse storage room in the San Fernando Valley. Out of all that documentation, though, one argument from attorneys for one of the defendants rankled sensibility above all others: the lawyers maintained that one reason the moviemakers were not liable for damages was because six-year-old Renee Chen had knowingly assumed the risk at Indian Dunes.

The testimony of the parents was important to the criminal investigations, helping to lay the foundation for the theory that the production team had been dishonest in its dealings with the families of the victims and reckless in its care of the children.

The parents were firm in their assertions that Folsey and Landis had not properly warned them about what was scheduled to happen during the children's scenes at Indian Dunes, and misled them with continual assurances that the children would be safe.

The parents' statements also served to add a special solemnity to the investigation. For example, when Daniel Le testified before the NTSB in early August, he began to talk about having watched someone carry the body of his son from the river.

NTSB investigator Abdon Llorente told Le he didn't have to continue with an explanation: "That's painful enough as it is."

"I couldn't cry, I couldn't cry," Le said in response.

The moviemakers would later claim that the parents had been kept fully informed, but there is no question that some *Twilight Zone* workers received important information only after the deaths. Dorcey Wingo was outraged when he learned for the first time, in a newspaper article, that My-Ca and Renee had been working illegally. He was already upset because Dan Allingham was not returning his telephone calls. Wingo told me that when he learned of the illegal hiring, he thought, "That was the stupidest thing I ever heard of. I had this high opinion of the production company before we worked for them. And then to find out about the children. I went, 'Oh, shit, here we all go marching right into the *Twilight Zone.*' I felt betrayed. I felt like cannon fodder at that point, that they used me. It was immoral not to tell me."

Indeed, George Folsey told me that drawing others on the set into the illegal hiring is "one of the things I regret most. We put a lot of people on the crew in a very compromising position: Elie Cohn, people in wardrobe, and assistant directors, anybody who had knowledge that the kids were going to be used illegally and had to go along with us, in effect, in breaking the law. That made me very uncomfortable. We did a very bad thing there."

The function of the National Transportation Safety Board was to determine the cause of the crash, whether it had been because of an error by the pilot or some other person, or the result of mechanical or structural malfunctions or weaknesses in the aircraft. Because of the premium placed by the public on air safety, NTSB investigations usually are performed with expedience, and the needs of the agency's investigators are given a priority by government.

To gather testimony about the flight—which would be coupled with a study of the helicopter debris and other physical evidence, including special-effects test explosions—formal hearings closed to the public and press were conducted by an NTSB panel. Thirty-four people on the set at the time of the crash were interviewed.

Tom Budds, whose agreement with NTSB chief investigator Don Llorente gave him immediate access to those interview transcripts, found the mass of evidence accumulated in the NTSB hearings valuable, providing a broad-based reference that he could not have accomplished on his own in such a short period of time. Still, the detective's investigative needs were different from those of the federal agency. While the NTSB could accomplish its task with only superficial conclusions about the actions of the moviemakers, Budds needed more. A criminal case against any of the participants at Indian Dunes would require detailed and substantial evidence.

Of course, Budds was not beginning in the blind. He knew that My-Ca and Renee had been hired illegally, so he was immediately suspicious of the production team. Within hours of the crash, he had heard Dorsey Wingo complain that unexpected special-effects explosions had resulted in the crash. From the beginning, Budds had heard of Landis's ill temper and tendency to bellow orders impulsively, changing directions spontaneously. Budds believed that those involved in the production were incriminating themselves every time they talked about the fatal night.

The detective had been alerted to wrongdoing by Dorcey Wingo's veiled allegations of poor communication and recklessness, which the pilot had made to Budds and Llorente six hours after the crash as the three men stood on the shore of the Santa Clarita River just a few feet from the overturned helicopter. Budds was eager to hear what John Landis and Paul Stewart would have to say when they appeared before the NTSB panel in early August.

Along with its own investigators, the NTSB allows involved parties to be represented on the questioning panel in any crash inquiry. The panel convened by the board's Los Angeles field office included representatives from the Federal Aviation Administration; Western Helicopters, Inc.; the Los Angeles County Fire Department; the Screen Actors' Guild; Bell Helicopters (manufacturers of the UH-1B); California State fire marshals; and The Burbank Studios.

Paul Stewart, who had not yet been interviewed by any investigator, entered the hearing room in Lawndale, a Los Angeles suburb near the international airport, on August 3. He had been drinking steadily since the crash and had not worked at all.

The special-effects worker was sober when he appeared before the NTSB panel, but he was physically tired and mentally exhausted, and he was overwhelmed by the number of questioners facing him. He had assumed that just Llorente, and perhaps one or two others, would be present. He wanted nothing more than to answer quickly the questions in any way he could and get out.

Stewart was an inarticulate man; he spoke quietly and sometimes obliquely. When specifics might better serve him, he had a habit of summing up a description or set of facts with the phrase "this and that and the other thing."

For example, when he was asked how many flights the helicopter had taken over the set that night, he answered: "I mean I flew it into rehearsal, and this and that and the other thing."

Stewart possessed a workingman's reticence that did not well serve him —or others under suspicion in the matter. He did, however, establish the foundation for one of the key arguments the moviemakers would use in defending themselves: that James Camomile bore the sole responsibility for any mistakes in judgment on the set.

Stewart told the NTSB panel that Camomile had been given specific instructions before he fired his 2:20 A.M. explosions: "I told him, 'Whatever you do, make sure you can see Vic Morrow visually with your eyes. Before you do anything, make sure the helicopter is in a safe place.'"

When Camomile was interviewed by both the NTSB and Budds, however, he said that he had been given no instructions concerning the position of the helicopter in relation to the explosions and had been directed by Stewart only to be concerned with the actors on the ground. In light of the emerging facts about the case, it seemed preposterous to place all the blame on Camomile alone.

Stewart's responses to many NTSB questions at first appeared direct and reasonable, but were actually quite ambiguous about his conversations with Landis, the instructions he had given Camomile, and the factors he had used to determine that the scene would be safe. His answers begged the important question of why the moviemakers had not been more specific in determining what distance the helicopter had to be from the mortars before it would be safe to detonate the bombs during the two-twenty shot—a particularly relevant consideration because of the problems the helicopter had encountered during the 11:30 P.M. scene, when it had been buffeted by the too-close fireballs.

Stewart did imply that common practice in the movie industry called for fireballs to be catapulted in the air close to helicopters: "We never set 'em up underneath the helicopter. It's always before he comes in or after he leaves, or off to the side." Using the proper camera angle, Stewart explained, can make a fireball blown to the side of a helicopter "look like it engulfs it."

One of the more astounding revelations of Stewart's testimony this day was that he had not even been informed of the problems the helicopter had encountered during the 11:30 P.M. scene. "Nobody discussed it with me," he said plainly.

Then he was asked by Llorente, "As far as the positioning of the helicopter during these practice shots: Were you ever consulted as to the position of the helicopter with relationship to the charge?"

"No, I wasn't," Stewart said.

"Is that unusual?" the investigator asked.

Again, Stewart did not answer the question directly: "I mean I've done bigger ones than this one. Even I think if it hit directly under the bottom of the helicopter it would never hurt it. Because all that's in that mortar is sawdust and you pour gasoline in." He did add, however, that despite his belief that it would be safe, he had never set off a gasoline and sawdust explosion directly underneath a helicopter.

Stewart's view about the destructive nature of gasoline fireballs was obviously much more benign than that of Wingo, who had vociferously warned Stewart before the crash that he didn't want special effects exploded anywhere near his aircraft.

"But you can stand next to these pots and blow 'em. We've done it for years with stuntpeople," Stewart told the NTSB panel.

Asked if he ever walked through the set with Wingo to show him the location of the mortars, Stewart said that he had not: "I just told him that they were all out in front of the huts and there was nothing inside any of the huts. And they're all gasoline and sawdust."

The NTSB investigators knew that a mortar had been found underneath the food-drying shack after the crash, and they suspected that debris from that explosion had disabled the helicopter. But Stewart was not even asked why he had told Wingo all of the mortars were outside the huts when clearly one had been placed beneath one. (Stewart's explanation to me was that he differentiated in name between "huts" with four walls and the open-walled food-drying "shack.")

Some members of the NTSB panel confused the definitions of mortars and bombs, sometimes using the terms interchangeably with the word "explosion." Stewart offered a quick course in special effects, explaining that a mortar was a steel container in which a black powder bomb was placed along with gasoline and sawdust.

Although not specifically pressed on the point, Stewart did refer negatively to Landis, hinting that the special-effects crew had been cautious in their dealings with the director: "You take your own cue, because what happens if you don't, our director gets so goddamn excited. That's why you stand up physically and look where everything is. You don't do anything you can't see."

Then Stewart placed Landis fully in the safety controversy by revealing that he had imparted to the director the information that at least one mortar had been placed under a structure.

"Did you ever discuss the shots and where the mortars were with the director?" Stewart was asked.

"Yes."

"So that he knew where all of the mortars were?"

"Yes. My discussion with John Landis was, I showed him where the mortars were. He wanted to put some of the mortars inside the huts, and I refused. Because I said if I put 'em inside the huts, then you might blow something away."

The panel did not pursue this surprising bit of information. Stewart was not asked to explain in detail the circumstances under which Landis had requested huts to be destroyed by explosives. More importantly, Stewart was not asked why he then directed that a mortar be placed under the food-drying shack when he had already told Landis that debris hurtling from exploding huts could endanger the helicopter and its occupants in the air, as well as the actors and crew members on the ground. (Stewart told me that while he recognized the danger of debris from a bomb in a hut, where gasoline vapors can accumulate and cause a more ferocious explosion, he assumed that the effect of the detonation under the open-walled structure would not have enough force to hurtle objects damaging to the helicopter.)

The haphazard questioning of Stewart may have met the needs of the NTSB investigation, but it only raised serious questions for Budds—fueling his speculation that the moviemakers had been reckless.

Budds believed that a case of negligence against members of the production team could be proven just by contrasting the conflicting statements of Stewart and Wingo. When he read the transcript of Landis's NTSB statements, made later the same day as Stewart's, the detective was even more convinced of his theory.

Throughout the course of the *Twilight Zone* case, Landis's attorneys worried about his volatility: his tendency to erupt with intemperate remarks. As with Stewart, the NTSB appearance was Landis's first interrogation on the matter.

Landis's imperious nature was not held in check when the questioning began on August 3. When asked the function of a director, his answer appeared steeped in the feelings of someone who believes he is being wrongly accused.

"The director is the one who gets the blame," he said, crediting the statement's author, the late Alfred Hitchcock. (Coincidentally, Landis's secretary, Alpha Campbell, had worked for Hitchcock for many years.)

The NTSB questioning in these early stages of the investigation was understandably imprecise, and naive about how movies are made. Landis reacted to some of the queries with derision.

"Was there any preplan developed for this sequence?" Llorente asked.

"Of course," Landis said, punctuating his answer, according to a sheriff's department transcript, by saying, "ha."

Landis confirmed that following the 11:30 P.M. shot, Wingo and Allingham had complained about the proximity of the helicopter to the fireballs, "and [we] decided that the helicopter should be much further over the river [for the two-thirty shot]."

Llorente then asked where Landis placed the helicopter for the 2:20 A.M. shot.

"It's not my responsibility to put the helicopter anyplace," the director said, toying with semantics. "I ask the pilot, uh, to place the helicopter in position for the shot." Contradicting his first snippy response, Landis did concede that he had chosen the spot in the air in which Wingo placed the helicopter during the rehearsal for the 2:20 A.M. shot.

The NTSB panel had not yet been able to confirm that Landis had ordered the helicopter to fly lower just before the fireballs disabled the aircraft, and this day they would not learn from Landis that he had given such directions.

"During the filming of the accident scene did you direct the helicopter to descend lower?" Llorente asked the director.

"During, I don't, truthfully, I don't know. I, I was, shall I describe what happened?"

In a response that did not answer the specific question, Landis said that at 2:20 A.M. he had been watching Morrow and the children, and once he had given the actor the cue to begin crossing the river with the children under his arms, he did not look at the helicopter. He had paid no attention to the helicopter or the special-effects explosions, he said.

"When Vic and the kids were about to me [in the river], the helicopter sort of landed in front of me. It didn't crash. It just sort of like sat down, And I was completely startled."

In a hesitant, jumbled answer, Landis said he didn't remember if he had communicated at all with the helicopter during the two-twenty shot.

"Dan and Dorcey were coordinating where the helicopter should be," he said, neglecting to say that the coordination was in conjunction with his directions on the ground being relayed by first assistant director Elie Cohn. In contrast to Wingo's statement that he had received from Landis precise instructions concerning where to fly, Landis told the NTSB that Wingo had had complete control of the helicopter's movements.

In a boastful comment, ill considered in light of the issues under discussion, Landis added: "[In] *The Blues Brothers* we did extraordinary helicopter stuff. In fact, I've made some of the biggest stunt movies of all time."

Landis grew more testy as Llorente's questioning continued. The director theorized that responsibility for safety on the set is well dispersed and is a function he as director does not shoulder alone, if he bears any such responsibility at all: "When a stuntman says to you, 'This is too dangerous,' or a pilot says, 'I cannot do this,' which happens a lot, then you say, 'Okay, we've got to think of something else.' I'm not God. I can't fucking say, 'Well, you know these visions of [movie director] Erich von Stroheim,' then blow them all up."

Wingo, the director implied, had had the responsibility to take charge: "I wasn't flying the helicopter and neither was Allingham."

Landis, fervently opposed to smoking, looked at Llorente, who had just begun to smoke, and asked: "Could you do me a favor and put out your cigarette?" The investigator readily complied. The incident might have remained a passing and unimportant request for courtesy but for Landis's laughing comment, which added a sharp edge to the exchange: "I don't allow people to smoke on my set."

(Landis was strict about smoking on movie sets he controlled. His aversion was at least partially the consequence of the death of *Schlock* coproducer Jim O'Rourke. "He smoked constantly and at age thirty he shriveled up and died of cancer," Landis had once told some film students. That Llorente took some offense at Landis's remark was indicated a few days later when Elie Cohn appeared before the NTSB panel. Early in the questioning, Llorente said to Cohn, "Well, I note that you smoke so you won't tell.me that you won't allow anybody on your set to smoke, will you?" Cohn was puzzled by the comment and said, "It's funny you asked, because John Landis hates smoking, he doesn't let anybody smoke on his set." Llorente replied dryly, "I know.")

None of the investigators involved in the case had yet turned their attention to Landis's *Twilight Zone* coproducer, Steven Spielberg. The evidence thus far suggested that, at most, Spielberg might have had knowledge that the children were being hired illegally, but there was certainly no indication that he had had any direct involvement in the planning of the scene. A rumor, begun by one disgruntled crew member who apparently had been drinking, that Spielberg had been at Indian Dunes at the time of the crash and immediately afterward had called for his limousine driver to take him away, had been quickly discounted by Budds.

When the questioning turned to the financing and authority structure for the movie, Landis was swift and firm in assuring the NTSB panel that Spielberg "had nothing and has nothing to do with the production of this particular episode at all."

"Okay," Llorente said, accepting the answer without hesitation and preparing to ask another question. Curiously, Landis interrupted defensively and added: "I mean it's true, he has nothing to do with this."

When the session was about to end, Landis's attorney, Joel Behr, said he believed that the director's answers had been "frank," and he wanted assurances that the transcript would not be given to the press: "Not because there's anything about it that anyone should have to hide. It seems to me, this is an inquiry that's properly being conducted by the various agencies, and let the media conduct their own inquiry, if they see fit, by their own means."

Llorente advised Behr that because the NTSB is a federal agency, the Freedom of Information Act required all NTSB hearing documents to be made public. Besides, Llorente speculated, the only question the reporters really wanted answered was whether Landis had ordered the helicopter lower just before the two-twenty shot. Then the NTSB investigator added: "My response to that, is that Mr. Landis's response for that was negative and the pilot had the absolute authority of the aircraft."

The NTSB record indicates that neither Landis nor Behr attempted to disabuse Llorente of that conclusion—which was correct insofar that Landis had responded in the negative, but false in its implication that Landis had not issued an order for the helicopter to fly lower.

On August 4, the day after he had appeared before the NTSB panel, Stewart was all the more eager to make short work of a late-afternoon appointment with Tom Budds.

Stewart, as he later told me, was then finding comfort only in his drinking, and he was decidedly still not in a clear-thinking frame of mind. As he walked into the tiny interrogation room at the county sheriff's West Hollywood substation, he was still troubled with thoughts of the deaths and now was beginning to feel abandoned by those from whom he wanted some support: "Oh, I had pulled Vic Morrow out of the water with his head chopped off, and I'm reading all the bullshit in the papers. And the studio was not supporting me. I mean, the studio, they didn't even want to know who we were. The paper says 'the special effects blew everybody out of the sky,' 'the special effects killed everybody.' I ran away from the press. I mean I just wouldn't answer the phone."

Budds, though, had little sympathy for Stewart when the bearded special-effects foreman came into the interrogation room. There was a prefatory conversation before Budds and Sergeant Thomas Finnegan turned on their tape recorder and began to question Stewart. Budds got quickly to the critical point.

"Okay, a couple of things, little gray areas here. Who was it that decided or directed where the charges would be placed?"

"It was uh, kinna uh, decided by myself and the director," Stewart replied.

"Did Landis know where all of the charges were?"

"He walked the set with me," Stewart said, implying that Landis had to have known where all the mortars were placed—including the one under the food-drying shack.

Budds confirmed that Landis and Stewart—who had information about where the bombs in the village were located—did not pass that information on to Wingo. Budds, of course, remembered that on the morning after the crash Wingo had told him that the village had been blown right out from under him and that the pilot had admitted that he had not bothered ahead of time to find out exactly where the mortars were located. All of this confirmed for the detective that on-set communications had been inadequate.

"Did anybody walk through the set with the pilot and tell him where all the charges were?" Budds asked.

"No," Stewart said, confirming Wingo's earlier statement.

Then Budds mentioned that he had heard that some live ammunition had been fired in one scene—a practice that suggested to the detective that the moviemakers had been willing to take unusual risks for the sake of effect.

Stewart, who didn't think that the shotgun blasts in the so-called banana plant sequence had posed a threat to anyone, quickly confirmed the point: "I did it. It's not common but I've done it before. Well, I wanted to see this plant get all shot up, so we put a bunch of squibs in it and I shot it up with a shotgun, but there was nobody in the scene."

It was true that there had been no one in the scene when the guns were fired, but Stewart didn't mention to Budds that Morrow had been in the proposed line of fire just seconds before the special-effects technicians fired the weapons.

Budds did not yet know about Stewart's drinking problems, but he did suspect that drinking or drugs may have played a role in altering the judgments of people on the set at Indian Dunes.

"Any drinking on the set?" Budds asked.

"No, because I won't put up with that," Stewart replied.

For now, Budds decided not to pursue the drugs and alcohol angle with Stewart. Instead, he decided to focus on an action that could more easily be attributed to the special-effects foreman. The detective knew that a suspected physical cause of the crash was debris from the explosion under the food-drying shack, and he wanted to know why a bomb had been placed in such an apparently dangerous location.

Stewart said that the bomb placement had been his idea: "I thought I could catch the thatched roof on fire, I tilted [the mortar] out." Budds wondered about the truth of that answer because when he inspected the mortar after the crash he found it pointing straight up, indicating to the detective that the force of the explosion had been directed up through the flooring and roof of the hut, and not back at the cliff.

"Did you have any idea that it may be a possibility that it's gonna throw that roof up in the air as an explosion?

"No."

Then, in contradiction to his earlier statement that he had pointed out all the mortars to Landis, Stewart said that he couldn't be sure whether Landis knew about the bomb under the shack. Nonetheless, Stewart talked about Landis's grand plan for a spectacular final scene: "He wanted to see the whole village blown up for the master shot."

Budds didn't show it, but he was growing furious at Stewart, whom he believed was lying in an attempt to cover up for John Landis. In light of other statements being made to him by others on the set, Budds couldn't believe that Stewart would have unilaterally made a decision to blow up a hut in the middle of the scene without the director's knowledge. In fact, Budds believed that Landis had ordered Stewart to place the bomb under the hut for a dramatic visual effect in the climactic rescue scene.

He was having a difficult time proving that, though.

The cluster of high-rise office buildings known as Century City, on the western border of Beverly Hills and built over what was once the back lot of Twentieth Century Fox studios, is a popular workplace for entertainment lawyers in Los Angeles.

On August 10, 1982, on his thirty-second birthday and eighteen days after the deaths, John Landis went to Century City to the office of his friend and lawyer, Joel Behr.

Landis, Behr, and two other lawyers were to discuss just how much trouble the director was in.

This private meeting was especially revealing of the director's moods, reactions, defenses, and concerns just after the tragedy, when it appeared that he would be the focus of much blame. In contrast to his public display of emotion at Morrow's funeral, Landis was now seemingly much more in control of his emotions, and expressing bitterness that he could be accused of any wrongdoing in connection with the helicopter crash.

The session, an intimate conference between lawyers and client, was transcribed presumably without thought that the contents would ever be made public. However, a copy of a transcript of at least a portion of that meeting, verified for me as authentic by attorneys involved in the case, was later given to me by someone who had been authorized by Landis and Behr to use the document.

The transcript is important for its illumination of Landis's view of his own role in the crash—a consistently adamant stance that he had done nothing at all that could have contributed to the sad events at Indian Dunes. The meeting was obviously one of several the director and his attorneys had conducted in recent weeks. In the 147-page transcript of this August 10 meeting, there is no mention of the illegal hiring of the children. The theme of this session was the question of who bears responsibility for safety on a movie set. Landis flatly excludes himself from such a burden.

The transcript shows that Landis can be as intolerantly quick-tempered in the privacy of his lawyer's office—even with men who are trying to keep him out of jail—as he is with crew members on the set.

Along with Behr and Landis, the other participants in the conversation were John Diemer, now a law partner of Behr's, and Harland Braun, a criminal defense attorney.

Behr handled civil matters for Landis, including his movie contracts. Now that it appeared Landis was facing the possibility of criminal charges, at least in connection with the illegal hiring of the children, Behr wanted Landis to have a criminal defense attorney.

Behr chose Braun, a thirty-nine-year-old former Los Angeles County prosecutor with a growing reputation for winning tricky criminal cases, particularly those that received a lot of news coverage. In one case, Braun had successfully defended two doctors on manslaughter charges after they had disconnected a terminally ill patient from life-support systems. Braun was also influential in the liberal Democratic politics of Los Angeles's affluent Westside neighborhoods.

Braun has an effusive personality. Within the constraints of being a proper Century City lawyer, he is something of a character. He is jovially brash, without self-consciousness. He is crafty enough always to use his press-attracting buffoonery to his client's advantage.

He graduated from the law school at UCLA and maintains his contacts within the district attorney's office, where he had served as a deputy for five years, beginning in 1968. His understanding of the politics of the office would prove important later in the *Twilight Zone* case.

In these early stages of the investigation, Braun was assuming that criminal charges would center on the illegal hiring of the children, although he recognized the potential for criminal negligence charges as well. Because of the various investigations under way by state, local, and federal agencies, the newspapers were continually reporting revelations about alleged misconduct on the *Twilight Zone* set, and Braun knew that continued publicity could put pressure on the district attorney's office to pursue the moviemakers aggressively. Braun well knew that any prosecutor would have a decided advantage in front of a jury because the death of two innocent children was particularly poignant.

Undeniably, the lawyers were dealing with a forceful personality in John Landis, and one who had limited insight into the negative impact his dominant personality could have on others—including jurors.

Landis was a man overflowing with creative energy to make movies, the ambition to rise to Hollywood success, and a keen understanding of the multimillion-dollar financing of films, including how to garner his share. Those who spent time with Landis saw a man of many shadings. He astounded friends with the breadth of his intellect, but he could also dismay them with superficiality and immaturity. He could be gently humorous or bitingly sarcastic, unduly humble or supremely arrogant, warmly consoling or impatiently intolerant. He was, in sum, a mercurial and demanding man.

Close friends, people who have known him since his teenage years, talked to me about contrasting streaks of generosity and insensitivity. One person recalled that, when growing up in Los Angeles, Landis would frequently kick the friend's dog into the swimming pool, thinking the act funny. The same person also remembered talking with Landis about what they would do if they were rich, and Landis produced from memory a list of gifts he would purchase for friends.

John Landis was attracted to making movies from boyhood. One of his first, only a few minutes long, was made with a sixteen-millimeter Bolex owned by a friend's father.

Schlock, which he made when he was twenty-one, was an amateurish paean to his obsession with gorillas. Eliza Garrett Simons, an actress who appeared in *Schlock* and *National Lampoon's Animal House,* remembered trips to the Los Angeles Zoo in Griffith Park during which Landis would spend hours watching the primates, describing with great understanding their patterns of behavior.

As an adult, he could afford to indulge himself with this hobby, buying original still photos from *King Kong* as well as gorilla toys, artwork, and other primate memorabilia, which filled a whole display case in his home. The prize gorilla possession was a life-size effigy, as realistic as any to be found in a natural history museum, a gift from Rick Baker, a longtime friend who went on to become a highly skilled special-effects craftsman. (Baker created the macabre makeup special effects that transformed David Naughton from a young American tourist into a drooling werewolf in Landis's *An American Werewolf in London.)*

After the crash, friends analyzed what aspects of his personality had led Landis to the tough spot in which he found himself.

Eliza Garrett Simons told me: "His brain goes very fast, rapidly, and he knows what he's going for. And he gets frustrated when the other elements aren't keeping up. Maybe the guys lighting the set don't share the vision and they're not in such a rush, and his mind is going faster than he is able to pull the company along."

Harland Braun, who had not met Landis before he became his lawyer in the summer of 1982, quickly began to realize that Landis's arrogance would be a detriment to a successful defense if criminal charges were filed against him. Landis once told Braun, "We're movie people. We don't follow the rules. We go into a city and we do what we want to do."

"Landis is the type of guy that says things honestly and positively, but about fifty percent of the time he's wrong. I mean, he has no sense of what he doesn't know," Braun told me. For example, it was proving to be indisputable that, prior to the 2:20 A.M. shot, Landis had been carrying a bullhorn and also had shouted for the helicopter to fly lower. "When I first met him," Braun recalled, "Landis said, 'I didn't have a bullhorn in my hand. I didn't shout 'Lower! Lower!' "

One of Braun's jobs was to try to prevent Landis from falling into incriminations created by his own words. For example, in the August 10, 1982, meeting with the three lawyers, Landis told how he had asked people to stand up before the two-twenty shot: "There must be two hundred witnesses to this, 'I don't want anyone sitting down. Everyone standing up during this take.' I did say that. I was very forceful about that, 'cause if something goes wrong, if you're sitting down, you can't run away. You know. And then I said, okay, which is what I do before any stunt or anything dangerous, no one sits, everyone's standing."

After an off-the-record conversation not in the transcript, Landis says to Braun: "Oh, I understand, am I saying dangerous?" Braun knew that a prosecutor would no doubt attempt to prove that Landis had a keen sense that a high level of risk was involved. The criminal lawyer explained that different meanings can be inferred from the same statement. "Doesn't mean the fact that you take precautions, that I drive within the speed limit, doesn't mean that it's dangerous," Braun said to the director.

With over two weeks having now passed since the crash, several of the investigating agencies were following a theory that the rotor blade had been damaged by a glue pot lid left near, or on, a mortar. Landis, who had asked Paul Stewart about blowing up huts and the sampan during the Vietnamese village scenes, now expressed to his lawyers a different viewpoint about the danger of debris: "The idea that someone would leave the lid of a glue pot can in an explosion is so unthinkable that it doesn't matter where the fuck it is. That's total unbelievable negligence.

"Now, I personally, I had no idea that there was an explosion inside a hut," Landis continued. "I wouldn't have let that happen. Just because it would have been dangerous to my, I mean, that's the only way that someone could get hurt, that is in fact, the only way that it did happen.

"I do not recall saying put an explosion inside a hut," he said.

"Whose responsibility is it to coordinate all of the safety elements?" Behr asked.

"To coordinate all of the elements is the production manager's job. To make sure everything's there, it's the assistant director's job to make sure everything functions," Landis said, apparently not satisfying Behr, who pressed with another question.

"Whose responsibility is it to make sure that all of the elements which could pose any kind of danger are sufficiently coordinated with all of the personnel?" Behr asked.

"It is a group responsibility," Landis said. "There is no such thing as a safety monitor. I do not perceive it as my responsibility to be an explosives expert, I'm sorry."

"Would you say that anyone on the set has any greater responsibility in terms of safety than you as a director?" Behr asked.

"Well, in fact, yes, the first assistant director's responsibility is to report to me that everything's ready."

A major theme of the session seems to have been Landis's insistence that safety responsibilities belong to others on the set, while the lawyers attempted to convince the director that, by his position and personality, he assumes a great deal of responsibility.

(In fact, at his appearance before the NTSB panel about this time, first assistant director Elie Cohn was also saying that there had been no warnings of danger prior to the crash. Unlike Landis, however, who was firm in his stance that his own judgment had been sound at Indian Dunes, Cohn was now suggesting in hindsight that the decision-making may have been flawed. Cohn told Llorente and others at the NTSB: "I never heard from anybody that it's dangerous, that we should, ah, especially after we did it at 11:30, I mean, you know, you know it sounds almost . . . foolish on a lot, part of us, not to think, you know, that it could be dangerous, I guess. But to my recollection . . . nobody ever said, you know, that it's, ah, we're planning it a bit too close.")

"It was safe, we had done it earlier," Landis said of the two-twenty shot. "It is clearly not the director's responsibility to ask if anything's safe. It is the assistant director's responsibility to ask if anything is safe.

"No safety coordinator in the world would have prevented this, unless we shut down production while he checked every single explosion. And checked every single aspect of this production, which would cost us five or six hours, and all movies would be made in Europe. I mean, you wouldn't get anything done.

"My responsibility is to make the best movie I can. It's that simple. I am consistently aided and hindered by everyone else. It's constant compromise. Actors aren't perfect. You want an actor to be perfect, you won't get one. Cameramen are not as good as you want them to be . . . it's not like a painter with a canvas where I can go, gee, I just dip there—I mean filmmaking is one of the most difficult arts purely because it's one of the most expensive and complicated arts. There's so many people between me and the image on the screen."

"When you say the best film possible, do you mean creatively?" Behr asked.

"Yeah, I mean creatively. What do you mean? Anything? Yeah, I hope it makes a lot of money."

The lawyers appeared to have a strong sense of the accusations Landis would face from the investigators, and also seemed to have a difficult time getting him to appreciate the import.

"Did you consider the sequences that you had written to be complicated, because it did involve explosions and helicopters?" Behr asked.

"Yes, it was complicated. Because, yes."

"And did you consider them to be potentially dangerous to people involved?"

"Sure, that's why you say, 'Can we do this?' " Then Landis added:

"Nothing was destroyed by those explosions, other than the helicopter and Vic and the kids."

Behr asked about his personality as a director: "So you get results by the process of intimidation sometimes?"

"If I have to, or seduction. It depends who you're dealing with."

"So sometimes is it fair to say that you get results by intimidation?"

"Emotional results yeah, yes, in performance and stuff, sure. If someone's doing something incorrectly. Because I'm the arbiter of what's correct, what's on the screen, and I try to get it the other way. If they don't deliver it then they're fired and replaced."

Behr pursued a point that promised to be an argument prosecutors would make if criminal charges were brought: "Do you have any reason to believe that people would compromise safety measures as a result of an intimidating personality? That you would express that you want something in a certain way creatively and, by God, you better have it?"

"No," Landis said, "I do not conceive that anyone in their right mind would do that, because now you're talking about something else. You're talking about safety."

"Well, I'm talking about margins of error," Behr said.

"I'm sorry, you're talking about margins of error affecting people's welfare. In fact, no one has ever been injured in any of my films. Which is astonishing. Until now, which sort of makes up for everything."

Landis, having had a taste of the investigation during his questioning by Llorente (presumably he was also reading the newspaper articles about the *Twilight Zone* probe), expressed the notion that his role was being misunderstood by those who wanted to blame him for the deaths: "What is shocking to me and my capacity for naiveté, is how ignorant people are. About how fucking movies are made. This issue has incredible potential to totally fuck the industry."

"Let me articulate it for you," Behr said. "The problem is that you appear to exert overall authority by personality, force of personality. That you at the same time have the title 'director,' which is in fact the most powerful authoritative figure on any movie set, generally speaking. That you have, in fact, selectively exercised your prerogative in certain areas which run the range from integration to smoking. What the problem is, is that people are therefore going to perceive you as the person who in a chain of command sense has the ultimate authority for and the ultimate responsibility for safety."

"But that is not correct," Landis replied.

"But that's the problem you're facing," Behr said.

Landis replied: "The idea that the director is responsible for safety on the set is one of colossal ignorance. Staggering. Breathtaking."

SEVEN

IN THE FALL of 1982, John Landis went to Philadelphia to direct the movie *Trading Places,* starring Eddie Murphy, Dan Aykroyd, Ralph Bellamy, and Don Ameche. Although several investigative agencies were questioning Landis's professional responsibility, there were Hollywood producers who did not share the misgivings about the director, a man who could make money for them.

Trading Places associate producer Irwin Russo told me: "There was a lot of directing talent but John Landis was bankable at the time. You get John Landis on it and you had a movie. Getting him certainly helped make the picture happen. John Landis was not far down on anybody's list in those days. He was probably one of the ten comedy directors in town who could make a movie happen. If John Landis is going to direct a good movie for you and bring it in on budget and do a good job, they're going to hire him. I don't think anybody's going to worry about this one mistake."

Irwin Russo's brother Aaron, the movie's executive producer, paid Landis a directing fee approaching $1 million, plus residual payments based on the movie's earnings. That, Irwin Russo said, was money well spent. The suggestions in California state agency reports—such as that of the California Occupational Safety and Health Agency—that Landis had acted improperly with regard to state regulations, as well as the speculation that Landis might face criminal charges, were not deterrents to the producers' hiring of Landis.

Irwin Russo said: "There might have been talk about his culpability, but everyone said, 'Let's wait for the trial.' Already rumors were flying around that kids were hired illegally. We all know we have to take chances at times, and you do things you're not sure about. The man is not a criminal. Most people saw it at worst as an unfortunate accident.''

Russo expressed a sympathetic view of Landis: "He's not a drunken, reckless guy. Maybe the only thing that's reckless about him is he uses a lot of cars [in crash scenes]. He thinks that's funny. I don't think that's funny, that juvenile humor that he has a lot of. He's a kid at heart in many ways. In many ways, his indiscretion is that he's a little childish. I don't think he wants to hurt anybody.''

Dan Allingham and George Folsey also worked on *Trading Places* and it was while in Philadelphia that they and Landis learned that criminal indictments against them might be sought. Although the top three members of the *Twilight Zone* production team continued to earn a great deal of money, the other two men under investigation—Dorcey Wingo and Paul Stewart—were not faring as well.

Western Helicopters had kept faith in Wingo, the company's director of operations, who continued to fly regularly on jobs but did no movie work. Western's president, Clair Merryweather, however, had heard prospective customers more than once retract a job offer when they learned Wingo would be the pilot.

Wingo had been emotionally distraught since the crash, with symptoms of sleeplessness and recurrent anxiety. He was finding his only solace in the routine and precision of flight.

Paul Stewart was a salaried craftsman who needed work to live; he had never made a lot of money, and divorce had drained his finances even more. For a long time after July 23, 1982, no job offers came to him. Part of the problem was his drinking since the accident. He had, however, stopped the binging several weeks after the crash. Driving home drunk one night, he rammed the rear end of a truck and was fortunate not to have been seriously injured. Stewart was unharmed, and a friend managed to get him home. The next morning Stewart awoke with the fearful realization that he had been destroying himself with his attempt to escape thinking about what had happened at Indian Dunes.

The special-effects foreman didn't believe that he was being shunned for work because of the alcohol. He attributed his unemployment to a type of class discrimination in the movie business. As experienced as he may have been, he was not a power, not someone whose presence assured huge profits to the producers. He earned $28.50 an hour—he was paid only for the time worked and did not receive residuals based on profits —and that, Stewart believed, put him in a category of employee easily expendable. He knew Landis and the others were still working, and thus he viewed himself as an easy scapegoat for the studios.

Stewart told me: "The people who I had worked with personally in years past—actors, technicians, camerapeople, and directors—all said after the accident, 'I'd still work with Paul Stewart.' Now, all of the people who don't know Paul Stewart, all the newcomers are saying, 'Well, Jesus Christ, that guy's terrible. He's a horrible person. We don't want to hire him.' They'd go out and do a show with explosives and the lawyers would come in and say, 'We can't hire Paul Stewart because of the liability. What happens if he hurts somebody? How is the insurance carrier going to cover us? We can't hire him now.' "

The California Occupational Safety and Health Administration (CAL-OSHA) completed its investigation by concluding that Landis, Folsey, Allingham, and Warner Brothers had violated dozens of state workplace regulations and levied more than $63,000 in fines.

In September, Landis's secretary, Alpha Campbell, received a letter from London from a woman named Trudy—Vic Morrow's girlfriend. The missive disturbed Campbell greatly, who later turned the document over to the district attorney's office. The letter said in part:

> I can't forget what Vic said to me. He thought some-
> thing was very wrong on the set. But he couldn't put
> his finger on it. The stunts bothered him. Especially
> with the shotguns, and you know, Alpha, they had real
> bullets. That made him very angry because he couldn't
> see the point of it.
>
> He really thought something was going on, if you
> get what I mean.
>
> I just wish I could close my eyes and wake up from
> a nasty dream. All I want is Vic back. But you can't
> have everything you want, can you?

If Morrow had singled out anyone for blame, including Landis, in his conversations with his girlfriend, that wasn't apparent from the woman's letter. Trudy asked if Campbell would pass on to Landis some of her modeling pictures. She wondered if there was a chance Landis would use her in a movie, even for a small role.

Campbell wrote back expressing a camaraderie born of their mutual sorrow over the death of Morrow—the secretary had become fond of the actor because he had treated her with a respect she felt she didn't always receive from others, including Landis. Campbell had reservations about Trudy's modeling pictures, though, and in her letter to Trudy said: "I do not think it would be such a great idea to present your picture to J.L."

By the fall, Tom Budds was convinced that he had a strong negligence case against five of the production team: Landis, Folsey, Allingham, Wingo, and Stewart. He recognized that his task to convince a district attorney prosecutor that criminal charges should be filed against the men would not be easy. Some sheriff's department colleagues questioned the detective's judgment in pursuing a matter they thought was better left to the civil courts.

Undoubtedly, Landis, Folsey, and Allingham could be charged with violating the state labor code for hiring the children illegally. But that offense was only a misdemeanor, and Budds thought that justice required more serious felony charges relating directly to the deaths of Morrow, My-Ca, and Renee.

The difficulty of the *Twilight Zone* case was that the determination of criminality required more discretionary judgment than in other crimes that resulted in death. Budds told me: "This was a subjective intellectual interpretation of what constitutes reckless and wanton conduct. Murder is murder, because—boom!—you shoot somebody and there's a bullet hole. In the opinion of my witnesses, who lived through the experience, [the actions of Landis and the others were] reckless and wanton."

Ready to make his presentation to prosecutors in November 1982, Budds carried three bulging binders into the office of Deputy District Attorney Gary Kesselman. The detective's "murder books" were a compilation of key interviews conducted by him and the NTSB, technological evidence about special effects and helicopters, and other documents that he believed laid the foundation for proving that the moviemakers had been criminally and egregiously negligent in their conduct.

Kesselman had been especially approved by District Attorney John Van de Kamp to monitor this high-publicity case. Kesselman came to the job with a reputation for integrity of the highest order. He had just successfully completed the prosecution of a man who had molested and then viciously murdered a ten-year-old boy named Danny Young.

The prosecutor had been emotionally drained by the murder trial but had won respect among his colleagues because he had voluntarily dismissed tainted evidence—an altered autopsy report and an improperly obtained tape-recorded confession—thus making the prosecution even harder for himself. The prosecutor had been especially saddened because his own son was about the same age as the young victim, and that identification added poignancy to the matter for him.

Kesselman had been so busy with the murder case that he knew almost nothing about the *Twilight Zone* matter. Once during the summer, when there was a television news report that mentioned My-Ca and Renee, he had asked his wife to turn off the set, saying, "I've seen enough dead children."

When he was called downtown for a meeting with top officials of the district attorney's office in September—Kesselman then worked in a branch office—he was surprised when one of his bosses quipped "We're going to make you famous" just before telling the lawyer that he was being assigned the *Twilight Zone* case.

Another lawyer had been monitoring the investigative paperwork since the crash, but now it was time to devote special attention to a decision about prosecution, a conclusion that would be based on Budd's evidence-gathering.

Although it might have been appealing for Los Angeles County district attorney John Van de Kamp, an elected official then campaigning for California attorney general, to seek the publicity assured by going after a Hollywood celebrity of Landis's standing, Van de Kamp was an unlikely politician to exploit his position. He is a man of impeccable character, and his appointment of Kesselman added credibility to the idea that the *Twilight Zone* matter would be dealt with professionally. (Van de Kamp won the November election and left the district attorney's office in December for his new job in Sacramento.)

As Budds sat down in Kesselman's office to make his presentation, he thought that a strong element of his case was that the moviemakers had not sufficiently heeded the warning of danger that the 11:30 P.M. explosions had presented when the helicopter and its occupants were endangered. In addition, the detective was convinced that Landis had then changed the helicopter's flight plan minutes before the 2:20 A.M. shot by ordering the aircraft lower—after also directing that Stewart place an explosive under the food-drying shack in contradiction to suggestions that debris could be dangerous.

Understanding the decision-making that had led to a mortar being placed under the shack just before 2:20 A.M. was important to the investigators. Significantly, the NTSB was nearing a conclusion that debris thrown up by that explosion had led to the tail rotor damage, causing the helicopter to spin out of control and plummet to the ground. The NTSB investigators had been met with some resistance. In October, a U.S.

district judge granted a request by an assistant U.S. attorney, on behalf of the NTSB, that Landis, Folsey, and Allingham, as well as the entities of *Twilight Zone* Productions and Levitsky Productions, be required to turn over materials such as scripts, notes, and graphic layouts.

Budds believed, based on the testimony of special-effects technician James Camomile, that after the crash someone (Paul Stewart, he suspected) had tried to alter evidence by moving a mortar. Camomile had told Budds that before the 2:20 A.M. shot he had placed a powerful round mortar under the hut at Stewart's direction. Budds, of course, during his survey of Indian Dunes had found under the shack a square mortar, a device that dissipates explosions less destructively than round mortars, which concentrate the explosive force. Budds's theory was that Landis and Stewart had conspired to create a spectacular bomb effect on film by using a round mortar without regard to the extra danger it presented.

Budds thought that the use of any type of mortar under the shack was dangerous, but he knew it would be especially incriminating if it were proven that someone had switched the mortars after the crash to hide the fact that a more powerful device had been used in the same scene as Morrow, the children, and the aircraft.

Budds had only circumstance and speculation to show that Landis and Stewart and the others had knowingly placed people at risk for the sake of a movie effect. However, the law did not require proof that a defendant had intended to hurt someone, or even was aware of the danger, in order to be found guilty of criminal negligence. The standard of guilt for a jury was only that under the same circumstances any reasonable person should have recognized the inherent danger. Still, Budds understood that a trial jury might not be comfortable with convicting a defendant without a clear understanding of the filmmaker's thoughts and intentions before the crash.

After Budds had made an oral presentation of the case to Kesselman, the prosecutor confirmed the detective's fears: The *Twilight Zone* case appeared to be best handled as a civil matter, already under way with the parents' multimillion-dollar lawsuits.

The detective, who had been immersed in the case for months and who was already wary because of the blackballing fears expressed by some witnesses, was not yet aware of Kesselman's reputation for prosecutorial integrity. Budds got angry and said: "Maybe there's something that I don't understand here." The detective wondered whether Hollywood influence (for example, rich members of the entertainment industry are big contributors to political campaigns) was affecting decision-making in the district attorney's office.

Budds slapped together his three notebooks, bulging with evidence documents, and started to leave the room. Kesselman, however, calmed him and the two talked some more. The prosecutor agreed at least to read through Budds's thick file.

The material did not convince Kesselman that he could successfully prosecute anyone based on what had been obtained thus far, but he believed the evidence was substantial enough to pursue further.

For much of the winter, Budds worked the case virtually alone. Kesselman had other matters to handle in the branch office where he was still assigned. Then in January 1983, a new district attorney, Robert H. Philobosian, took office. One of his first acts was to declare a war on street sales of drugs. For the task, he marshaled a force of district attorney staff investigators, including the man who had been assigned to Kesselman and the *Twilight Zone* case.

In March, Budds and Kesselman decided to present the *Twilight Zone* case to the Los Angeles County grand jury—a body that deliberated in secret. The investigators had found that many witnesses were avoiding them, and when questioned expressed a great reluctance to testify, some out of fear of being blackballed and others in loyalty to the moviemakers. Some witnesses hedged in their answers, and others just lied.

Kesselman assumed that the mystique of the grand jury might compel many witnesses to be more open and truthful than they had been so far. Evading a grand jury subpoena, or being caught lying to the investigative body, could result in severe consequences. The grand jury's power of indictment could be an effective prodding device. But the prosecutor needed to act soon. Grand jurors, appointed by Superior Court judges, sit for a specified term of office, and the current jury's term would end in June. The district attorney's grand jury adviser told Kesselman that it would be wiser to present his complicated case to a seasoned panel of jurors than a new group unfamiliar with the legal process.

Since the deaths, the investigation had been awash in speculation and rumors that alcohol and drug use had contributed to the crash. The allegations were formalized in a civil suit that had been filed in October 1982 by Morrow's daughters, Carrie Morrow and Jennifer Jason Leigh. Named as defendants were virtually every entity involved in the making of the film, from Warner Brothers to the company that leased the land. (The suit was later settled out of court with an unpublicized payment, estimated to have been $850,000, by the defendants' insurance companies to Carrie and Jennifer. Because the matter never went to trial, the attorneys who had filed the lawsuit were never pressed to substantiate the drug allegations.)

The question of whether drugs or alcohol had impaired the judgment of any of the moviemakers before the crash eventually became a fruitless object of investigation. There were only rumors.

Budds knew that Stewart was a drinker but had concluded that even if Stewart had had some beer while working, drunkenness was not the root cause of the events at Indian Dunes. In a similar vein, Budds had heard the suspicions that Landis, because of his frenetic pace, was a cocaine user. Again, though, proof was unconvincingly circumstantial.

The detective's suspicion about Landis was fueled by knowledge of the director's friendship with John Belushi, a drug user who often sought the companionship of other drug users. A number of witnesses, though, even those with a strong bias against Landis, countered the rumors that Landis abused drugs. Donna Schuman said that based on her six months of working with Landis and what she had been told about Landis by Folsey, whom she had trusted, she was convinced that the director did not.

Schuman later testified: "One of the first things I was told about John Landis is that he does not smoke, he doesn't allow smoking in the office, he doesn't drink, and he does not allow drugs. Anybody ever caught under the influence anyplace is automatically fired. No questions asked, no matter who you are, you're fired."

A notable exception to that rule was Belushi, a man who had drawn special forgiveness from many people close to him.

Alpha Campbell told Budds about lengthy meetings between Belushi and Landis in Landis's office. After one of the comedian's visits to the production office, she said she found what appeared to be a cocaine spoon on her desk in the office's reception area—an item that Landis later instructed her to throw away, she told investigators.

Budds pursued his suspicions by compiling a collection of observations others had made about Landis, including his physical movements, appearance, and emotional moods. Without naming his suspect, Budds asked narcotics detectives to evaluate whether the mannerisms indicated a drug influence. (He was told that they appeared to, but the detective knew such speculation was meager proof.)

The issue was not mere curiosity for Budds. If he could prove that drug or alcohol use had affected the decision-making on the night of the crash, that would be compelling proof of criminal negligence. The bulk of the hard evidence gathered by the detective, however, spoke against the likelihood that drugs or alcohol were a relevant factor. Kesselman calculated that he and Budds devoted more than one thousand investigative hours solely to the issue of drug and alcohol use.

Intimates of the director, some of whom have known him since he was a teenager, told me that Landis is adamantly opposed to drug use. Robert Liddle, a long-time friend of Landis, who worked as Morrow's stand-in in *Twilight Zone,* told investigators that in a conversation some months after the crash Landis told him that his feelings were hurt because some people suspected him of abusing drugs. Eliza Garrett Simons, who spoke to Landis the day Belushi died, said the director was devastated by the comedian's pitiful overdose death but not surprised by the occurrence. "He had been scared by Belushi before," she said.

The references to Landis in Bob Woodward's biography of Belushi, *Wired,* a journalistic investigation that emphasized Belushi's drug world, depict Landis's violent reaction to Belushi's frequent drug use on the set of *The Blues Brothers.* Even with that, the director remained supportive, although discouraged by his inability to help Belushi with his addiction.

When Landis began work on *National Lampoon's Animal House* in 1977 he knew little about Belushi, even though by that time Belushi and his colleagues among the "Not Ready for Prime Time Players" had a large, devoted following across the country because of their innovative and daring comedy on NBC's *Saturday Night Live.*

Landis respected Belushi's significant comic charms, describing him as a cross between Harpo Marx and the Cookie Monster. Largely because of Belushi's drug abuse, though, the director also had trying times with the actor in the two movies in which they worked together.

In *National Lampoon's Animal House,* Landis injected an undertone of sweetness in some of his characters—Belushi included—to counteract their distasteful fraternity antics. Belushi played "Bluto," who became famous with his cries of "food fight" and "toga party." Landis correctly recognized that Bluto's presence in the movie could be overdone, and he restricted Belushi's screen time, but not without struggling with the forceful actor over the issue.

One significant scene in the movie involved several of the fraternity brothers making a carousing trip that includes a visit to a black nightclub. Belushi thought his character should go on the trip, but Landis resisted. George Folsey, Jr., the editor of *Animal House,* told me that Landis and Belushi had "quite a battle about that." Landis prevailed.

The movie was filmed in Eugene, Oregon, where Landis was concerned about Belushi's off-screen partying. "John Landis was heartbroken about John Belushi's self-destructive nature and he was very protective," said Eliza Garrett Simons, who had a role in the movie. "Most of us stayed in a hotel, but Belushi and his wife had rented a house. There was a lot of partying that went on there and John Landis tried to enforce some kind of [discipline]. The problem with Belushi is that no matter what he did [in the off-hours], he always managed to show up for work on time and he'd be great."

When Landis and Belushi worked again two years later on *The Blues Brothers,* Belushi's drug abuse had increased and was seriously damaging his work, which disheartened Landis even more.

"I got the pretty strong impression that John was having a lot of trouble controlling Belushi, and I know a couple of nights getting him out of his trailer to work was hard," Folsey recalled. "I think it just caused John Landis to have a terrible time. All the pressure was on him to try and get the movie made and for a reasonable price and he's having these problems with one of the big stars of the film, trying to get him to work and shoot the movie."

In January 1982, two months before Belushi's death, Landis spoke to a group of film students and was asked about his plans for the future. He mentioned a number of projects. He named some actors with whom he would like to work. He said, for example, that he would like to do another movie with Dan Aykroyd, Belushi's best friend and the costar of *The Blues Brothers.* Landis did not, however, say that he would like to work again with Belushi.

For all of Steven Spielberg's fame and influence, plus the fact that he was the coproducer of *Twilight Zone,* Spielberg was of little interest to the investigators. He had not been on the Indian Dunes set, and Budds suspected that his knowledge of the illegal hiring was peripheral. Adding to the disinterest was Spielberg's apparent disinclination to cooperate with any investigations. A man of Spielberg's stature could easily insulate himself from investigators, and Budds concluded that he had neither the time nor the energy to pursue a reluctant witness who would likely be of minimal value to his case.

Spielberg's resistance to participation in any inquiry was indicated by a letter he had sent to the National Transportation Safety Board—in effect a diplomatic announcement that he did not care to be involved.

> In response to your request, I was never at the Indian Dunes location of "Twilight Zone" on the night of the accident or any other time.
>
> I declare under penalty of perjury that the foregoing is true and correct, executed at Los Angeles, California this first day of December 1982.

Spielberg's signature was written in clear and bold script.

While Budds saw little reason to question Spielberg, he had a different opinion about Spielberg's top assistant, Frank Marshall, who had been on the set the night of the accident and, Budds believed, must have known about the illegal hiring. Marshall was not a candidate for prosecution, and Budds and Kesselman let that be known to Marshall's lawyer, explaining that they only wanted to question the movie executive. Budds, especially, grew increasingly disdainful of Marshall as he evaded the detective at every turn.

Once, Budds went to The Burbank Studios unannounced, hoping to surprise Marshall in his office. The detective had made an appointment with someone else at the studio, but once he was inside the gates he went directly to the Spielberg production office. Budds remained convinced afterward that when he announced himself to the receptionist, Marshall went out the back door.

In the spring of 1983, when Kesselman finally learned from Marshall's lawyer that Marshall had decided not to cooperate willingly, the district attorney's office issued a subpoena. In an attempt to serve the legal document, sheriff's deputies began a surveillance of Marshall's home in Malibu. The investigators soon learned that Marshall had left for Europe, where he worked on Spielberg movie projects.

As he prepared for the grand jury, Kesselman was stymied by the conflicting statements of the special-effects crew. Because Paul Stewart was one of his primary targets, the deputy district attorney decided he would grant immunity from prosecution to the four assistants, including James Camomile, who had actually detonated the explosions with his firing board. Having been granted immunity, the four would then be forced to testify before the grand jury. Otherwise they could plead their constitutional right against self-incrimination. Kesselman needed statements from the special-effects team to resolve the conflicts about the planning for the 2:20 A.M. scene and the controversy over whether a mortar had been switched after the crash in an attempt to fool investigators.

Kesselman made his decision to grant immunity after a meeting with James Camomile and his attorneys at Seasons restaurant in the San Fernando Valley on March 23, 1983, two months before the grand jury would hear the case. Paul Stewart was neither invited nor told about the meeting, although he was represented at the time by the same attorneys as the four special-effects crewmen.

* * *

By May, Kesselman was pressured by the dwindling time remaining before his presentation to the grand jury. Budds, too, was maintaining a full schedule. On May 11, Kesselman went to the home of Dr. Harold Schuman, the psychiatrist who, as a favor to George Folsey, Jr., had used his contacts in the Asian community of Los Angeles to obtain the children for the movie. Kesselman had met neither Harold nor Donna Schuman before, and it was only through a casual conversation that the prosecutor learned that Donna Schuman harbored intensely negative feelings toward Landis because of the deaths.

Although disillusioned, she maintained a friend's loyalty toward Folsey. She offered to help Kesselman with background information and investigative leads but said that she did not want to testify, particularly against Folsey, who had been a longtime friend.

"I know the people. Can you give me a break? If you've got stuff elsewhere, is there any reason I have to say it?" she asked Kesselman, who promised that if he could find other witnesses who could testify to the same material, he would do so. Over time, she provided the prosecutor with insight into the way the Landis production office functioned, and her opinion of the personalities and ethics of the film's principals.

The idea that a grand jury would be investigating the crash was a frightening concept to many who had been involved in the production of the movie. Anderson House, for one, had been deeply affected by the deaths, and told friends that he felt he had been an innocent victim of someone else's scheme. Now he worried whether the grand jury might indict him. Kesselman, to encourage full and honest testimony, assured House in writing that he was not an investigative target.

Kesselman's prosecutorial interest was focused on Landis, Folsey, Allingham, Wingo, and Stewart, the men he believed had had full authority and responsibility over what happened. He later told me: "If I were to go on a theory that you're going to indict and prosecute every person on that set who knew that there were children who were being used, I would have indicted two hundred people."

On May 31, the secret proceedings of the Los Angeles County grand jury began. Kesselman concisely explained the case to the twenty jurors: "While interviews have been contradictory, and many witnesses appear to have been less than candid, evidence indicates that director Landis desired to have explosives placed under or inside the huts constructed on the set to simulate the destruction of the entire village in the final scene.

"Landis was apparently told by Paul Stewart that it would be dangerous to place these explosives under or inside the huts because the debris, including pieces of bamboo, would fly in all directions, thereby creating substantial hazard for the helicopter as well as to the spectators on the set. In spite of these warnings, explosives were placed under one of the huts."

Dorcey Wingo was the first witness.

His culpability, Kesselman argued, rested in his lack of caution, seemingly admitted to Budds the morning of the crash, when the pilot said that he had not determined the specific locations of the special-effects explosions before any of his flights.

Wingo and his lawyer knew that he faced indictment and concluded that there was now nothing to gain by answering Kesselman's questions in front of the grand jurors.

"Mr. Wingo, were you hired as a helicopter pilot in July of 1982 in connection with the John Landis *Twilight Zone* production?"

"Yes, sir, I was," Wingo replied.

"Who hired you, sir?" Kesselman said.

"I wish to make a statement at this time sir. I respectfully refuse to answer on the grounds it may tend to incriminate me and subject me to the risk of forfeiture of my pilot's license on which I base my livelihood."

The pilot, in refusing to testify, asserted his constitutional rights under the Fourth, Fifth, Sixth, and Fourteenth amendments.

Kesselman tried one more question: "Did you, in fact, pilot a helicopter on July 23 at approximately 2:20 A.M. at Indian Dunes in connection with the filming of the John Landis segment of the *Twilight Zone*?"

"I respectfully refuse to answer that question on the grounds that it may tend to incriminate me," Wingo replied.

After ascertaining that Wingo would answer all questions with the same response, Kesselman excused him from the session. When the pilot had left the room, Audrey Collins, a deputy district attorney assisting Kesselman, told the jurors that they should draw no inferences from Wingo's decision to remain silent.

During six days of testimony, the jurors were presented with the details of the production at Indian Dunes from thirty-six witnesses. Narrated by an assistant cameraman who had worked at Indian Dunes, the jurors saw all the film that had been taken of the early Friday morning crash and the scenes before, which had been filmed on Thursday night. The collection of film segments lasted about twenty minutes and, along with the 2:20 A.M. scene, showed several views each of the 9:30 P.M. scene in which Morrow runs from the huts with the children in his arms, the

11:30 P.M. scene when Connor confronts the helicopter (the scene in which the aircraft is buffeted because gasoline and water mortars were exploded too close to it), and the 2:00 A.M. rehearsal in which Landis can be seen standing in the river and using arm gestures to position the helicopter in the air above.

Kesselman had finally decided that he needed Donna Schuman's testimony, and she told the grand jurors about the illegal hiring of the children. She also described the Landis production office as "Chaos. Total and complete. The emphasis was on doing things cheaply rather than correctly."

Second assistant director Anderson House testified: "I knew it was against the law to have children working after hours, and, second, it didn't seem to be the kind of thing young children should be working in." House also described the efforts of the production team to prevent fire safety officer Jack Tice, who was also a teacher-welfare worker, from seeing My-Ca and Renee on the set.

Renee's uncle Peter Chen and the parents of both children told of their sorrowful experience, asserting that they had been deceived by the production team about the true danger the children faced.

"What would you have done if you had known the children were being used in the filming?" Jack Tice was asked.

Tice was bitter about the tragedy and said: "I would have shut the set down. Because the children shouldn't be working in an area that dangerous. No one that I knew in the [California] labor board would permit it. Neither would I."

Cynthia Nigh, the assistant who had been engaged to marry Allingham (they had since broken the engagement), suggested that some production team members had been well aware beforehand that their actions in connection with the children were questionable. She quoted Folsey as having said in the days before the filming at Indian Dunes: "We'll probably be thrown in jail after this, just because of the kids."

Kesselman wanted to show that not only did the moviemakers willingly violate state child labor laws by hiring My-Ca and Renee to work after hours, but also that they had known ahead of time that the scene with the helicopter and special effects was especially risky. Nigh helped Kesselman make that point by telling the grand jurors that just before the 2:20 A.M. shot Landis turned to the gallery of spectators and crew and ordered them to "be ready to move in case anything goes wrong."

Veteran helicopter pilot John Gamble, who described the care he takes in planning a scene with special effects, stated that Wingo had not exercised ordinary caution.

First assistant director Elie Cohn was unsure of some events in the final moments before the deaths but confident that Landis had given the order for the helicopter to hover at a lower altitude than had been rehearsed, a last-minute change that may have contributed to the crash. "To the best of my memory," Cohn testified, "John Landis started saying 'lower, lower.' I think he was using the bullhorn but I'm not completely sure about that."

Although Landis denied that he had directed Stewart to place a mortar under the food-drying shack, or even knew that a bomb was placed there, Kesselman argued circumstantially that because of the authority structure on a movie set, especially one governed by the forceful Landis, it was illogical to believe that a special-effects foreman would place a large explosive in the middle of a scene without the director's knowledge and approval. Cohn, an experienced assistant director, corroborated that theory for the jurors.

Harry Stewart was the first of the four special-effects crewmen to testify. He and his three colleagues had not yet been actually granted immunity from prosecution by Kesselman. The prosecutor, unwilling to make such concessions until he absolutely had to, wanted to see what the men would do when they entered the jury's chamber, unaccompanied by their attorneys, who were not allowed into the closed session.

Not surprisingly, Harry Stewart, as well as the three others who appeared later, refused to answer even introductory questions. Once their reticence had been established on the record, Kesselman then presented each with a letter of immunity, which he had prepared in advance on behalf of District Attorney Robert Philobosian.

> In view of the fact that you have just invoked your constitutional rights against self-incrimination at this Grand Jury hearing called to investigate the circumstances surrounding the deaths of Vic Morrow and two child actors on July 23, 1982, and in order to facilitate a thorough investigation into the facts surrounding this incident, I hereby agree and promise on behalf of the District Attorney's Office as follows:
>
> That you, ———, will not be prosecuted for your involvement in any act or circumstance which lead (sic) to the deaths of the aforesaid individuals. In return for this promise, it is expected that you will testify truthfully before the Grand Jury, and in any further court proceedings which may arise in this matter.
>
> It should also be understood, ———, that if you

> deviate from the truth and testify falsely at any time,
> you can and will be prosecuted for perjury.

One of the key points Kesselman made through the testimony of these men was that the special-effects crew had not been advised that the explosions at 11:30 P.M. had caused problems for the pilot and the other occupants of the helicopter. The importance of this communication omission is that the information could have provided them with a warning to take extra care at 2:20 A.M.

Harry Stewart told the grand jurors that the prohibition against detonating structures in proximity to aircraft and people is "common knowledge to any powderman [special-effects technician]. That's why we put sawdust in the mortars and keep them clear, so that there can't even be a little rock or anything flying up. That's the whole point."

The jurors heard about Landis's anger and flippancy during the preparations for the final scene.

Assistant cameraman Randy Robinson, who had been in the helicopter, attributed the tragedy to the director's spontaneity and exuberance over obtaining a more thrilling shot: "I think they just got carried away and wanted us in the shot to make it more dramatic, I think."

Robinson, who had participated in the revealing press conference three days after accident, also talked about industry blackballing: "I think people feel that way generally, that anytime anything happens it's best not to say a word. I was rather nervous about having spoken out. I was a little concerned about safety because I've been around a few other accidents where people have died and it's been something I don't like to see. And this was too outrageous for us to let go on. I had to say something. A lot of people said, 'Well, you're crazy. You'll never work again.' I may have a real bad name in the industry because I'm a loudmouth. I don't know. I get a lot of real good positive reaction."

Camera operator Steve Lydecker believed in the power of blackballing. He had worked regularly in the movie industry for twenty-two years and believed that his six months of unemployment was due entirely to his outspoken criticism of the production after the crash. His 2:20 A.M. position on the crane across the river from the village had offered the most complete view of the set. "I would say it was probably lack of information and timing that was probably the largest contributor," he said.

Paul Stewart arrived at the downtown courthouse ill informed and believing that he, like the other men on his crew, would receive immunity. He was surprised when he was excused from the session after invoking the Fifth Amendment.

During the week, a court clerk read aloud to the grand jurors the transcripts of both his and Dorcey Wingo's National Transportation Safety Board testimony from the previous July.

James Camomile, after being granted immunity, surprised Kesselman when he said that he had been wrong when he told Budds that he had placed a powerful, round mortar under the food-drying shack before the 2:20 A.M. shot at the direction of Paul Stewart. He said that actually he had placed a square mortar, the one Budds found several hours after the crash.

Camomile said that his mistake had been pointed out to him in conversations with others on the crew, including Paul Stewart. Kesselman thought that Camomile was lying in an attempt to protect his friend Paul Stewart, now the only special-effects man who could face prosecution because of the grants of immunity to the others.

Kesselman, however, didn't know that a sheriff's department analysis of photographs and sound recordings of the explosions, using sensitive technical equipment, had confirmed that the mortar under the food-drying shack at 2:20 A.M. had indeed been square. Camomile's testimony was accurate. In previous statements to Budds he had confused in his memory the mortar under the food-drying shack with a round mortar he had placed in an open area nearby.

Camomile's testimony took Kesselman off stride, and the prosecutor went so far as to warn Camomile about perjury statutes before he moved on to other issues.

One important point made by Camomile was about the instructions Paul Stewart had given him before the 2:20 A.M. shot. Camomile said that he had not been told anything about where the helicopter should be when he detonated his bombs, only that Morrow and the children should have reached a certain spot in the river away from the village: "It was a visual and audible instruction situation. As to the exact flight path, I was not, once again, given a complete verbal dissertation of it. It was established that the helicopter would be coming in, holding its position, the machine guns would begin to fire."

Allingham, Folsey, and Landis all testified voluntarily, but under an agreement between their attorneys and Kesselman they were not asked questions about the illegal hiring, the offense Braun assumed was the most likely with which they would be charged.

Allingham, in contradiction to the testimony of others, said that after the eleven-thirty shot he had not been upset by the proximity of the helicopter to the special effects, nor had he tried to communicate displeasure about the flight to anyone on the ground.

Later, even the defense attorneys would joke about Allingham's extensive memory lapses, to which he referred frequently during his grand jury testimony.

"I truly don't remember whether I went to John and really said anything," Allingham testified in relation to his actions after the 11:30 P.M. shot. "I strongly believe that we were as safe as one could be. We hired the very best people. And I think to really top it off, I thought it was so safe that I went up in the helicopter. And I think if I would have had any idea that it wasn't safe, or any recollection that there was any more safety factor than walking across the street—I am not suicidal—I don't think I could have gotten in that helicopter."

Allingham—unwittingly, no doubt—supported Kesselman's contention that the scene had been poorly planned.

"Were you ever present for a meeting between Mr. Stewart and Mr. Wingo, with or without Mr. Landis present, to walk the set and view each special-effect mortar?"

"I was not with anybody. No."

Folsey, whom the prosecutor recognized had no substantive function in the planning of the Vietnamese scenes, was a target because of his participation in the illegal hiring. He testified that no one ever suggested to him that it was unsafe to have the children in proximity to explosives or a helicopter.

John Landis did not help himself with his testimony, which was contradictory to that of others and sometimes had a hostile, petulant cast to it. Poor communication was central to Kesselman's theory of negligence, and Landis said little to indicate that he had adequately monitored vital coordination between or among others.

"Was there any substantial conversation then between Mr. Stewart and Mr. Wingo regarding the helicopter vis-à-vis the explosions in the upcoming scenes?"

"I'd have to assume so. Because I left. I didn't stay."

Regarding the problems of the eleven-thirty shot, which, Kesselman believed, should have been thoroughly discussed by everyone involved in a single group, Landis said: "On the ground, I'm unaware of Paul and Dorcey actually having a specific conversation about that specific shot."

"Did you set up a meeting?" Kesselman asked.

"When I say to someone, 'Go talk to someone,' I don't take them by the hand and lead them over there. Did I take him by the hand to Paul? No, I did not. I asked both men if they were ready, they both said 'Yes.' I assume if these men are experts, licensed by the state to do their jobs, they've done their jobs."

Landis expressed his nervousness to Kesselman and the jurors: "I must tell you, this whole thing scares me. The whole grand jury investigation, because I'm very concerned. Please forgive me for being uneasy and uncertain."

Landis did finally give in to his anger as Kesselman pressed him about how he positioned the helicopter for the final shot: "On the last rehearsal I'm not certain. I don't know if—is that—you know more about this film than me. Was that the one that was filmed by Frank Marshall?"

"Mr. Landis, unfortunately I can't give testimony here. I can only ask the questions."

"I'm sorry," Landis said.

Testimony from others that Landis had repositioned the helicopter at the last minute was overwhelming. But Landis was firm in his account.

"Did someone to your knowledge say the words 'lower, lower, lower' at any time?" Kesselman asked.

"Absolutely not. And might I add, if they did, no one could have heard them."

"Did you see the helicopter begin to lower at that time, begin to descend?"

"No, sir. It was stationary," Landis said, in stark contradiction to what the jurors had already observed themselves when they saw the film of the helicopter's descent just before the 2:20 A.M. scene began.

"Did you say the words 'fire, fire, fire'?"

"No, sir. Again, let me repeat what I did."

"Mr. Landis, you can just, in the interest of time at this point . . ."

"I'm sorry. I apologize. This is the worst experience of my life and it's very emotional."

Landis was Kesselman's last witness. Just before the director was excused, he firmly denied having had a discussion with Stewart about placing mortars in huts for the two-twenty shot and said that he had "absolutely no knowledge" that a bomb had been placed under the food-drying shack.

Because of the uncertainty of the testimony that the week of grand jury hearings would elicit, district attorney supervisors had not given Kesselman authority to ask grand jurors for indictments until the day of Landis's testimony. Landis had testified in the morning, and during the lunch break, Kesselman made final adjustments to the closing argument he would make in the afternoon. Tom Budds, who, after all, had now devoted close to a year of his life to the *Twilight Zone* case, wanted to hear

Kesselman's speech, which he knew would be distinctively compelling. By law the proceedings were secret to all but the jurors and prosecutors. Budds, however, stood near a door to the grand jury chamber that was slightly ajar and allowed him to listen, an innocent enough reward for his hard work.

Budds's professional gratification came when he heard Kesselman request the indictments alleging the serious charges that Budds all along had believed were warranted.

"I am requesting that the grand jury bring indictments against five individuals for involuntary manslaughter," Kesselman began. "And those individuals are John Landis, George Folsey, Jr., Dan Allingham, Dorcey Wingo, and Paul Stewart."

For Budds and Kesselman, the case was finally in its proper focus. Indictments for involuntary manslaughter signified that at least one arm of the state's judicial system was not satisfied with the explanation that the deaths had resulted from an unavoidable accident, or even simple negligence. The indictments represented the conclusion that the lapses in the professional responsibility of the moviemakers had been so wantonly reckless that the men responsible should go to jail.

In a real sense, the indictments questioned whether the deaths were products of modern moviemaking's continual quest for more realism and bigger stunts—all with an eye to box office receipts.

The charges Kesselman sought were divided into two categories: one based on the illegal hiring of the children and the other based on the allegedly reckless behavior the night of the accident.

Landis, Folsey, and Allingham, based on their participation in the illegal hiring, were each named in two counts, one for each child. Bringing the children to Indian Dunes, Kesselman said, was an act of child endangerment.

Landis, Stewart, and Wingo were each named in three counts—one for each child and Morrow—for their allegedly negligent behavior on the movie set in the hours before the crash.

The prosecutor explained that for the jurors to indict Wingo, Landis, and Stewart, they would have to conclude that their acts, of omission or commission, had been committed "without due caution and circumspection. That is a negligent act which is aggravated, reckless, or gross. It would be such a departure from the conduct of an ordinarily prudent or careful man under similar circumstances to show a disregard for human life that the consequences, namely, the death, was foreseeable, and that the death resulted as a natural and probable result of the reckless act."

Kesselman left the room as the jurors deliberated on his remarks. In late afternoon, they voted to issue the indictments against the five men. The documents were then presented to a Superior Court judge for review. Kesselman asked that arrest warrants for the five defendants be delayed for a time, giving him the opportunity to notify defense attorneys so that the men could surrender voluntarily for arraignment.

Stewart, who was working in Albuquerque, New Mexico, was called by his lawyer and told that he had been indicted.

Incredulous, Stewart yelled back into the telephone, "For what?"

A week after the grand jury had voted, the five moviemakers appeared in a Los Angeles courtroom for their arraignment—on the same day that *Twilight Zone: The Movie* premiered in movie theaters across the country.

The Landis segment, starring Vic Morrow, remained the first of four tales in the movie. Omitted entirely, however, were the Vietnamese village scenes with the children. The sheriff's department had long before confiscated all of that film for evidence.

Thus, without a scene to display his humanity and morality, the character of Bill Connor remained unredeemed, as viciously shallow a personality as had been portrayed at the opening of the film.

If the climactic scene had been completed without incident, that probably still would not have changed the views of movie critics who, for the most part, found the movie as a whole, and the Landis segment in particular, mediocre at best.

Even Rod Serling's namesake *Twilight Zone* magazine, published by his widow, Carol Serling, who had enthusiastically granted name authorization to the producers, could find little to praise in the film. The magazine's reviewer said of the Landis episode: "In its understated way, [it is] one of the most appalling bits of moral idiocy I've seen in some time on the silver screen, for it takes as its essential premise the idea that it would be a fine and good thing to round up those afflicted with racial prejudice and anti-Semitism and send them to Nazi death camps. Landis seems to think that would be one hell of an idea."

Of all the reviewers, Richard Corliss of *Time* magazine came to the singularly most compelling conclusion about the movie's artistic value: "Hardly looks worth shooting, let alone dying for."

EIGHT

THE WORRIES of defense attorneys that John Landis would be unable to contain his volatile temper during the legal proceedings were first realized seven months after the grand jury indictments.

Under a California Supreme Court decision, persons indicted by grand juries—because defense attorneys may neither be present nor cross-examine witnesses in the secret deliberations—have the option of conducting a preliminary hearing before a judge, who determines whether the evidence on which the indictments are based is sufficient for a jury trial.

The preliminary hearing for Landis, Folsey, Allingham, Stewart, and Wingo, before Magistrate Brian D. Crahan, took nineteen days in January and early February 1984. The defense, led by Harland Braun, used the forum to create a minitrial, fighting vigorously to break Kesselman's case before it could be presented to a jury.

The outburst from Landis that the defense lawyers feared happened one day during the hearing. Braun, Landis, Kesselman, and others were in a makeshift storage room adjacent to the court, reviewing trial exhibits: the broken tail rotor, pieces of bamboo from the huts, special-effects equipment, photographs, and other items and documents.

Landis asked the prosecutor if he truly believed that he was guilty. Kesselman replied that he did not believe that Landis had intended to hurt anyone, but if he had not been fully convinced that the director was criminally negligent, he would not pursue the case.

"I hope you don't take this personally, I'm just doing my job," Kesselman said.

"You're fucking with my life!" an enraged Landis yelled back.

Leonard Levine, who recently had been hired to represent Allingham, later told me the exchange "was a tense moment"—calmed only because Kesselman quietly walked away.

Landis, though, did not repress expressions of his antagonism toward Kesselman, one day belittling the physical appearance of the prosecutor, who typically dressed in dressy boots and suits that were awkwardly tight-fitting. "There goes the midget in high heels," Kesselman told me he heard Landis remark.

Levine, then thirty-six, is, like Braun, a graduate of UCLA law school and a former Los Angeles County district attorney prosecutor. He is a gentlemanly person with a quick, legal intellect.

Two other attorneys, in addition to Levine, were also new to the defense team.

Arnold Klein, a forty-one-year-old Buffalo, New York, native, who had graduated from Golden Gate College School of Law in San Francisco, was the third member of the defense team to have been a former Los Angeles County prosecutor. He had been in private practice only two years and had moved into a new office the same day Paul Stewart telephoned and asked him to take the case. Stewart, who had heard of Klein through a mutual friend, felt comfortable with the lawyer's down-to-earth nature. Klein is unpretentious, inheriting from the streets of Buffalo an ability to speak to the workingmen of the special-effects team, which quickly won their trust.

Eugene Trope, then sixty-seven, has built a prosperous civil law practice—he drives a gleaming white Rolls-Royce with red leather interior and dresses immaculately—with an emphasis on the legal affairs of aircraft pilots and Federal Aviation Administration licensing matters. He quickly developed a fatherlike affection for Dorcey Wingo, and even took a few helicopter lessons, so he could better understand Wingo's function as a pilot.

As the preliminary hearing approached, Harland Braun had been concerned not only with the demeanor of John Landis during the proceedings but also whether Landis's uncle, Benjamin Landis, a prominent, retired Los Angeles County Superior Court judge, would improperly affect the court. Ben Landis was described by acquaintances as a friendly man, a proponent of the "old-boy network" who was especially fond and proud of his nephew.

After retiring, Ben Landis maintained friendships with sitting judges and visited the courthouse frequently. Braun didn't worry that Ben Landis would be so foolish as to make an overt and improper request of another judge to dismiss the charges. But the defense lawyer did wonder whether he might attempt some subtle, informal lobbying on behalf of his nephew. Braun later told me that although Ben Landis no doubt would have thought he was doing the right thing, "I was always afraid that Ben would pick up the phone and try to influence the case."

In early 1985 a group of Superior Court judges once had a discussion about potential conflicts of interest they might encounter in the *Twilight Zone* case because of their relationships with Ben Landis—this at a time before a trial judge had been selected, and any of the criminal jurists was eligible to hear the case pending assignment by the court's presiding judge. The specific issue that concerned the judges involved Ben Landis's occasional invitations to them for Hollywood screenings of his nephew's movies. When one such invitation was received after the grand jury indictment had been handed up, some questioned the propriety, as well they might.

When Ben Landis attended the preliminary hearing one day, Braun asked him to leave so that the defense could not be attacked for attempting to bias the proceedings, although the retired judge's presence had already been noted by the hearing magistrate and others in the courtroom.

Budds wondered about the effect of Ben Landis's presence on other court officials: "It can't hurt to have a retired member of the Superior Court sitting there and it being recognized that he's a relative. Throughout that whole criminal courts building that day, everybody knew that John Landis had an uncle who was a retired judge. That's just the way the grapevine works in the building."

Kesselman, for the most part, followed a course of argument similar to that which he had taken in the grand jury. Under the scrutiny of cross-examination, however, the testimony of prosecution witnesses lost some of the certainty with which it had been imbued in the secret grand jury proceedings. Such challenges, of course, were an accepted component of the adversarial judicial system, and Kesselman was capable of holding his own in contest with the defense team.

In one important area, though, Kesselman's witnesses failed him, with almost disastrous results to the prosecution. The issue was the precise nature of the damage sustained by the helicopter.

Indisputably, the helicopter had been damaged in flight because of a special-effects explosion. While the aircraft's tail was engulfed in a rising fireball, one of two tail rotor blades broke in half. This created such stressful pressures on the remaining assembly—called an aerodynamic imbalance—that the entire rotor gearbox began to vibrate violently and snapped off—all within a matter of seconds. Wingo was then incapable of controlling the helicopter because the necessary stabilizing force of the tail rotor had entirely disappeared.

The critical question about this sequence, however, was what had caused the tail rotor blade to break into two pieces.

The prosecution's witnesses testified that the blade had been hit and dented by a piece of debris shot up from the ground, thus setting up the aerodynamic imbalance. Defense experts, however, theorized that the extreme heat of the fireball had instantaneously loosened the adhesive on the thin metal skin that covered the blade, causing it to peel off (called delamination). With one tail rotor blade missing its outer skin, the defense said, a new weight differential created the stress on the metal.

Whether the tail rotor had been damaged by debris or heat was important to the arguments of both sides.

Kesselman, basing his conclusion on the reports provided him by his technical experts, argued that the last-minute placement of a mortar under the food-drying shack—even after Landis and Stewart had discussed the danger of debris—was criminally negligent because when the bomb detonated beneath the shack's raised platform floor the explosion sent chunks of bamboo soaring, one of which struck a tail rotor blade.

The prosecutor, however, watched the testimony of his technical witnesses invalidated by the defense. Kesselman still believed that debris had caused the crash, but his scientific evidence was not sufficient to counter the more convincingly detailed delamination studies of the defense experts.

For example, an FBI technician had concluded through tests at a government missile range in New Mexico that a six-ounce bomb would not be strong enough to send a piece of debris flying twenty-four feet in the air with enough force to cause the dent in the blade. The FBI agent, however, had based his calculations on only one trajectory and didn't take into account that debris hitting the blade from a different angle might have sufficient force to cause the damage. At this stage of the proceedings, though, Kesselman could not compensate for the limited testing.

With doubt raised about whether debris could have been a factor in the crash, Braun argued that since there were no records of any helicopter crash ever having been caused by delamination, nor had the manufacturer ever warned owners of the aircraft about delamination, then the failure of the glue was an unforeseeable event. The defendants, Braun concluded, could not then be held accountable for the unknown. Legal precedent concerning personal liability did make Kesselman's argument vulnerable to challenge.

Thus Kesselman's negligence case was jeopardized by an argument that, to a layman, sounds flimsy indeed. (Is it not reasonable to expect someone to recognize that the searing heat of a fireball twenty-five feet in diameter might cause some sort of serious damage to a hovering helicopter or endanger the aircraft's occupants?)

The government lawyers did not surrender the point, though. Kesselman, using material other deputy district attorneys familiar with appellate law had discovered, successfully argued to the magistrate that legal precedent in liability cases did not require that the prosecutor prove the specific, technical cause of the crash. Kesselman needed only to demonstrate that the defendants had placed people in a knowable "sphere of danger" likely to result in some disastrous event.

The hearing ended in early February, and lawyers for both sides began research for legal briefs to be submitted to Crahan for his review before he rendered a decision.

In late March—Crahan had not yet ruled—Braun called Kesselman and said he and other defense attorneys wanted to meet with the prosecutor. The request for a discussion was not out of the ordinary, but when the defense team arrived at Kesselman's office, the deputy district attorney was not persuaded by their presentation. Braun and the others tried to convince Kesselman that he should drop the charges. The meeting quickly deteriorated into a shouting match, and the defense attorneys left.

Within a day, Landis's business attorney, Joel Behr, who had been told about the imbroglio, called Kesselman and asked for a meeting of his own. The prosecutor disliked Behr's client, Landis, but had a professionally cordial relationship with Behr and readily accepted. Behr went to Kesselman's office in downtown Los Angeles.

"Do you know what this is doing to these men?" Behr asked, according to Kesselman's account of the session. "Do you know how this is destroying their lives? Isn't there some way that we could resolve this?"

Kesselman later related to me that the discussion then turned to voluntary guilty pleas the defendants might make in order to avoid a trial. Kesselman says that Behr expressed concern that such admissions would affect Landis's defense of the parents' still-pending civil suits.

Kesselman was not skilled in civil law, he told Behr, but assumed that if Landis, Allingham, and Folsey pleaded guilty to a felony conspiracy to hire the children illegally, that plea might have no legal impact on the civil case, in which the defendants were accused of recklessness and negligence for their actions on the movie set.

Kesselman supported a plea bargain—although he did not say so to

Behr. The prosecutor assumed that a voluntary plea would likely result in some jail time for the defendants, and he planned to argue vigorously for that. A plea also avoided the risks (acquittal by a jury) and cost of an expectedly long trial. For the defendants, voluntarily pleading guilty to the hiring charge promised a jail term undoubtedly shorter than the maximum state prison term they would face upon conviction by a jury on the more serious involuntary manslaughter charges.

"He didn't pick up on it. And I wasn't pushing because I wasn't authorized," Kesselman told me later of Behr's lack of response to a plea bargain. Nor did Behr mention the conversation to Harland Braun and the other defense attorneys.

On April 23, 1984, Magistrate Brian Crahan issued his ruling. The decision was a blow to Landis, Wingo, and Stewart, who were bound over for trial for their actions at Indian Dunes on the night of the crash.

Crahan, however, dismissed the involuntary manslaughter charges against Folsey and Allingham. The two counts in the indictment in which they were named had been based on their involvement in the conspiracy to hire the children. (The two counts of involuntary manslaughter against Landis based on his participation in the hiring prior to filming were also dismissed. The three counts for his actions on the set remained.) Crahan concluded that the moviemakers would not necessarily have known at the time of the hiring that they were placing My-Ca and Renee in mortal danger, although they must have recognized that they were putting the children at some risk:

> Although there is undisputed evidence that each of these three individuals [Landis, Folsey, and Allingham] were aware that the children would be placed in both an illegal working condition and proximate to possible dangerous materials, to wit, a hovering helicopter and exploding mortars on the Vietnam-style village set, the evidence does not in and of itself, appear to create that type of foreseeability as to these individuals that the mere act of child endangerment would lead to their deaths.

Crahan took a harsh view of not only the production team but the parents as well for endangering the children.

> This court finds it difficult to believe the parents were totally unaware that the children would be exposed to

some type of helicopter and/or explosive action since the matter was to take place in a Vietnamese village under siege.

However, the law is not quite so clairvoyant as to impute knowledge where none actually exists. In this situation the parents of the deceased children, the principals involved on this set, and anyone who knew their presence, could reasonably be assumed to have endangered the children with respect to the night working conditions, that is, that they might catch a cold or suffer fatigue . . . that they might in fact be burned by some flying debris from mortars placed proximate to the river bed . . .

With regard to the three counts of involuntary manslaughter against Landis, Wingo, and Stewart for the deaths of the children and Vic Morrow, Crahan found that there was culpability:

Where three people die and the cause of death is not an act of God, a reasonable inference can be drawn that some human connection and some human error led to those deaths. It has been argued that the delamination of the tail rotor is legally unforeseeable simply because it has never previously occurred. This line of defense begs the essential question as to whether or not the hovering helicopter in close proximity to the explosives was not in and of itself an act reckless in nature and exposing innocent parties to grave danger. The court believes that a crime, to wit, involuntary manslaughter, was in fact committed by certain principals on the set during the early morning hours of July 23, 1982, in the filming of the final segment of *Twilight Zone: The Movie.* Whether [a jury] will come to the conclusion of guilt, beyond a reasonable doubt, is a question beyond this court's jurisdiction.

Crahan noted that the application of involuntary manslaughter statutes to the facts in this case was "unique in the annals of California criminal legal history," and most cases that even resemble the *Twilight Zone* matter have been tried in civil courts.

While it was obvious that none of the principals had any intention to harm, "let alone kill, two children and one adult actor . . . Unfortunately, the attempt to obtain visual truth led to death without any articulated specific rhyme nor reason."

Although the defense suggested that James Camomile was to blame for firing the explosives too soon, Crahan said that even if Camomile had acted improperly, that did not relieve the defendants of their responsibilities. Neither was it a mitigating factor that they themselves could have been injured or killed. Their innocent intent was not at issue, only their alleged negligence.

Crahan ruled that Stewart bore responsibility as the supervisor of the special effects, Wingo for flying his helicopter so close to the explosions, and Landis for his direction of the entire sequence in a "quest for cinema vérité":

> In achieving such absolutism, he appears to have gone beyond the realm of simple mechanical direction, but in fact set up, among other things, the combination of circumstances which in the final seconds of filming, caused death and destruction.
>
> There were ample warnings to these individuals prior to the 2:20 filming episode, which made their conduct from the time of such warnings calculating and unreasonable, and therefore criminal in nature.

Kesselman was confident that the district attorney's office could win any appeals of Crahan's decision, the next step in the legal process before the matter finally reached a jury trial. Both sides had issues on which to seek redress: The defense sought a higher-court dismissal of the charges against Landis, Stewart, and Wingo, and the district attorney's office sought the reinstatement of the charges against Folsey and Allingham. Even though the prosecutor had overcome the delamination fiasco in the preliminary hearing, Kesselman concluded that he would have to be prepared with a stronger technical argument in a jury trial. He believed that a group of jurors, average people not studied in the nuance of law, would want a prosecutor to tell them exactly what happened at 2:20 A.M. Closer to trial, he decided, he would ask district attorney supervisors to approve the large expenditures necessary for sophisticated scientific analysis of the delamination issue. He believed he could use to his advantage a conclusion that the helicopter was damaged either by debris or heat. But he had to be able to tell a jury which one it was. Allowing the defense to do so instead would weaken his position.

The first concerns for both sides, though, were the appeals of the magistrate's rulings. A hearing before Superior Court judge Gordon Ringer was set for November.

In March, a month before Crahan's ruling, the National Transportation Safety Board announced its finding in a document Kesselman now knew was flawed because it had been based on the same incomplete testing that had been used by his experts at the preliminary hearing. The NTSB investigators had reported that debris caused the damage to the tail rotor blade.

Defense attorneys did not let the NTSB conclusion go unchallenged, and they provided the federal agency with the work of their technical experts in a request that the board review its study. The NTSB investigators agreed, and later issued a revised report adding as fact that one of the tail rotor blades had delaminated because of heat. But the new report only added more doubt about whether it was debris or heat that had been the primary catalyst for the aerodynamic imbalance. Neither was identified by the federal investigators as the primary cause:

> The National Transportation Safety Board determines that the probable cause of the accident was the detonation of debris-laden high temperature special effects explosions too near a low flying helicopter leading to foreign object damage to one rotor blade and delamination due to heat to the other rotor blade, the separation of the helicopter's tail rotor assembly, and the uncontrolled descent of the helicopter. The proximity of the helicopter to the special effects was due to the failure to establish direct communications and coordination between the pilot, who was in command of the helicopter operation, and the film director, who was in charge of the filming operation.

On July 3, 1984, Tom Budds was at work when he received the worst news of his life.

His youngest son, 3½-year-old Michael Francis Budds, had wandered into the backyard and drowned in a hot tub that Budds had surrounded with a gated fence and a small brick wall in an attempt to protect his son. Budds never learned whether the gates had been accidentally left open by someone or if the boy had undone the latches himself.

Budds had been separated from his wife since June and had not been living in the house. The child, one of Budds's five sons, had been home with the family's trusted housekeeper. Budds's estranged wife was at work at the time.

Budds suffered from nightmares afterward and missed his son with deep, emotional pain. Defense attorneys believed that the death of the boy added an emotional prejudice to the detective's zeal for a conviction in the *Twilight Zone* case. At the time of Michael's death, however, Budds had all but completed the substantive part of his investigation and had already formed his opinion about the guilt of the defendants.

Budds believes that the death actually helped the defense by distracting him from his work. "It was one of the toughest things in my life to keep focused on this case," the detective told me.

The loss of his son did heighten his sensitivity to the importance of the case: "It made me feel more strongly what I'd known all along: that children are precious and you have a higher responsibility and should guard them more carefully. Kids don't have the experience. That's why they have parents and guardians and teacher-welfare workers."

A curious turn of events took place on November 3, the Saturday before Judge Ringer was to hear the appeals of Magistrate Crahan's ruling.

For three years, Kesselman had been a financial investor in a downtown Los Angeles taxi dance hall called the Club El Gaucho, a place employing and frequented primarily by Hispanic immigrants, where men paid a fee (usually thirty cents) by the minute to dance with female hostesses.

That Saturday night, the Club El Gaucho and several other similar establishments in the city were raided in a joint effort of the Los Angeles Police Commission, the city police department's vice squad, and the U.S. Immigration and Naturalization Service. Several hostesses at Kesselman's club were arrested and turned over to the INS as suspected illegal aliens. One of the ten, according to police reports, had been observed performing a lewd act, and Kesselman was later warned by a police commission official that his club was a potential location for prostitution. Another hostess had been arrested earlier in the year and fired. Kesselman said he was a financial investor and did not have a function in day-to-day management, but he promised to ensure that any problems would be corrected.

Of course, the raid could only embarrass Kesselman and harm the credibility that his integrity as a prosecutor had won for him. Although there were several establishments targeted in the raid, Kesselman was convinced that he had been set up. The police commission, the agency that licensed establishments such as the Club El Gauco, was a politically influenced group. The prosecutor was convinced that Harland Braun, using his ties to the city's Democratic Party structure, had set the raid in motion.

Kesselman often went to the club on Saturday nights for a cup of coffee with the staff. (By law, no liquor was sold at the club.) He assumed that the plan had been that he would be caught at the club during the raid, surely generating negative news accounts about him. The prosecutor's connections with Latin American immigrants was not unusual. He had served in the Peace Corps in Central America, and his wife was a Mexican national. Kesselman, however, happened not to be at the club when the raid took place.

The following Tuesday the hearing before Ringer took place as scheduled, with still no news reports about the Saturday night raid. On Thursday morning, however, the *Los Angeles Times* ran the story under a large headline, embarrassing to both Kesselman and the district attorney's office: "Deputy D.A. Draws A Warning After Dance Hall He Co-Owns Is Raided."

Gilbert Garcetti, who has since been appointed chief deputy district attorney, told me that office supervisors had concluded that Kesselman had done nothing illegal or unethical in connection with the club, and the matter was not pursued.

Braun, who apparently had not been involved, nor had any prior knowledge of the raid, later told me that he was convinced, however, that someone "connected to the Hollywood side of the *Twilight Zone*" had been instrumental in its timing. He would not, however, point to anyone in particular. Neither did Garcetti nor others in the hierarchy of the district attorney's office make any substantial effort to determine if someone had tried to influence the prosecution by means of the raid.

Ringer's ruling, announced orally to the lawyers and the defendants at the conclusion of the hearing on November 5, devastated the production team. The judge found that the magistrate's order to send Landis, Wingo, and Stewart to trial had been proper. In addition, Ringer concluded that Crahan had ruled erroneously regarding Folsey and Allingham and reinstated the charges against them.

> This is a classic case of a situation where on the basis
> of the evidence contained at the preliminary hearing,
> the defendants, and all of them, should stand their
> trial.
> This isn't nickelodeon time anymore. I'm not ex-

pressing a personal opinion, but I should have thought that after seventy-five years somebody might have thought it inappropriate to put Lillian Gish on an ice floe and send her into the middle of Niagara Falls to make a movie.

Whether a jury will determine that's what happened, whether the jury will determine that one or more of the defendants was simply civilly negligent, or whether a jury will determine that they were all criminally negligent is not for me to say.

This is a case to be tried.

The defense, as expected, appealed Ringer's decision to a state court of appeals and lost. Their request that the California Supreme Court review the case was turned down by a margin of one vote.

The appeals took months. Finally, in August 1985, the *Twilight Zone* case appeared close to a jury trial.

In a routine preliminary session that month before Superior Court judge Arturio Muñoz, who had since been assigned the case as the trial judge, Muñoz suggested that this complicated matter might better be handled with a plea bargain negotiated between Kesselman and the defense team. Muñoz offered to assist the negotiations.

Soon afterward, Harland Braun, representing Landis; Leonard Levine, representing Allingham; and Richard Rosen, representing Folsey, met with Kesselman and Budds. Braun was concerned that a jury conviction of involuntary manslaughter could result in state prison sentences for the defendants. He offered a compromise: Landis, Folsey, and Allingham would voluntarily plead guilty to a felony conspiracy to hire the children illegally, provided the district attorney would not argue for a sentence longer than one year in a county facility.

The proposed negotiated plea would include that all charges would be dropped against Wingo and Stewart, who had played no role in the illegal hiring.

Kesselman was surprised by Braun's offer, because it mirrored the alternative he had suggested to Behr a year before, and he told Braun so. Braun, who is a skilled criminal defense attorney, found the offer appealing, and was angered that Behr had not discussed it with him many months before. So the defense lawyer asked the prosecutor to consider the deal.

"I will take it up with the powers that be," Kesselman told the defense lawyers in reference to his supervisors.

Budds was furious that Kesselman would consider a plea bargain. In the detective's view, the compromise demeaned the reason for pursuing the case because it did not speak directly to culpability for the deaths.

"Well, two kids are dead," the detective sputtered.

"Calm down, Tom," Kesselman said. The prosecutor explained the tricky legal problems of pursuing the matter before a jury.

As Braun and his colleagues had to consider the worst that could happen to their clients in a trial, Kesselman also had to presage his chances for success. The result, Kesselman believed, was that even if he went to trial and won, a Superior Court judge, Muñoz in particular, would be unlikely to imprison first-time offenders, who were arguably decent people otherwise. Kesselman wanted Landis and the others to spend time in jail but had concluded that they probably would serve no longer a sentence after a trial than they would after a plea bargain. Kesselman also recognized the possibility that a jury would acquit them, leaving them criminally unpunished for any of the misdeeds he believed they had committed—including the indisputable illegal hiring.

Kesselman brought the proposal to District Attorney Ira Reiner, a publicity-conscious politician who had been elected the year before. Reiner, previously the elected Los Angeles City controller, had limited courtroom experience, and had never prosecuted a major felony case. Colleagues, however, and defense attorney Braun credited Reiner with sharp prosecutorial instincts sometimes weakened by political motivation. Kesselman went through the pitfalls of the *Twilight Zone* case in detail. Involuntary manslaughter would be quite difficult to prove, Kesselman said.

"You've got three dead people, a helicopter, and explosions. What else do you need?" Kesselman, in an interview with me, quoted Reiner. Kesselman believes that Reiner had not paid attention to the presentation and was primarily attracted by the positive publicity such a high-profile case might garner for the office.

Kesselman called Braun and said there would be no deal.

Unknown to the prosecutor, Reiner and his top aides had quickly made a decision to replace him. There is no reason to doubt that Kesselman would have prosecuted vigorously if he had gone to trial. However, other lawyers in the district attorney's office told me that Reiner—who has a penchant for frequent press conferences in which he talks tough about stopping crime, but not always with a full grasp of the facts—believed that Kesselman had "gone soft."

Career prosecutors in the office said that the decision to refuse the plea bargain was not necessarily a mistake, but any prosecution still required a lawyer of skill, sensitive to the case's subtlety and nuances, and a trial presentation convincing enough to counter what would no doubt be a skilled defense.

In the seven-hundred-lawyer district attorney's office—a political and gossipy place—it was inevitable that word would get back to Kesselman that Reiner and two of his top aides, Garcetti and Richard Hecht, were seeking to replace him.

Kesselman heard the news on the elevator one day when a fellow prosecutor innocently said, "Gary, I hear you're off the *Twilight Zone* case."

In the nine months since the Club El Gaucho raid, Kesselman had gone to Garcetti several times and offered to be taken off the *Twilight Zone* case so that the office and the case would not be tainted by bad publicity. Kesselman had attempted to sell the club, but the transfer was stuck in escrow, and he worried that his continued association with the establishment could be used by the defense to publicly embarrass the *Twilight Zone* prosecution again. Kesselman also cited, among other factors, his lingering fatigue from the Danny Young murder case. Garcetti always declined Kesselman's offers to leave the case. Now that all of the *Twilight Zone* appeals had ended, though, and the case was close to trial, Kesselman assumed he would remain prosecutor for the duration of the case.

He viewed Reiner's decision to replace him as an unfair rebuke. Instrumental in the move had been Richard Hecht, the office's director of central operations and a man with whom Kesselman did not get along. Colleagues of Hecht told me that he had always disapproved of Kesselman's links to the Club El Gaucho. Hecht had been promoted when Reiner took office in January. One of his first acts had been to move Kesselman, without explanation, from the special trials division to the complaints division, effectively a demotion in office stature.

Angered by the surprise news of his replacement in the *Twilight Zone* case, Kesselman went back into his office and called Budds.

"Jesus Christ, come down here," he said.

By the time Budds arrived, Kesselman had learned the name of the deputy district attorney, a woman, who would replace him.

NINE

Lᴇᴀ Pᴜʀᴡɪɴ D'Aɢᴏsᴛɪɴᴏ is a physically tiny woman of precise and immaculate personal style. In 1986 her job was prosecuting career criminals, a task the forty-nine-year-old woman performed with unrelenting fervor, winning praise from police and the victims of crimes. Some adversaries, however, saw her passion for her work as all too vengeful. Since she was exposed daily to the terrifying results of criminal violence perpetrated unmercifully by the people she prosecuted, a hard approach to recidivists was understandable and commendable. Nevertheless, her critics say that sometimes Lea D'Agostino doesn't know when to stop.

In ways similar to John Landis, D'Agostino is a demanding personality whose combativeness in professional relationships is, to say the least, not always endearing to others. Although she is only five feet, one inch tall and weighs ninety pounds, there is nothing frail about her.

She is unrelenting in the courtroom and when she is challenged elsewhere. While serving as the assistant prosecutor in the trial of Muharem Kurbegovic, known as the "Alphabet Bomber," for his execution of a terrorist-style bombing at Los Angeles International Airport in 1974, the defendant nicknamed her "The Dragon Lady." She accepts the appellation proudly, suggesting that it signifies her prosecutorial tenacity. On her office wall hangs a plaque presented to her by a group of Los Angeles Police Department robbery detectives, whose cases she prosecuted. It reads: "For 'hard nose' tactics, untiring enthusiasm and dedication."

D'Agostino has a tough exterior, her will strengthened by childhood struggles. She was born in Tel Aviv, in what was then Palestine, in 1937. Her mother, Berta Purwin, had made her way from Nazi-controlled Lithuania in the late 1930s, marrying Monik Sheinbein, a Polish Jew, ten days after meeting him. Sheinbein was a member of a Zionist group. He was shot in the stomach by an Arab, and later died from complications of the wound when Lea was five years old. Her mother later married a British sailor, and the family moved to England where Lea attended a girls' boarding school. When her mother's second marriage ended in divorce, the two moved to the United States, staying briefly with relatives in Boston before moving to Chicago where other family members lived. They used Berta's maiden name, Purwin. America was a fascinating revelation to Lea, who was amused by the bubble gum her cousins gave her and awed by visits to the first supermarkets she had ever seen.

Upon graduating from high school she was accepted into the school of speech at Northwestern University, but the lure of an income from a steady job was more appealing. She went to night school for one semester and did not graduate from college.

Only nineteen years old, Lea Purwin moved to Los Angeles and soon talked her mother into joining her. They remain loyal to each other and inseparable, often conversing several times a day. Berta Purwin is a proud, determined woman who obviously passed on her strong will to her daughter.

In the 1960s, Lea Purwin worked as an executive secretary to movie producer David O. Selznick (whose films include *Gone with the Wind*) and later for talent agent Freddie Fields. For a time, she dated one of the office's famous clients, the late British comic actor Peter Sellers. She also worked as manager of some trendy nightclubs, including the Marina City Club and The Factory, whose owners included Peter Lawford, former brother-in-law of the late John F. Kennedy, and Pierre Salinger, JFK's White House press secretary.

In 1972, feeling professionally unfulfilled, she and a friend, on a whim, decided to go to law school. Three years later Lea had graduated from the unaccredited West Los Angeles University School of Law (a college degree is not required for admission to an unaccredited law school in California).

She had only wanted to be a prosecutor, and was offered a job in the Los Angeles district attorney's office, where she soon made a reputation for her industriousness, winning promotions quickly. She is said to be the first female prosecutor in California to win a death penalty conviction. When appointed to the *Twilight Zone* case she held the second highest ranking a deputy district attorney can attain.

In one office evaluation during the time she was prosecuting career criminals, a supervisor wrote: "Ms. D'Agostino is a uniquely dynamic and tenacious advocate. Through her experience and hard work she has developed into an outstanding trial lawyer, capable of prosecuting any case. During the past year Ms. D'Agostino tried a four-month-long murder case against two vicious prison gang members, and obtained an unexpected conviction, in spite of opposing counsel being most difficult and obstructionist."

"I would not practice law if I could not be a DA," D'Agostino told me. "The gratification that I get comes out of helping victims through what I know is probably the most traumatic part of their lives, and from knowing that I have put rapists, murderers, kidnappers, and robbers behind bars where they belong. I know it sounds soapbox but it really is true you have made the streets a little safer. I get an enormous satisfaction out of doing that. I sleep like a baby."

While in law school, Lea Purwin met Joseph D'Agostino and the two were married during her third year of study. The license plate on the prosecutor's car reads "HRH-LEA" (her royal highness), a gift from her husband, who is general manager for Epicurean, Inc., a food service company operating the dining and concessions at the Hollywood Park and Los Alamitos race tracks. The couple also own a fast-food chicken franchise in Burbank. Friends describe their relationship as loving, and for all the harshness attributed to her public life, Lea D'Agostino says she enjoys traditional romance at home: "I still like the common courtesies. I enjoy being a woman. I have an old-fashioned husband and I enjoy that. And I adore my husband cherishing me and treating me like a lady. I don't ever want to give that up. I cut my husband's hair, I iron his shorts. My one extravagance is clothes. I do my own nails."

She has her superstitions. A piece of gold jewelry—a queen bee—is always pinned rakishly on her shoulder, and whenever she goes to trial she carries six blue felt-tip pens, a holdover omen from her bar examination days. She never removes a Star of David, the only item she has that belonged to her father and which she wears on a necklace. Her upswept black hair is always perfectly in place and she wears elegant designer clothing, favoring the work of Louis Feraud.

When Budds arrived at Kesselman's office after the lawyer's angry telephone call, they decided to call D'Agostino on the pretext that Budds needed to know if he would be working with a new prosecutor—but the two actually hoped to learn more about Reiner's plans for Kesselman.

Budds told me that D'Agostino, who then worked in the district attorney's San Fernando Valley office, denied that she had been given the job and was hesitant about revealing that she had already been downtown for an interview with district attorney supervisors. (Although Reiner talked to D'Agostino in September about taking the case, it wasn't until six weeks later that it was confirmed for her. Before the meeting she thought she had been called downtown to be offered a supervisory position in a sexual assault division, a promotion she desired.)

The first encounter with D'Agostino had not resulted in good feelings toward her by either Kesselman or Budds.

Kesselman was not the only attorney being replaced in the *Twilight Zone* case.

Landis and Behr, in the summer, had begun a cross-country search for a new criminal defense lawyer to replace Braun, whom they did not tell about their quest. Overtures were made to some of the most prominent attorneys in the country, including Alan Dershowitz and Edward Bennett Williams.

It was not surprising that Landis would be concerned. He had heard Harland Braun speak confidently of acquittal from the beginning of the case. Nonetheless, Landis had been indicted by a grand jury, bound over for trial by a magistrate after a lengthy preliminary hearing, and lost all of his court appeals. And now even the offer of a plea bargain had been rejected by the district attorney's office. The movie director was headed to trial by jury.

Behr and Landis were finally successful in retaining a defense lawyer with national stature.

Few lawyers in America could match the accomplishments—on both sides of the counsel table—of James Neal of Nashville, a slow-speaking, cigar-smoking southern man of liberal persuasion.

As a prosecutor, he had been instrumental in two of the more remarkable federal prosecutions of the past twenty years. In the early 1960s he became a special prosecutor in the Department of Justice under then-Attorney General Robert Kennedy. There he won an important conviction—for jury tampering—for the government against the pervasive corruption of Teamster president James Riddle Hoffa.

Both Neal and Hoffa were tough and tenacious, barrel-chested men who had struggled to success from humble backgrounds, and Neal's confrontation with the union man established the lawyer's reputation.

Neal had left the poor farmlands of rural Tennessee with a football scholarship to the University of Wyoming. He returned to Nashville to attend law school at Vanderbilt University, where he graduated at the top of his class.

In his workingman's world, Hoffa had clawed his way up the ranks of the Teamsters, which he had joined as a rough street enforcer, a "goon" for the union bosses.

Neal went toe to toe with Hoffa in the 1962 trial, taking in stride the Teamster president's daily attempts at physical intimidation when he would direct a sneer and an obscene gesture at the young prosecutor. Neal faced courtroom pressures rarely endured by lawyers. A man intent on assassinating Hoffa burst into the courtroom one day brandishing an air-powered pellet gun. The gunman first aimed at Neal, apparently mistaking the square-jawed lawyer for his target, then quickly turned toward Hoffa. But the air pressure on his weapon was too low, and Hoffa stood seemingly unperturbed as the pellets bounced harmlessly off his chest.

A streak of insecurity in Neal, formed in his farmland youth, was the basis for his overachieving energy, which fit well in the highly motivated presidential administration of John F. Kennedy. Attorney General Robert Kennedy used Neal's legal skill in his determined campaign against Hoffa, and Neal's athletic talents in the famous touch football games on the sprawling lawn at Hickory Hill, Kennedy's Virginia home.

Neal's courtroom determination was never more evident than when he became a Watergate special prosecutor and chief trial lawyer in the 1975 prosecution of President Richard Nixon's inner circle: former Attorney General John Mitchell and former White House aides H. R. Haldeman, John Ehrlichman, and Robert C. Mardian. Neal won convictions in stunning fashion and was credited by some observers for a brilliant closing argument to the jury. During the presidential administration of Jimmy Carter, he was a leading candidate for Director of the FBI.

Neal enjoyed equal success as a defense lawyer, winning acquittals for Elvis Presley's doctor, accused of illegally prescribing drugs, and for the Ford Motor Company for allegedly manufacturing the Pinto model with the knowledge that a faulty gas tank structure could result in an explosion in a collision. Most recently, he had successfully defended Louisiana governor Edwin Edwards, who had been indicted on public corruption charges.

Neal was the target of a persuasive campaign on the part of Behr and Landis. At first Neal didn't want the job. He had been away from his home in Nashville much of the previous several years. He was just beginning his second marriage. He had already turned down a Texas oil company's civil case that would have guaranteed him a fee of millions of dollars. A Boston attorney named John Flint, who had worked with Neal during

Watergate and who also had Hollywood connections, convinced Neal to at least meet with Landis and Behr, which he did, in Washington, D.C.

"I was not charmed," Neal told me of his first session with the brash director. "I didn't like him at all." Neal was repulsed by Landis's unremitting arrogance. He declined to take the case. Over time, there were more entreaties. Behr and Landis went to Nashville. Neal was still resistant. Finally Neal was flown to Los Angeles and agreed to represent Landis.

The Tennessee lawyer did make one point abundantly clear to his new client: Landis would have to change his attitude.

"When you didn't have a permit," Neal told Landis sternly, "which is a violation of the law, you're out there at two A.M. with helicopters and special effects and they get their heads cut off on film, John, nobody's being outrageous in questioning your conduct there."

From the beginning, Landis had been incredulous that he could be accused of wrongdoing. His longtime friend Eliza Garrett Simons recalls a conversation in which Landis said: "Eliza, do you realize what they're accusing me of? Do you remember the man who put his hands around Dominique Dunne's neck and deliberately squeezed the life out of her? That's called manslaughter. That's what I'm being accused of. How can it be?"

Neal's plan was to defend Landis using the same principles he applied in the Ford Motor Company case, arguing that whatever mishandling may have taken place, such as the illegal hiring, it did not rise to the severity of a criminal act. He would suggest that any misdeeds were more appropriately resolved in the civil courts.

Neal's hiring created an unsettling dilemma for the defense team. Neal and Braun agreed that they could not be cocounsel. Braun was not willing to become Neal's assistant. Braun and others viewed Landis's unannounced search for a new lawyer as an effective firing.

Still, Braun was vitally important to any defense effort. He was intimately familiar with the complex facts and issues involved and, as a former deputy district attorney in Los Angeles, had a keen understanding of the prosecutor's office. He was friendly with Richard Hecht, the office's director of central operations. Braun and Levine had been responsible for Garcetti joining the office years before. None of this meant that Braun would receive any favors from his former government colleagues, but he represented an important communication link between the defense team and the district attorney's office.

In a reshuffling of jobs that everyone on the defense team viewed as a necessary compromise, Braun became George Folsey's lawyer.

Joining Neal from Nashville was one of his law partners, James Sanders, also a Tennessee native and top-ranking Vanderbilt Law School graduate. He was forty-one years old, and, many believed, possesses an even sharper legal mind than Neal's.

Dealing with Kesselman had been a struggle for the defense attorneys, but they soon realized that the relationship with the new prosecutor would be even more trying. The defense attorneys recognized that D'Agostino would be uncompromising in her prosecution and equally unforthcoming in her personal dealings with them. Joe Ingber, a defense attorney and friend of Paul Stewart's lawyer, Arnold Klein, warned that D'Agostino had a reputation among defense attorneys for becoming embroiled in personalities. She did win cases—every one she had ever tried as a prosecutor.

"But winning convictions," Ingber told me, "is no criterion for the esteem with which you are held by your contemporaries, both those who work with you or against you."

D'Agostino, a person who is not easily dismissed, inspires fierce loyalty or abiding disdain. She would not let the defense team steal the spotlight of the press, precisely the role District Attorney Ira Reiner intended she would play. Important to the thinking of Gil Garcetti, the chief deputy district attorney, and others in the office, was the recent acquittal of auto magnate John Delorean on federal cocaine charges. Garcetti and some colleagues believed that the daily press conferences by defense attorneys, while assistant U.S. attorneys prosecuting Delorean stood mum, had damaged the government's position.

The district attorney's office expected that *Twilight Zone* defense lawyers, particularly Harland Braun and Jim Neal, would aggressively seek publicity to attack the prosecution.

In November 1986, Harland Braun tried to embarrass the district attorney's office into expanding its investigation, suggesting to Reiner and others that they would be remiss if they did not consider that Steven Spielberg and his associates Frank Marshall and Kathleen Kennedy had also been criminally culpable in the illegal hiring of the children. Braun sent a letter to Garcetti attacking the prosecution's limited efforts to question the movie executives.

Landis, Folsey, and Behr were furious when the issue was reported in the newspapers because they did not want to attack Spielberg publicly. They debated whether Braun should be fired, but they realized that his knowledge of the details and nuances of the case was invaluable. Braun remained, but the tensions between him, Neal, Landis, and Behr increased.

The Spielberg organization was at the peak of its influence in Hollywood. The previous July, Spielberg had been on the cover of *Time* magazine, seated next to a movie camera on one of his sets, with the headline, "Presenting Steven Spielberg, Magician of the Movies." The magazine estimated that the gross income of *E.T.* and *Jaws* was $835 million on a $19 million investment.

The *Time* magazine writer, Richard Corliss, the man who had dismissed *Twilight Zone* in his eloquent review, had more positive statements to make about Spielberg and his close associates.

He referred to Kennedy and Marshall as Spielberg's "parents" in his Amblin Entertainment movie production company:

> They share executive producer credits on the films he presents; they keep four sharp eyes on a dozen or so film projects; they grease the tracks that connect Steven with the studios and the press; they act as a DEW line to monitor the unguided missiles of his imagination. . . . In private life, Kennedy and Marshall live together.

By the late spring of 1986, with the trial only weeks away, D'Agostino had concluded that the district attorney's office would be attacked in court for giving up their pursuit to subpoena Marshall.

If the investigators could find Marshall in order to present him with a subpoena, it didn't matter how he might testify. Marshall would be forced either to admit knowledge of the child labor law violation or say he didn't know anything about it. If he denied knowledge, he would just further confirm the prosecution theory that Landis conspired to conceal the illegal act.

Budds's investigative pride was also at stake. Marshall's evasion of him had made "a mockery of the system," Budds told me. "We decided that we can't let anyone in our society get away with that."

Once the decision to subpoena Marshall was reached, Budds made an anonymous call to Spielberg's multimillion-dollar office building located in a hidden corner of Universal Studios and learned that Marshall was in London working on a movie.

Using Interpol and Scotland Yard to trace Marshall's whereabouts, Budds located the studio in London where Marshall was working and the movie executive's residence, the St. James Club.

The normal protocol of serving a subpoena through diplomatic channels would have taken several weeks or longer, time Budds and D'Agostino did not have. Instead, Budds presented an affidavit to a federal magistrate with the request that he issue an international subpoena. Budds alleged that Marshall was a material witness in a criminal prosecution and was evading questioning. U.S. magistrate Volney Brown in Los Angeles issued the subpoena and Budds flew with it to London, where he made contact with Scotland Yard and the Federal Bureau of Investigation legal attaché at the U.S. embassy.

It took a few days to coordinate paperwork between the American and British authorities. Finally, U.S. embassy vice consul Karen L. Christensen went one morning to the St. James Club, subpoena in hand. Budds, who was not authorized to act in a law-enforcement capacity in Great Britain, did not accompany her. At the St. James Club, the woman identified herself to the receptionist, who then called to Marshall's room. The receptionist quoted Marshall as saying he was going out to lunch but would meet Christensen later in the afternoon.

Within an hour of Christensen's call, Budds later learned, Marshall had checked out of the St. James Club, entered a chauffer-driven Mercedes-Benz, and been driven off, presumably to an airport.

Scotland Yard detectives could not find Marshall's name on any manifest for commercial flights from the London airports. The investigators speculated that Marshall had been flown out of the country that afternoon on the Amblin Entertainment corporate jet. Steven Spielberg, Budds said, had been in Paris at the time with director Richard Benjamin, promoting the movie *The Money Pit.*

Dejected by Marshall's disappearance, Budds called D'Agostino and Garcetti in Los Angeles to ask what he should do next. They suggested he head on to Paris, but the detective, who had already spent five days traveling, argued that it would be futile to pursue the matter. He returned to Los Angeles. His was the last attempt any government authorities made to question any high-ranking member of Spielberg's production office about the *Twilight Zone* case.

District attorney investigator Gerald Loeb told me that the effort to find Marshall had had one discomforting effect on Kathleen Kennedy. Because of her relationship with Marshall, and the likelihood she would know his whereabouts, a "stop and hold" request was made through Interpol, requesting that she be regarded as a "suspicious person" and detained for questioning while the international subpoena for Marshall was in force. Some months into the trial, Loeb said he was contacted by federal authorities and told that Kennedy had been stopped at customs in Madrid. He sent back word, however, to say that investigators were no longer interested in speaking to her.

George Folsey told me that the defendants, too, wanted Marshall to testify, to corroborate Landis's statements about the decision to hire the children illegally. He said that Landis talked to Spielberg after the preliminary hearing and asked him to intercede with Marshall. "Whether [Spielberg] attempted it, I don't know. Obviously, Frank went out of the country and avoided the subpoenas," Folsey said.

Spielberg had had little to say publicly about the *Twilight Zone* case since his 1982 letter to the NTSB. *Los Angeles Times* reporter Dale Pollock, however, quoted the director twice. In the spring of 1983, before the grand jury indictments, and the morning after the Academy Awards, at which his big hit *E.T.* had not been honored with major category Oscars, Spielberg appeared to direct criticism at Landis.

The paper quoted Spielberg: "This has been the most interesting year of my film career. It has mixed the best, the success of *E.T.*, with the worst, the *Twilight Zone* tragedy. A mixture of ecstasy and grief. It's made me grow up a little more. The accident cast a pall on all 150 people who worked on this production. We are still just sick to the center of our souls. I don't know anybody who it hasn't affected. A movie is a fantasy—it's light and shadow flickering on a screen. No movie is worth dying for. I think people are standing up much more now than ever before to producers and directors who ask too much. If something isn't safe, it's the right and responsibility of every actor or crew member to yell, 'Cut!' "

In another article written by Pollock a year later, the reporter wrote that Landis remained a close friend of Spielberg, who still declined to comment extensively about the deaths. "The experience is still clearly painful," Pollock wrote. Curiously, in the one quote from Spielberg, the number of people he connected with the production had risen from the quote the year before: "It was tough on all of us, all 390 people involved in making the movie, and it continues to be." Apparently, in the first interview Spielberg had referred to only those who had worked on the Landis segment of the film.

Jim Neal knew that a successful defense would require a cohesive, concise explanation of the events at Indian Dunes. Prior to Neal's involvement the defense lawyers had not always made their arguments with a focused strategy in mind. Neal thought that the way to defend the case was to show that the moviemakers had had a well-thought-out plan for the final shot, that they had reasonably assumed it was safe, and that unforeseen circumstances beyond the control of the defendants had intervened to cause the crash. To make his point, he focused on a statement previously made to investigators by cameraman Randy Robinson, who said it had been his understanding from Allingham that the plan was for the helicopter to be positioned well across the river before the shoreline explosions were detonated.

On July 11, 1986, with jury selection scheduled to begin in just a few days, Donna Schuman wrote a long memo to D'Agostino, detailing her knowledge of the defendants and what they had done during the movie's production.

The two women had developed a friendship and talked frequently on the telephone. D'Agostino saw Schuman as an ally and one of her most important witnesses, one whom the prosecutor had decided would be the first the jury would hear.

On Monday, July 21, eight lawyers, five defendants, a sheriff's investigator, a bailiff, a stenographer, and a court clerk were grouped in front of Superior Court judge Roger Boren for the beginning of the trial. Boren had been assigned the case after Muñoz had been promoted to the position of presiding judge of the Superior Court.

Boren, forty-five as the trial began, is an even-tempered man who wears a thick, bushy mustache. While serving as a California deputy attorney general, he was the coprosecutor in the lengthy "Hillside Strangler" case, in which he won a conviction against Angelo Buono Jr. He was appointed to the bench in 1984. Throughout the *Twilight Zone* trial, Boren's calm would be sorely tested by the lawyers appearing before him.

Even before the trial's start, petty bickering among the adversaries injected a sour mood into the proceedings. Reminiscent of the diplomatic pettiness at the Paris peace talks during the Vietnam War, the lawyers argued about seating arrangements and whether the prosecution or the defense would sit closer to the jury.

"Maybe we could eliminate the prosecution's table," Harland Braun said, smiling.

"I think you would like to eliminate the prosecution altogether," D'Agostino snapped back.

Boren directed that D'Agostino would sit closer to the jurors.

If there had been any doubt about the depth of D'Agostino's conviction that the defendants had committed heinous acts, that was dispelled in her courtroom comments on Wednesday, July 23. The day was the fourth anniversary of the deaths, and routine legal motions were being discussed. Braun suggested that the district attorney's office had made a tactical error by charging Folsey with involuntary manslaughter in the deaths of the children but not similarly charging him in the death of Vic Morrow.

D'Agostino had a quick and firm response.

"Frankly," she said, "I wish second-degree-murder charges were involved here. I believe if I had been the district attorney I would have, in fact, charged second degree murder."

The admission was publicly supported by Chief Deputy District Attorney Gilbert Garcetti, showing that D'Agostino had the strong backing of her supervisors to pursue an aggressive trial strategy. Garcetti's pronouncement also signaled to Gary Kesselman that district attorney supervisors would sanction public criticism of him.

The next day, July 24, Donna Schuman wrote a second memo to D'Agostino, listing three quotes she attributed to the defendants. The statements, presented without further explanation in the note, read in full:

> I asked George Folsey the penalty for using children without permits. He said: "A slap on the wrist and a little fine . . . unless they find out about the explosives and then they'll throw my butt in jail."
>
> I asked George Folsey why he made such a point of telling everyone about the explosives on the set. He said: "With all these explosives on set you should advise everyone so that you're covered in case something were to go wrong."
>
> John Landis also made the statement: "We're all going to go to jail."

The memo contained information to which Schuman had not testified before, either in front of the grand jury or at the preliminary hearing. If true, the comments were quite incriminating. Thus it was all the more curious that such damaging evidence would be emerging just before trial in a case that had been investigated for four years.

Schuman's memoranda were promptly turned over to defense attorneys according to the rules of discovery—the procedure by which the prosecution must make all of its evidence available to the defense prior to trial. Real courtrooms do not live up to the pervasive myth of the trial as a theater of dramatic Perry Mason-style surprises—a falsehood perpetuated by movies and television.

Also on July 24, a pool of more than 150 prospective jurors was called, and jury selection began, not to be completed until four weeks later.

Of the more than one hundred people questioned in nineteen days of *voir dire,* the process during which the lawyers and the judge question potential jurors, all but a few had but the vaguest knowledge even that the deaths had occurred during the making of a movie. Limited public memory of a high-publicity incident like the *Twilight Zone* is common: It is not a testament to the lasting impact of press coverage on the general population.

The Nashville team of Neal and Sanders had spent a considerable sum of money to engage a mock jury in an attempt to determine their effectiveness. (D'Agostino, while in law school, wrote a law review article that suggested critically that such expensive, psychological review could lead to a system in which defendants who could afford the expense could, in effect, buy knowledge that enables them to select a jury likely to be biased in their favor.)

The lawyers later agreed that the *Twilight Zone* jurors had been chosen with reliance on their experience-bred intuition. Not unexpectedly, D'Agostino and the other attorneys said what they really wanted were jurors with "common sense," and, when asked by reporters, said that is what they got.

No one, of course, wanted to be quoted as saying they were disappointed in a particular juror, or in the jury as a whole. Boren ordered the jurors not to read newspaper stories or watch television broadcasts about the trial. Still, everyone recognized that such bans are not always obeyed.

As a group, the jurors were a collection of decent, middle-class people who led hardworking, honest, and orderly lives—people of neither affluence nor poverty. The youngest was in his thirties, the oldest in her seventies, an ethnic mix of blacks, whites, Asians, and Hispanics.

Lauretta Hudson, sixty-seven, was a retired supervisor at Kaiser Permanente Hospital who went to few movies and watched little television. She drew laughter in the courtroom when she said the mention of *Twilight Zone* brought to mind the name Alfred Hitchcock. She read about astrology but said she would never use astrological predictions to decide a criminal case. "It may have been God's plan for this to happen," was her thought when she had heard the news of the helicopter crash in 1982. "I don't like to dwell on unpleasantness," she said.

Lois Rogers was a sixty-one-year-old former secretary with three grown children, including a daughter about to take the California bar exam. Her son owned a Cessna airplane, in which she refused to ride, out of fear. She was a "somewhat conservative" registered Republican who enjoyed target shooting with her husband. Her hobby was compiling her family's genealogy on her home computer. She would become the jury's foreman.

Wilbert D. Fisher, a retired Army colonel, had served in the Corps of

Engineers for twenty-two years. The sixty-four-year-old man was a fan of classical music and public television. He was a Democrat whose father had been a Los Angeles County deputy sheriff, and his former brother-in-law was a judge. He was one of two jurors who had seen *Twilight Zone: The Movie.* "It was good," he said.

Roger Aker had been a maintenance man and repairman at a lumber firm for thirty-four years and had served on a criminal jury in 1980. The last book he had read was *Cyco-Cybernetics,* the Scientology tract on positive thinking. Of *Twilight Zone: The Movie* he said: "I didn't like it. I think it was better before on TV." There was a wisecracking vein in his humor: "It only bothers me when people say 'no problem.' Then I know something bad is going to happen."

At seventy-three, Mary Strohm was the oldest juror. The mother of five children, she had just read *The Death of Innocence,* about the effect of sexual freedom on children, and *A Texan Looks at Lyndon.* She knew the effects of violent death on the survivors of the victim; a relative of a close friend had been murdered. She agreed with the philosophy that it was better that ten guilty people go free than that one innocent person be convicted.

Beulah P. Wilson was a divorced mother of three grown children. She worked in the supply department at the Los Angeles County-University of Southern California Medical Center. Her reading included the *The Wall Street Journal* and the Bible. She was a Baptist Sunday school teacher and a member of her neighborhood watch program.

Arizona Watkins, a fifty-eight-year-old secretary for the Los Angeles Community College District, had previously worked for KNBC. Two of her husband's children from a previous marriage had been killed in a 1957 house fire caused by their playing with matches. She had been a purse-snatching victim.

Paul Gonzales, fifty-three, had been a maintenance painter at Sears for twenty-five years. He didn't read newspapers, magazines, or books, but enjoyed listening to country music and "The Bible Answer Man" on radio. He candidly admitted that he didn't think he was a very good judge of character.

James W. Ross, fifty-four, the father of three children and grandfather of three, had been a shipper for Aluminum Company of America for twenty-seven years. He had an auto mechanic's degree and had used explosives in the Army.

Junus Rachal was a fifty-nine-year-old machinist and grandfather of four. He had grown up in Louisiana and was proud of his Cajun background. He was a "very liberal Catholic Democrat" who liked to fish, hunt, and square dance.

Robert F. Belmonte was a thirty-seven-year-old budget analyst for the Los Angeles Department of Water and Power, and father of two children. He liked a wide variety of movies and television shows, and his brother was a clerk of the Los Angeles County Superior Court. (He was not involved with the *Twilight Zone* case.)

Crispen R. Bernardo, a native of the Philippines, was a chemist for the state of California, analyzing samples for toxicity. He once taught chemistry at UCLA, and his television viewing was limited to public television.

On Thursday, August 28, the twelve jurors and four alternates were sworn in, with testimony scheduled to begin the following week.

TEN

THE *TWILIGHT ZONE* courtroom on the fifteenth floor of the county Criminal Courts Building in downtown Los Angeles was a theater of ego. The clash of personalities, particularly the running skirmish of insults between D'Agostino and Braun, created an unprofessional and undignified atmosphere.

"If we could sell tickets, *Twilight Zone: The Trial* would make more money than *Twilight Zone: The Movie,*" joked Arnold Klein, Paul Stewart's attorney.

There was entertainment in the charged standoff between Lea D'Agostino and her adversaries. But the sour personal confrontation between her and the defense lawyers also threatened to impede a reasoned study of the criminal charges.

The courtroom is spare and plain, with panels of light wood on the walls. The California state seal hangs above the judge's bench. Fluorescent bulbs cast a harsh, faintly yellow light in the windowless room. The unflattering illumination was in marked contrast to the bright, color-enhancing lights these filmmakers worked with on their movie sets.

In the left rear of the room, space was reserved for a television camera and its operator. Occasionally, still photographers, their motor-driven cameras covered with sound-muffling cloaks, leaned against the wall close to the jury box. The spot was perfect for photographing the witnesses, who faced the spectators from a seat at the front of the courtroom, but provided a poor perspective for the faces of the defendants and lawyers at the counsel table.

About fifty spectators could be accommodated, and three long rows of benches were often filled. Court bailiff Larry Breazeale reserved the front row for *Twilight Zone* families by taping a hand-lettered sign to the three-foot-high wooden partition running the width of the court, called the bar, that separated the spectators from the restricted front half of the room.

Regulars in the front row were the wives of John Landis and George Folsey, Jr. Deborah Landis had a resolute air about her, exuding determined support for her husband and resentment about his plight. Belinda Folsey is a soft-spoken person with delicate features whose emotional pain over her family's ordeal was evident. Landis's mother and stepfather were frequent spectators. Joel Behr, Landis's business attorney, often attended the sessions. Sometimes seated at the far end of the front bench was Berta Purwin, a feisty, outspoken woman of strong will and limitless faith in her prosecutor daughter, Lea. The parents and other relatives of My-Ca and Renee attended only on the few days of their testimony.

Two shorter benches on the right side of the courtroom were reserved for reporters. Depending on how sensational any particular day's testimony promised to be, the press corps could swell. A group of regulars provided the bulk of news coverage. They included Linda Deutsch of the Associated Press, Michael Harris of United Press International, Andy Furillo of the *Los Angeles Herald Examiner,* Paul Feldman of the *Los Angeles Times,* Paul Dandridge of KABC television, Barbara Palermo of the Los Angeles *Daily News,* Barbara Riegle of KFWB radio, and Rebina Luther of City News Service. I sat with this group.

In the wide hallway outside the courtroom, the television crews set up a bank of monitors and often watched the proceedings out there.

One group of people noticeably absent from this trial were producers and screenwriters seeking to obtain rights from the participants for a television movie or feature film. For example, a highly publicized child-molestation case being tried in a courtroom on the same floor as the *Twilight Zone* case was receiving a great deal of attention because of a former prosecutor's involvement in a proposed screenplay. In Santa Monica there was jockeying for position for a television film about the "Billionaire Boys' Club" murder case.

The industry's distance surely could not have been because the *Twilight Zone* case is uninteresting fare for film. The elements of power and money, the tragic deaths, and the dynamic personalities provide a meaty foundation for a dramatic retelling. More likely, the case of movie director John Landis was just too close to home.

The jurors—twelve regular members and four alternates—sat in two rows of chairs along the left wall at the front of the room. Boren sat at an elevated bench facing the courtroom from beneath the state seal. Just beyond the bar was the long counsel table. D'Agostino sat at the far left, closest to the jury, and Tom Budds sat next to her. Continuing on to the right were Dorcey Wingo, Eugene Trope and his assistant William Anderson, Jim Neal, Jim Sanders, Leonard Levine, and Harland Braun. Arnie Klein and Paul Stewart sat at the end, directly facing the jury from the opposite side of the room. Bailiff Larry Breazeale sat at a desk against the wall behind Klein.

One other much-used location was near clerk Sylvia Felien's desk. Here, frequent, whispered conferences between the judge and the lawyers were held beyond the hearing of the jurors, defendants, reporters, and spectators. For these sessions, Boren stepped down from his bench and leaned forward toward the attorneys, who, because of their number, crowded close together, straining to hear and be heard without allowing their voices to carry. These conferences were used to debate points of law during testimony, as well as for each side to make frequent complaints about the deportment of the other. Some of the most important work of the trial was conducted at these sidebar, or bench conferences.

Three of the attorneys—D'Agostino, Neal, and Braun—chose to make opening statements to the jury.

During the morning of September 3, D'Agostino stood up to face the jury for the first time. Her good luck charms were in place: the gold bee pin on her shoulder and six blue felt-tip pens wrapped in a rubber band nearby on the counsel table. Her rich, dark hair was upswept, folding into a French twist with not a single strand astray. Her personal manner reflected the unvarying flair and resolve of her lawyering.

She began with the admission that she was nervous.

D'Agostino established the theme of her prosecution: that the children were hired illegally not merely to evade state rules about late hours but also to ensure that no bureaucrat could learn of the inherent danger presented by the helicopter and explosives and bar the children from being used at all.

In her all-encompassing style, she promised much detail to come: "You're going to be required to absorb a great deal during this trial. In the process you may, in fact, find out how movies are made. So it's almost a whole new world for you. That's why we want to try and make it as easy as possible."

The jury was alerted to a central allegation of her case: that even after the buffeting of the helicopter by explosions during the 11:30 P.M. shot, which should have provided a sufficient warning of danger, Landis still demanded massive explosions for the final shot with the children, Morrow, and the helicopter in proximity to each other. Furthermore, she said, Landis had made the scene even more dangerous by ordering that a mortar be put under a hut, even after discussions that such explosions could create threatening debris. "Paul Stewart permitted himself to be talked into placing a mortar under a hut," she said.

The jurors could not know at this stage that there were flaws in the prosecutor's comments. For example, she dramatically related how, in the fatal scene, the concussion from initial explosions tipped the helicopter, "almost causing it to fall" into the camera crane across the river. A sheriff's department analysis of the film had long before proven that the movement she described had not taken place.

Another signal that the prosecutor was not fully prepared came when she quoted some statements Dorcey Wingo had made to the National Transportation Safety Board. At a sidebar conference out of the hearing of the jurors, Levine and Klein rightly argued that because of a previous ruling by Boren, D'Agostino was not yet free to present to the jury those comments of the pilot. The prosecutor asked for a recess to go to her eighteenth-floor office to check her files. She said she was "one thousand percent positive" that the statements had been made to Tom Budds, which would make them admissible as evidence. Boren, however, said no: "I think it is up to you to be prepared on the opening statement, as to the origin of the statements."

Throughout the trial, the jurors heard dozens of times from Boren that they were to disregard statements they had already heard. The first such caution by the judge was delivered on this point: "As to the quotation that counsel was stating to you just a few minutes ago, at this time the jurors are admonished to disregard that part of the opening statement and not to consider it for any purpose."

D'Agostino continued with her opening statement, which established the prosecution's contention that the defendants had taken unacceptable risks. The fatal scene, she argued, "could have been done without sacrificing any artistic reality, without sacrificing any human life."

The most compelling moments of D'Agostino's presentation came when she described the evolution of make-believe moviemaking into numbingly tragic actuality:

"You're going to look at the film and you'll hear witnesses tell you that there was nothing in that final scene, ladies and gentlemen, that was an illusion. You'll be told that the fireballs that were created on the set were very, very real fireballs, and they created some very, very real fire that had to be put out with very, very real water. It was not an illusion. You will hear that the helicopter that was used in this scene was not a toy. It was not a figment of anyone's imagination. It was not an illusion but it was a very, very real helicopter. These were not deaths from which someone could get away and wipe the blood-looking catsup and say, 'I'm alive.' These are very real deaths. They were not an illusion, ladies and gentlemen. You are not going to be able to see Renee Chen coming from the back of the courtroom, or My-Ca Le, or Vic Morrow. They are not going to say, 'Look, we put our heads back on, it was an illusion.' "

Levine quickly objected to her last comment as overly emotional and inappropriate argument. Boren agreed, telling the jury to disregard the remark. But such vividly descriptive statements are not easily forgotten. (D'Agostino's melodramatic comment about the dead children was a paraphrase of the concluding paragraph in a 1983 *Rolling Stone* magazine article about the *Twilight Zone* case.)

The defense attorneys were well aware that D'Agostino could easily win the jurors' emotions by combining testimony about the deaths of the children with evidence of Landis's immature and domineering personality. Their counterattack stressed that however compelling the emotions may be, they were irrelevant to the underlying law of the case. The defense would also present technical data in an attempt to portray the tragedy as an unavoidable accident.

"As often happens in life," Jim Neal said in his folksy tone, "unforeseen, unforeseeable, and even bizarre events combined to produce the very tragic accident. Not one of these gentlemen intended to hurt anyone. Not one of these gentlemen thought the scene as planned and rehearsed was dangerous. Not one of these gentlemen is guilty of criminal negligence."

He emphasized a phrase he would repeat often during the trial: "The scene as planned and rehearsed was not reckless." He seemed careful, however, to mention only the planning and rehearsal and not the actual execution of the plan. Neal made a quick, and obviously imprecise, reference on a chart to the aircraft's proposed position a "safe distance away" from the explosions. This lack of specificity, Klein later told me, was necessary because the production team had never discussed a specific distance the helicopter needed to be to ensure safety.

"When the helicopter had moved to a safe distance away," Neal said to the jurors, "that was the cue for the special effects up near the shore to go off. Then the helicopter was to go across [the river], turn around, raise up in the air, become a camera platform, and let the camera in the helicopter film the supposed burning of the Vietnamese village.

"Ladies and gentlemen, man proposes, God or fate, depending on your point of view, disposes," Neal said. The lawyer suggested that the jurors look to others than the defendants to place blame, especially James Camomile, who had detonated the bombs: "He failed to look where the helicopter was."

Expecting Donna Schuman's testimony to be forcefully negative toward Landis and the others, Neal put the jury on notice that he did not believe she was to be trusted: "Donna Schuman simply is not telling the truth."

The Nashville lawyer ended powerfully, with a bold attempt to persuade the jurors to set aside the deep emotions they would no doubt experience. "It will be your feeling to sympathize terribly with these parents, as we do, but it will be your duty to put that sympathy aside and determine what the truth of the matter is. Had the helicopter tilted the other way we wouldn't have had a trial of Mr. Landis and the others. They wouldn't have been defendants here. They would have been dead."

From the very first day of the trial, grand themes about the trial's meaning were discussed in the press. Joe Morgenstern, a local columnist writing in the next day's *Los Angeles Herald Examiner*, said:

> The prosecutor was a theatrical creation in her own right . . . [she] looked like a heroine from some 1930s or 1940s melodrama: upswept cheekbones and hairdo à la Sylvia Sidney, fashionable shoulder pads à la Joan Crawford . . . as powerful a director as John Landis has been in the movie industry, and as powerful an authority figure as any director is on his or her own set, it's possible to see Landis as a prisoner of that industry, and its insatiable demands for "lower, lower, lower" and "more, more, more." In that sense, the industry is on trial, which may have been the main point all along.

There was some truth in Morgenstern's assessment. The alleged crimes involving breaches of professional conduct had implications for others than the defendants because the jury's verdict could drastically affect industry safety standards. The *Twilight Zone* case, though, was not the industry on trial. D'Agostino insisted that it must be viewed as an examination of five men whose alleged acts, if true, deviated egregiously from what is acceptable, not only within the movie industry, but also in society as a whole.

D'Agostino's most difficult task was to prove that the defendants, prior to the filming of the village rescue scene, had had a clear sense that they were courting great risk.

The defense team was well equipped to raise doubt in the minds of jurors about the validity of D'Agostino's theories—if the lawyers could maintain at least a superficial unity.

A divisiveness among the defense team members was always simmering just below the surface. There was mistrust. No one expected that Allingham and Folsey would betray their allegiance to Landis, but Landis was vulnerable if either Paul Stewart or Dorcey Wingo decided to say that he had been tricked or forced into doing dangerous things on the set. Neal once referred to the defense as "the five-headed monster," because no lawyer knew exactly what any of his colleagues might do. A common disdain for D'Agostino, however, created a certain solidarity, although not a harmonious one.

D'Agostino seemed not to recognize the fragility of the defense team's superficial harmony. Early in the trial she said to me: "If they're working at cross-purposes it would be wonderful, but right now they're presenting an extremely united front. I would have to believe that Mr. Neal, as clever as he is, and he is an extremely clever man, and as long as he continues to be the master puppeteer, it will continue to be that way."

If Braun, Klein, and Trope, particularly, were puppets, they were recalcitrant ones. One of the more foolish episodes exacerbating the underlying discord among the defense lawyers began one day in September as all seven men posed for a portrait in the courtroom. (Free-lance photographer Curt Gunther and I were preparing an article about the *Twilight Zone* attorneys for *People* magazine.) Unknown to Neal, during the first few shots Braun leaned over and raised two fingers behind Neal's head in a schoolboy "rabbit ears" trick. When the unflattering photograph was published Neal was incensed, not only because it had been chosen by the magazine's editors, but also at Braun for his childishness. Braun, without shame, laughed off the incident.

By her aggressively sniping posture, in which she presented the defendants as men of limitless evil and their lawyers as devious perverters of justice, D'Agostino allowed herself to become a target of deep-rooted and genuine animosity.

Klein told me early in the trial: "Since D'Agostino has come onto the case, the defense has to work twice as hard. One, to exonerate our clients, and two, to see D'Agostino eat it. She isn't respected for her ability. She isn't respected for her personality. She may have been assigned because she was a woman, but I don't think she's portraying the motherly type who can grieve for two lost children and thereby display empathy. I think she's coming across as a hard-core, two-fisted prosecutor who will do anything and say anything to make a case. I think that's self-destructive in front of a jury if you're a prosecutor."

D'Agostino viewed the expressed animosity of the defense lawyers merely as a tactic of diversion, seemingly unwilling to accept that she did generate genuine ill will. She told me: "What they're trying to do basically is focus the issue and the press away from the facts of the case which are devastating to their clients. I find it really amusing, and in a sense somewhat flattering, that seven top, highly paid defense attorneys have to stoop to these tactics to try and eliminate me. I do not intend to engage in a contest because I don't think I could stoop that low. My mother always taught me one thing: If you can not say something nice about someone, say nothing." D'Agostino, however, did not follow her mother's advice and was often openly derisive of her opponents.

At the outset, the defense admitted that Landis, Folsey, and Allingham were guilty of having violated the state's child labor laws by illegally hiring My-Ca and Renee to work after hours. There was strategy in the confession. Under the law, merely hiring the children to work in off-hours was not sufficient grounds to support a conviction of criminal negligence. Since it was obvious that the men had violated the law on the hiring point, and D'Agostino would undoubtedly prove that easily, the voluntary confession, the defense lawyers theorized, could add credibility later when the more serious charges were denied.

Central to D'Agostino's theory of prosecution, however, was that the illegal hiring laid the foundation for the involuntary manslaughter charges because the men allegedly knew that they would be placing the children in a dangerous situation. The prosecutor told me: "They did not hire these children to appear in a schoolroom having a cup of tea. They did not hire these children to appear in a scene at a picnic. They hired these children with full knowledge that they were going to be placed in the situation in which they, in fact, were placed; that is, under a helicopter in the proximity of explosives at night, or in the early morning hours. Now, I don't think you have to be a Phi Beta Kappa to agree that whenever you have these three things, explosives, low-hovering helicopter, and human beings, let alone two tiny babies, there is a potential, it is certainly foreseeable, that something can go wrong. They took a calculated risk. And they lost."

* * *

After a brief opening statement by Harland Braun Thursday morning, Boren turned to D'Agostino and said, "Call your first witness."

"Thank you, Your Honor. The people call Donna Schuman," the prosecutor said confidently.

Guided by D'Agostino's questions, Schuman appeared, at first, just as the prosecutor had hoped: strong and knowledgeable, describing the inner workings of the production company, Landis's relationship to Steven Spielberg, and the movie's economics. Schuman, a tall, blond woman in her fifties who had been secretary to George Folsey, Jr., during the production, said that the preparation for filming was marked by rushing and chaos.

"I was told that the *Twilight Zone* segment would be done cheaply, as cheaply as possible. It was going to be quick. It was going to be simple."

Schuman appeared to be unraveling a despicable conspiracy of the moviemakers. She told of her discussion with Landis's secretary, Alpha Campbell, about the secrecy of the script, and Folsey's allegedly misleading phone calls to parents. She confirmed that in telephone conversations she overheard that Folsey did tell people—the parents, she assumed—that there would be no permits for the children: "And then he'd always say: 'Oh, by the way, I want you to know that we are going to have some explosives on the set, but that doesn't have anything to do with the kids.' "

Schuman said she never heard Folsey mention a helicopter in those conversations, in which he was always specific about the money being offered: $500 if the child was hired, $100 to stand by, and $25 for an audition with Landis.

The former *Twilight Zone* production secretary said she once asked Folsey why he told people about the explosions if the special effects were not to have any impact on the children. "It is the right thing to do," she quoted him as replying. "When we are going to have explosions on the set . . . you ought to tell everybody up front. I mean, you know, God forbid anything goes wrong, and then if you tell everybody up front you are covered."

Through Schuman, D'Agostino laid the foundation of her argument that the men knew the chance they were taking. On this point, Schuman began one of the trial's most important running controversies when she alleged that Folsey conspired to keep the illegal hiring of the children secret not just to avoid a monetary penalty because of the late hours, but also because he knew it was criminal to expose the children to such danger. Schuman recounted a conversation she said she had with Folsey prior to filming: "I asked him: 'What is the penalty for working kids without a permit?' He said, 'A slap on the wrist and a little fine, unless they find out about the explosions and then they will put my butt in jail.' "

D'Agostino, knowing that Schuman would then implicate Landis in the same manner she had just done with Folsey, asked Schuman if she had heard any other comments by any of the defendants. Schuman answered: "It was Mr. Landis, and I was coming out of the Xerox room into the hallway. He was at the other end of the hallway and he had his back in a door and he was saying, 'You know, I want it big. I want it big.' And then he turned around and he started up the hallway toward me, and as we passed, he threw his arms up and said, 'Arrghhh, we are all going to jail.' "

"You assume he was kidding at the time?" D'Agostino asked.

"Yeah, of course," Schuman said.

Schuman confirmed a large number of the incriminating incidents that were central to D'Agostino's prosecution. For example, Schuman talked about discussions concerning the use of dummies rather than children. "Prior to the day of the fatal crash I was sitting with George [Folsey, Jr.] in the office and Allingham came in and said, 'Andy [House] is worried about the kids and wants to use dummies or midgets.' Folsey laughed and said, 'You know, don't be ridiculous. You know John [Landis] wouldn't go for that. It's going to be the real thing or nothing.' It's the real thing or no go. Words to that effect."

The witness was also instrumental in helping D'Agostino establish that the production team had tried to hide from others the information that they were using children illegally. The witness said she knew about Allingham's deceiving Warner Brothers vice president Ed Morey on the afternoon of the accident, when Allingham had said he didn't know anything about the children. After the call, Schuman testified, Allingham reported the incident to Folsey.

Schuman, whose friendship with George and Belinda Folsey was now long over, told the jury that immediately after the accident Folsey was astonished that anything could have gone wrong: "He insisted that it was an accident. That they had rehearsed it about thirty times. He said, 'We just had this accident. Like an act of God. You don't think John and I would have tried it if we didn't think it would be safe?' "

Key to the prosecutor's plan was to demonstrate that Landis exerted unusual control over others, and Schuman laid the foundation for that argument.

One of the last questions to Schuman in the prosecutor's direct examination of her first witness was: "How did you know John Landis was the boss?" Schuman replied: "He told everybody else what to do."

When D'Agostino leaned back in her chair, the butterflies had long since passed. Her case had begun strongly. But D'Agostino had only to wait until the first questions of cross-examination before she saw her star witness in trouble. Nettlesome issues, unanticipated by D'Agostino, arose.

Jim Sanders began the defense's cross-examination of Schuman by asking the witness, who had appeared before the grand jury and at the preliminary hearing, why she had not before testified about these important Landis and Folsey comments—known collectively for the remainder of the trial as the "going-to-jail statements."

"I wasn't asked the question by any of the attorneys," Schuman answered.

Since July, when according to the rules of evidence discovery D'Agostino had provided the defense with copies of Schuman's memorandums containing the quotes, the defense had been skeptical about Schuman's truthfulness. Some, Braun chief among them, theorized that as the trial approached, D'Agostino had concluded that she needed more substantial proof that members of the production team had had a clear understanding of the criminality of the hiring—and the danger of the scenes —prior to July 23, 1982. The only way for the government to prove that foreknowledge, the defense now would argue, was to fabricate evidence.

There is no doubt that in 1982 Folsey had made joking comments about going to jail, but he told me they were uttered only in relation to having the children work after hours. Cynthia Nigh had heard those remarks by Folsey and had told investigators years before. But until Schuman's recent revelations, there had been no substantiation from any witness that Folsey or Landis had talked about the criminality of their actions in relation to the physical danger in which they were placing the children at Indian Dunes.

Pressed by Sanders, Schuman began a series of answers that permanently disrupted D'Agostino's prosecutorial strategy.

Sanders asked Schuman why she had not even told D'Agostino about the important jail statements in her detailed memorandum to the prosecutor on July 11, but had waited two weeks and then written a second memorandum, on July 24. Schuman hesitated, and then said she had omitted the comments from the first memo because she had already given the information to other investigators in the past.

"When had you revealed it?" Sanders asked, knowing that the discov-

ery rules would have required that the previous prosecutor, Gary Kesselman, divulge such information to the defense.

"Four years ago," Schuman answered.

"To whom?" Sanders asked, believing he was chipping away at an
implausible chronology.

"There were other investigators before Mrs. D'Agostino got here. I
was asked questions by about a million people. I talked to an attorney
over here for the first time, I would presume it would be Gary Kesselman."

"You are pretty sure you told Mr. Kesselman four years ago?"

"Yes."

The drama of this confrontation between lawyer and witness was building, but unlike television portrayals of courtrooms where the denoue-
ment always comes just at the end of the hour, the day ended
unclimactically for Sanders.

Boren ran the court on a regular schedule, beginning each morning at
ten or ten-thirty and ending each afternoon at four or four-thirty (with
ten-minute breaks in midmorning and midafternoon and a ninety-minute
lunch break—all designed not to overtax the jurors' concentration). The
Twilight Zone case, which Boren initially anticipated would last several
months, was conducted Monday through Thursday so the judge could
attend to unrelated court business on Fridays.

The end of the session this day, a Thursday, left the attorneys with a
long weekend to ponder the unexpected development of Schuman's
veiled allegation that Gary Kesselman had withheld evidence from the
defense—a felony violation of the state evidence code, if true.

Before adjournment, though, Jim Neal asked Boren to order that no
attorney could talk to any witness during the period when the witness is
testifying. Neal didn't want D'Agostino and Schuman to discuss strategy
for the remainder of Schuman's cross-examination. "I have wrestled with
this in many cases," Boren said, "and my feeling is that it doesn't serve
any great purpose. Cross-examination can determine if the witness has
been coached."

That night, Kesselman learned he was embroiled in a controversy when
Barbara Palermo of the Los Angeles *Daily News* made a routine call to him
for comment.

Kesselman said that he didn't remember Schuman ever attributing any
such quotes to Landis or Folsey.

On Friday morning, D'Agostino called Kesselman and asked if he had
heard about Schuman's testimony. When he said he had, D'Agostino said
she didn't think the issue would be a problem since "you know Donna

Actor Vic Morrow on the set of *Twilight Zone: The Movie.* Photo courtesy of Globe Photos

Child actors Renee Chen and My-Ca Le, in costumes and makeup just before their last scene. *Photo courtesy of AP/Wide World Photos*

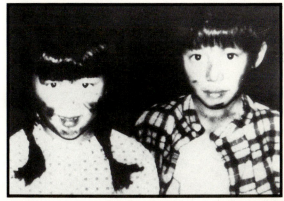

Director John Landis, in hip boots and waving megaphone, helps position helicopter during rehearsal flight just prior to the fatal scene. *Trial exhibit photo courtesy of Arnold Klein*

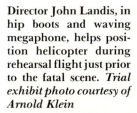

View of the fatal scene from the cliff-top camera seconds before the deaths. Morrow and the two children are to the right of the spotlight beam as special-effects explosions begin in the village. *Trial exhibit photo courtesy of Eugene Trope*

Seconds after the crash of the helicopter, Director John Landis, arms outstretched, is at the rear of the aircraft. *Trial exhibit photo courtesy of Arnold Klein*

The defense lawyers, despite disagreements, publicly present a unified front as the trial begins (left to right): Eugene Trope, William Anderson, Leonard Levine, James Sanders, James Neal, Arnold Klein, and Harland Braun. *Photo by Curt Gunther*

Prosecutor Lea Purwin D'Agostino, the focus of continual attacks by defense lawyers, who proudly accepted the disparaging nickname "Dragon Lady" as a sign of her unrelenting courtroom style. *Photo by the author*

Sergeant Tom Budds, the Los Angeles County Sheriff homicide investigator who constructed the *Twilight Zone* case. *Photo by the author*

D'Agostino fielding reporters' questions at Indian Dunes, February 10, 1987, just before the jury arrived to inspect the crash site. *Photo by the author*

Superior Court Judge Roger Boren (right, facing camera, with sunglasses) telling defendants and attorneys he will not grant the prosecution request for a demonstration helicopter flight at Indian Dunes. *Photo by the author*

A reunion of *Twilight Zone* jurors in November 1987 (left to right, standing): Annie Luckey,* William Lottman,* Polly Farina,* James Ross, Crispen Bernardo, Arizona Watkins, Wilbert Fisher, Paul Gonzales. (Seated): Robert Belmonte, Roger Aker, Lois Rogers (foreman), Junus Rachal, Lauretta Hudson. (*Alternates.) *Photo by the author*

Director John Landis at Indian Dunes as the jurors survey the area during the trial. *Photo by the author*

Defendant Dan Allingham, the production manager, standing on the shore of the Santa Clarita River waiting for the jury to arrive. *Photo by the author*

Deborah and John Landis with defendant George Folsey, Jr., associate producer, at Indian Dunes. *Photo by the author*

Paul Stewart, special-effects coordinator for *Twilight Zone*. *Photo by the author*

Helicopter pilot Dorcey Wingo at the Rialto, California, airport in the summer of 1987 after his acquittal. *Photo by the author*

Schuman told you those 'going-to-jail' statements." Kesselman replied that there was a problem because he didn't remember that Schuman had done so.

Still, he couldn't be absolutely sure, and he asked D'Agostino if she had checked the notes he had made when he interviewed Schuman prior to the grand jury appearance in the spring of 1983. When Kesselman was taken off the case by District Attorney Ira Reiner the year before, Kesselman had turned over to D'Agostino all of his documents in the case, which filled a number of file drawers. D'Agostino said she had never seen those notes.

Later that morning, Kesselman walked to D'Agostino's office and asked his colleague why she had not asked him about the statements when Schuman had first mentioned them the previous July.

"C'mon, Gary, you know that Donna Schuman told you that."

"Lea, that is the problem. I should remember even without notes a Landis statement like that. I remember a Folsey quote in the record, but not from Donna Schuman." (Cynthia Nigh had testified to that in the grand jury.)

Then D'Agostino stood up from her desk and closed the door.

"Look, it's the two of us in the office. You are not important, I'm not important, the only thing that is important is this case," D'Agostino said.

The prosecutor later told me that she had been appealing to Kesselman to put aside his pride and admit that he may have forgotten that Schuman had given him the incriminating information. Kesselman, however, bristled at D'Agostino's words and assumed that they had darker meaning: "Lea, if you are even implying that I would commit perjury for this case, you've got the wrong guy." Then he headed for the door.

"Well, just make sure you don't commit perjury the other way," D'Agostino retorted, in a warning that he not aid the defense out of bitterness with her.

Meanwhile, the defense had wasted no time in moving to exploit the dispute between the two deputy district attorneys. On Friday afternoon Kesselman received a subpoena that Leonard Levine had issued. The former *Twilight Zone* prosecutor was being summoned as a witness for the defense.

The defense couldn't lose on the issue. If Kesselman confirmed that he had been given those statements in 1983, then the defense attorneys had a substantial argument that a mistrial be declared because they had been improperly denied information they should have had long ago. Neal, Braun, and the others, however, assumed Kesselman would say he had not been provided the statements by Schuman in 1983. That testimony would circumstantially support the defense contention that D'Agostino's first witness lied in an attempt to strengthen the prosecution's case.

Out of professional courtesy, Kesselman called D'Agostino Friday afternoon to advise her that he had been subpoenaed as a witness. D'Agostino told him that she had just spoken to Donna Schuman, and the witness had said that Kesselman had an obligation to confirm the truth of her testimony. D'Agostino also said that Harold Schuman was "a head doctor" and that he would help Kesselman remember that Donna Schuman had provided the "going-to-jail" quotes in 1983.

"That's enough. It's absurd," Kesselman said angrily. He slammed down the receiver of his telephone. Apart from one courtroom confrontation that would take place the following Monday, Kesselman did not speak to D'Agostino again.

Schuman returned to court on Monday for further cross-examination. First, however, Boren allowed defense attorneys to question Kesselman, without the jury present, to delve further into the question of whether the defense had not been properly provided with discovery evidence.

The jurors remained in their waiting room, adjacent to Boren's chambers, while Kesselman took the stand.

"I have no recollection of having these statements imparted to me," Kesselman said firmly to a question from Harland Braun.

Braun continued: "Is it a fair statement that not only did you not receive that information from Mrs. Schuman, but also not from any investigators?"

"That's a fair statement," Kesselman answered.

D'Agostino was now in the unusual position of cross-examining a district attorney colleague. She suggested an alternative to the theory that someone was being deceitful. Perhaps Kesselman had just forgotten that Donna Schuman had said those things to him.

"Your memory is like everyone else, fallible to forgetting?" D'Agostino asked.

"Probably worse than most, yes," Kesselman answered. He added, however, that he was convinced that he would have undoubtedly remembered evidence as important as "going-to-jail" statements attributed to Landis and Folsey. He said unquestionably he would have written the statements in his notes of his 1983 interviews of Schuman.

The disappearance of Kesselman's notes was now another mystery the defense sought to exploit.

Braun enthusiastically pursued the Kesselman-D'Agostino controversy and asked Boren to allow the jury to hear about the dispute now, not when the defense presented its case which was at least a few months away: "Now, if [D'Agostino] believes Mr. Kesselman, she is presenting evidence [by Schuman] she believes is false. If she believes the witness, she believes her own fellow deputy district attorney is not telling the truth."

Trial strategy was now reversed. The prosecution, which had hoped that the defense would crumble in internecine attacks, was now dissembled with its own internal warfare between deputy district attorneys.

Boren, however, rejected Braun's request and the issue was left unresolved for the time being. The jury was called into the courtroom to hear more testimony from Schuman.

Jim Sanders began by attacking the apparent lack of logic in Schuman's testimony. If in early July 1982 she had learned from Folsey's own comments that the production team thought the children would be endangered, why did she not warn her husband, who was playing an instrumental role in procuring the children for the movie?

"You are saying very somberly. I better clarify all of this. When they talked about their butts getting thrown in jail, they were quite obviously joking. I never meant to imply that they grabbed me, threw me in a dark, smoke-filled room, and said, 'You know if anybody finds out about this . . .' It was a joke, it was just a joke."

"You didn't favor us with that piece of information last Thursday," Sanders said.

"You didn't ask me," Schuman responded.

Finally, Sanders broached the subject of whether Schuman had fabricated this crucial portion of her testimony. Referring to Schuman's July 24 memorandum to D'Agostino in which the quotes were first mentioned, Sanders asked: "Did somebody call you up and tell you to add some things?"

Schuman explained: "Mrs. D'Agostino called me at my home to ask me a question about something. She also asked me about the 'butt in jail' statement. I said, 'Yeah, well, I know that.' And I was shocked that she didn't know, and then she started saying, 'Well, did you ever tell [Kesselman]?' And I said, 'Yes, I did.' And she went to question me further, and I told her the other two things and she said words to the effect: 'Oh, my God, get it down on a piece of paper and get it to me right away. I have to get it to the defense attorneys].' "

Sanders and the others on the defense team were astonished by this answer, which raised a new question of logic. If D'Agostino had never been advised of the "butt in jail" statement, as the prosecutor had thus far maintained, how could she have have posed a question about it to Schuman? That contradiction would go unanswered for a time.

When Leonard Levine questioned Schuman, the witness made the strongest accusation challenging Kesselman's truthfulness thus far. She claimed that in 1983 he had told her he would withhold the evidence he had in order not to tip his hand to the defense before the trial. In effect Schuman accused the former prosecutor of admitting to a felony violation of the discovery rules.

"He told you he had intentionally violated a court order to turn over information?" Levine asked.

"Yes," she answered.

"When?"

"Prior to the grand jury. He told me he was only going to ask a few questions because the purpose of a grand jury is not to put on a trial. Only to get an indictment. He said there were a lot of reasons. One was some of [the testimony] was not very good and you would kick the crap out of me."

"Did he tell you why he would not ask questions regarding the Folsey and Landis 'jail' statements at the preliminary hearing?"

"I don't remember his exact words. It was something more or less like tipping his hand. I would prefer not to call another person a liar. I think he's a nice man, he worked real hard. He got canned and I'm sorry. I feel bad."

Schuman had now tainted the district attorney's office in testimony before the jury.

Levine asked Schuman whether her credibility should be in question: "Those statements were never said, were they?"

"No," Schuman responded, "I'm sorry, you're wrong, sir. I am not a liar. Sometimes you really do forget, because three people have been killed and you just don't want to go over it and over it."

As her time on the witness stand neared an end, Schuman was forced to concede that she had not heard Landis or Folsey ever specifically say that they thought the scene was dangerous.

There was one remarkable occurrence outside the courtroom affecting this issue. Tom Budds had sat in the courtroom dismayed at watching the Schuman controversy distract attention from what he believed were more important and relevant issues of the defendants' culpability.

He wanted to take the witness stand to say that they did not have such testimony in 1983 from Schuman and that he and Kesselman had been overjoyed when Cynthia Nigh told them she could testify that she had heard "going-to-jail" statements. D'Agostino wasn't about to put Budds on the witness stand to say that. So Budds surreptitiously spoke to Allingham's attorney, Leonard Levine, in a courthouse stairwell and said: "Put me on the stand. I can clear this thing up."

It is not unusual for investigators, and often prosecutors as well, to maintain professionally cordial relationships with their adversaries during trial. And Budds was certainly not trying to aid the defense. He believed if he could just resolve the controversy, the trial would then focus more clearly on the case he had built. D'Agostino was furious at Budds when she heard about his conversation with the defense attorney. Boren, however, told the defense attorneys they had to wait until the prosecution's case was entirely finished before they could call witnesses.

With the jurors out of the courtroom, Neal again asked the judge to allow Kesselman to testify in front of the jury now: "We have an extraordinary situation that's gotten curiouser and curiouser." Again Boren refused. The defense would have to wait, probably several months, to present Kesselman as a defense witness.

That night on the television news and in the next morning's newspapers the reporting was disastrous for the district attorney's office. "Two Versions of Twilight Zone Story," read the headline in the *Los Angeles Herald Examiner.*

"I believe the witness one hundred million percent, because I can't count any higher," D'Agostino told the *Los Angeles Times,* referring to Schuman and effectively accusing Kesselman of lying.

The defense attorneys knew that to win they only had to raise reasonable doubt in the minds of the jurors about the prosecution's evidence. They were pleased when they learned Tuesday morning that the jurors were, indeed, already confused and had sent a note to the judge: The panel members did not even know to whom the testimony presented so far related.

When Schuman's testimony was over, D'Agostino bolstered the credibility of her witness with testimony from two of Schuman's friends and Harold Schuman, all of whom said they had heard her refer to the "going-to-jail" statements prior to the previous July.

Kendis Rochlen Moss, a television scriptwriter and longtime friend of Schuman, said she had first heard the statements when she and Schuman were picketing the CBS studio, during a writer's strike, on March 15, 1985. Moss said she asked Schuman why she had not revealed the statements at the preliminary hearing. "She said she wasn't asked, but had told people in the district attorney's office about it."

Gail Wellens, a psychotherapist and friend of Dr. Harold Schuman, recalled a lunch with him and his wife at the Los Feliz Inn the day after the crash in 1982: "Donna Jean said that Mr. Folsey had said that if they found out about the explosives, that his ass would land in jail."

Wellens had only recently come to D'Agostino with her confirmation of Schuman's testimony. Wellens said that when she read about the controversy in recent newspaper stories, she recalled her own conversation with Schuman, particularly because the quotes used in court by Schuman contained the word "butt," and she specifically remembered Schuman having said "ass."

"It was one of the grimmest luncheons I have ever attended," Wellens said. "I just know that Donna Jean looked like death, and they both were very somber."

Harold Schuman, a psychiatrist for thirty-five years, inadvertently alerted defense attorneys to what they perceived as more illogic in the sequence of events the prosecutor was offering. Attempting to corroborate his wife, Schuman confirmed that she had given Gary Kesselman the jail statements on May 11, 1983, but then added, however, that that was the first time he had heard them.

Defense attorneys thought it suspicious that Dr. Schuman did not testify that he had heard his wife refer to the Folsey and Landis comments at their lunch with Wellens. They also found it suspect that Donna Schuman, in a year following the accident, did not mention these important statements to her husband who, after all, had played an important role in finding the children for the job.

Levine pointedly asked Dr. Schuman if D'Agostino had asked him to corroborate his wife.

"Absolutely not," he said, "It was my own idea that I remembered some of the information in question."

Out of the presence of the jury, Braun pressed hard for a court investigation of whether D'Agostino had coached Donna Schuman to lie during her testimony.

"It is a fraud on the court," Braun said.

Boren, however, who had already instructed the defense that Kesselman could be called as one of their witnesses to rebut Schuman, said he didn't want to hear any more about it. The judge said the controversy was "derivative of the principal issue," which was whether the defense had received discovery of the Schuman statements prior to trial, which they had in July.

D'Agostino's pride, however, kept the issue alive: "I'm assuming an implication that I, not Mr. Kesselman, am attempting to perpetrate a fraud on the court," she said defiantly. "If that is true, I am willing to take the witness stand and answer any questions Mr. Braun has to present to me."

"Yes, Your Honor, we accept the challenge," Braun responded cheerfully.

Forced to continue with the issue, Boren told Kesselman that he, too, could make a statement to the court if he wished. As intensely protective of his integrity as D'Agostino, he chose to take the witness stand under oath.

"Mr. Kesselman," Neal asked, "did you ever tell Mrs. Donna Schuman that you were going to conceal or withhold relevant information she had given to you, as a matter of trial tactics?"

"Sir," Kesselman said firmly, "I never said that or anything like that. That is absolutely not true."

The jury, of course, remained secluded, unaware of the proceedings in the courtroom. D'Agostino's supervisors were chagrined when they learned she had decided to become a witness herself. It was an unnecessary action that potentially threatened her ability even to continue as prosecutor in the trial. Garcetti, for one, wanted D'Agostino to push on with more prosecution witnesses. Although he was publicly supporting D'Agostino in comments to reporters, he quite unsuccessfully tried to reason in private with his headstrong colleague.

D'Agostino began her under-oath statements to the court with an explanation of how Schuman had come to write the July memorandums containing the incriminating jail statements.

Recognizing that Schuman's version of their conversation was illogical, D'Agostino testified that it had been Schuman who first mentioned the "butt in jail" comment.

The prosecutor said that in a discussion with Schuman about the upcoming trial, she asked if Schuman had heard any statements similar to those Cynthia Nigh had testified to concerning Folsey's joking about jail: "She said, 'Did I hear them? I heard a lot more. Didn't Gary Kesselman tell you about it?' And I said, 'No, he did not.' She was absolutely aghast. 'If he didn't tell you, than I wonder who else he didn't tell. Let me go over some of the information.'"

Braun asked D'Agostino why she didn't then go to Kesselman and ask about this.

"Why should I?" D'Agostino asked, defiantly staring back at Braun from the witness chair.

"Did you not recognize that something was wrong?" Braun asked.

"Oh, I realized there was a problem. I figured someone was trying to withhold information from me so I wouldn't be adequately prepared," D'Agostino said without elaboration, although the import was clear: She was accusing Kesselman of deliberately sabotaging her case by having withheld from her the evidence Schuman had provided him in 1983.

When D'Agostino had completed her testimony, Neal said to Boren: "There is really something terribly wrong here. I urge the court, I beg the court, really, to get all the facts in. Make a decision for us."

Boren remained firm: "I don't believe, as far as the jury is concerned in this case, what Mrs. D'Agostino believes or thought as to those particular times is relevant. And I feel that going into any of these areas at this time is a waste of the court's resources and the case ought to go forward."

"Mrs. D'Agostino is lying," Harland Braun said in a speech even more fiery than was his custom. "And we can prove that because if anyone knows anything about Mrs. D'Agostino, if she had been told in July that someone was withholding evidence from her, or she didn't have something to use against the defense, she would have been in to [her supervisors] in fifteen seconds. I don't want to borrow from one of Mr. Neal's cases, but she sounds like Ron Ziegler saying 'it's nothing but a second-rate burglary.' We will prove to the jury that when Mrs. Schuman testified, she made the story up about Mr. Kesselman and that Mrs. D'Agostino went along with the story. So we will argue to the jury that the prosecutor is a liar and perjurer and suborns perjury."

Neal, perhaps playing the role of southern gentlemen on behalf of John Landis—thus allowing Braun and the others to be seen as the flamboyant, dislikable members of the defense team, drawing attention away from Landis—was more cautious in his accusations: "I do not look at Mrs. D'Agostino as putting on perjured testimony, or suborning perjured testimony. I do say that there are some strange circumstances here."

Harland Braun wrote to California attorney general John Van de Kamp (who had been district attorney in 1982 and had assigned Kesselman to the case) and asked him to begin an investigation of impropriety in the Los Angeles district attorney's office. A Van de Kamp subordinate replied that the matter was appropriately under Boren's jurisdiction during the trial.

A week after D'Agostino had been on the witness stand, the mystery of Kesselman's missing notes was solved. D'Agostino said that they had been in her files all along, unnoticed by her in a folder she thought contained unimportant material. Kesselman's notes of his interview with Schuman were written in outline form. There were no references to specific quotes by either Landis or Folsey. There was one comment, tantalizingly incomplete in light of the controversy, that said without reference to anyone: "get a little fine working past 6 P.M. having them on set with explosives." An explanation would not be forthcoming for some time.

Nonetheless, the entire series of events was a boon to the defense. The controversy had not only distracted the prosecutor from her case but also had brought an unnecessary, doubt-raising issue before the jury. The fight had also helped unify the defense team.

Neal's defense table colleagues Trope, Braun, and Klein, however, were hardly admiring of the man from Tennessee. Klein and Trope particularly, whose clients' fortunes were not tied to Landis in the same manner as Allingham and Folsey, were always prepared to abandon the team if their own acquittal depended on it.

Klein told me at the time: "I would believe there is a tacit agreement that when it becomes necessary to protect your client's full interest, you will do what you have to for your client without regard to the other defendants in the case. Our gentlemen's agreement, again, is tacit, that if we're going to point the finger at another defendant just tell the other attorney first."

The Kesselman-Schuman controversy disintegrated harmony among the prosecution team. District attorney supervisors were left to wonder about the quality of D'Agostino's work and the soundness of her judgment. A number of fellow deputy district attorneys were embarrassed by D'Agostino's public attack of Kesselman. Most important, Budds and district attorney investigator Jerry Loeb, who was assigned to D'Agostino for the trial, were discouraged by the turn of events.

Tom Budds, whose professional investment in the case was extensive, went to his supervisor in the Los Angeles County sheriff's office to say he was considering not attending the trial so he would not have to sit next to D'Agostino and be associated with her. Out of pride in himself and the case, however, he chose to stay. He concluded that if D'Agostino were left alone, her sagging credibility would reflect devastatingly on the evidence —and the case he had built would surely be lost.

Budds told me: "I felt it was very important for me to be there, to show the jury that it wasn't a spurious prosecution. Here's a legitimate cop and he did a legitimate investigation and he's a reasonable man and he's still sitting here."

ELEVEN

WITH THE background of four years of investigation in the *Twilight Zone* case, Tom Budds viewed a disturbing incident early in the trial as emblematic of Landis's moral character and immaturity. On the morning of September 10, Budds and all the lawyers gathered in front of Judge Roger Boren for a whispered conference out of the hearing of reporters and spectators. Budds was upset as he talked:

"Yesterday while I was escorting Ms. Rochlen back upstairs in the elevator, she indicated to me that during the break, while she was still sitting on the witness stand, Mr. Landis looks at her and goes like that toward her. Like she was being shot." The detective extended his right hand, as if in the shape of a pistol, index finger straight out, thumb raised, and the remaining fingers closed. "My concern is it's been difficult enough getting these witnesses here, let alone having them put under . . . what I feel is intimidation."

Jim Neal angrily interrupted Budds, saying, "I would like the court to hear from Mr. Landis on that. I mean, I deny that."

Boren quickly concluded Landis's gesture was "not in contempt of court at this point, because I did not see it. If, in fact, it occurred, that would be cause for grave consequences," the judge said to Neal, and advised him to warn Landis.

"I wouldn't even finish the trial if he did something like that, and I'm satisfied that he didn't," Neal said.

What Neal and Landis apparently didn't know is that Eugene Trope

156

could easily have put the Nashville lawyer to the test on that rash promise.

"Yes, I saw the gesture," Trope later told me, characterizing Landis's finger-pointing as that of "an arrogant individual who seemed to want his own way all the time." Paul Stewart's lawyer, Arnold Klein, who had not seen the gesture, said to me of Landis: "Wasn't that the most pitiful display? Here's a guy fighting for his life, doesn't even have the brains to just sit there. That just boggles my mind why he would even do that. He was one hair from going away to state prison."

Trope's courtroom silence about what he had witnessed was an instructive example of the relationships that had developed among the lawyers in the case.

Neal's curt manner in defense strategy sessions had already antagonized Trope, who felt loyalty neither to him nor Landis. Trope found John Landis particularly offensive and always believed that his client, Dorcey Wingo, was on trial only because of the director's misdeeds. Still, Trope considered himself a defense attorney through and through; he had acceded to a publicly unified defense posture promoted by Neal and, philosophically, he was inclined not to aid the prosecution. D'Agostino, particularly, was an unlikely recipient of any Trope largess.

Trope's disdain for the prosecutor was profound because of her suggestion in a secret session the previous August that the defense lawyer was incompetent to provide Wingo with an adequate defense.

Over the summer, D'Agostino had become increasingly upset at Trope because of his cooperation with other defense attorneys, particularly Neal. In 1982 after the crash, a lawyer had filed a civil suit on behalf of Wingo against Landis, Warner Brothers, and others, alleging that they had placed the pilot in dangerous circumstances. Wingo had never signed the lawsuit, but neither had he had it withdrawn, and it stagnated as the criminal case dragged on over the years.

D'Agostino knew that Trope always had the option of defending his client by asserting that Wingo had been deceived by Landis and the others about their true plans to detonate spectacular special effects near the helicopter in the final scene. In fact, prior to Neal's entry in the case, Trope had prepared a legal brief—which he never filed with the court—that placed blame on other members of the production team in its assertion that at the last minute "an unwritten change occurs in the script."

Also included in the brief was Wingo's recounting that he believed that the plan for the scene called for the helicopter to be on the opposite shore of the river when the mortars were fired. In one of Neal's first meetings with other defense attorneys, he seized upon that account, supported by the testimony of Dan Allingham and cameraman Randall Robinson, and said: "Gene, I've looked at your brief and your story is going to be our story."

D'Agostino asserted that Trope's agreement to join with the other defense attorneys was unprofessional capitulation. She had been further incensed by Trope's cooperation in a motion to prevent her from presenting testimony about the banana plant scene in which live ammunition had been used. In the meeting with Trope and Boren, held in the judge's chambers in late afternoon on August 19, she said that such testimony would be helpful to Wingo because it showed that Landis was prone to put others at risk.

D'Agostino said to Boren in that secret August meeting: "I guess there really is no polite way to do it. But I feel as an officer of the court, it is my ethical duty to bring [it] to Your Honor's attention. [I] believe that maybe the pilot is not getting an adequate defense or adequate representation."

Trope, and the other defense attorneys who learned about the session afterward, believed that D'Agostino had been moved not by concern for Wingo or legal ethics but by an opportunity to intimidate Trope, a man who admittedly had little criminal defense experience. Trope and Wingo were the lobbying targets of D'Agostino and Budds, who wanted the pilot to agree to testify against the others. Wingo, of course, would have made a powerful prosecution witness if he alleged that he had been deceived by Landis about the real plans for the two-twenty shot.

Trope bristled at D'Agostino's attack on his legal abilities and integrity, telling Boren: "Your Honor, the years have flowed for a long time. I have never heard such a charge in my life." The prosecutor replied: "Gene, it has been very difficult for me to do. I cannot tell you the sleepless nights I have had because of this."

Trope asserted that he had not compromised himself or his client: "All the defense counsel are unhappy with me because I am the maverick, simply because I feel our defense is independent of theirs."

D'Agostino's misreading of Trope's reaction to her claims was consistent with her misunderstanding of the relationships among the defense attorneys. Boren took no action other than to seal the meeting transcript from public view and order that Wingo be allowed to read it.

Although the finger-pointing incident quickly passed as a courtroom issue and remained unpublicized during the trial, another Landis expression of antagonism to Kendis Rochlen Moss did not go unnoticed, however. Andy Furillo of the *Los Angeles Herald Examiner* reported that during a trial recess, after Moss had been told by the judge to shorten her lengthy answers, Landis said to her, "Do you get paid by the word?"

The jurors would have photographs; charts; film of the actual accident; and a three-dimensional, five-foot-wide, three-foot-high (from river to clifftop) scale model of the Indian Dunes set made by Los Angeles County deputy sheriff John Shannon, who had surveyed the area the morning after the accident. The model was complete with black scorch marks from the fireballs on the cliff, tiny mortars, a model helicopter lying on its side, and fragments representing the tail rotor components that had been strewn about the set. The huts were constructed from paper and broom straw. There was even a tiny director's chair, toppled over just as Budds had found it.

A controversy over still photographs lingered throughout the trial. D'Agostino had lobbied vigorously to enter into evidence photographs of the victims, both before and after death. In a motion paper to Boren she wrote, "The photographs in this case which show the decapitated and mutilated bodies of the victims are the best evidence that the victims were placed in a situation fraught with peril: underneath and in very close proximity to the low-hovering helicopter." She also wanted to show the jury the on-set photo taken of My-ca and Renee, wearing their costumes and smudged with the dirtlike makeup, as well as a flattering picture of Morrow. In addition, D'Agostino asked the judge to allow her to present the autopsy reports of the three victims.

Defense attorneys argued that such material, particularly concerning the children, would be "an improper and unduly prejudicial effort to appeal to the jury's sympathy." Case law heavily favored the defense position and Boren refused D'Agostino's requests. The jurors saw none of the photos.

The defense, however, did accuse D'Agostino of misusing the pictures outside the courtroom. The prosecutor kept in her office, propped up on a table facing her desk, a large matboard display of the photographs—including the police pictures of the torsos and heads after the crash—she had sought to show the jury. Harland Braun and others complained that the pictures were intended to prejudice witnesses when they went to the prosecutor's office for discussions prior to their trial testimony.

D'Agostino told me that the photographs were her constant reminder that she was working on behalf of three people who died violently. Braun said the photographs transformed the prosecutor's office into a "grotesque chamber of horrors" and he asked Boren to order her to remove the pictures from sight. The judge said it would be inappropriate for him to police the prosecutor's interviews but that defense attorneys certainly could cross-examine witnesses about whether they had been unduly influenced.

D'Agostino had a habit of making sounds or facial gestures during defense cross-examination that finally annoyed Neal so much that, during his cross-examination of Shannon, whom the lawyer was questioning about the set's dimensions, he complained to the judge. Neal said the prosecutor's responses were becoming "tedious." Boren, whose view of D'Agostino was blocked by the scale model that had been placed in the center of the courtroom facing the jury, instructed her not to make any facial expression that would indicate dissatisfaction with the proceedings. "I represent to the counsel that I didn't do it either," she said, "and I hope it's okay if I breathe, counsel."

Marci Liroff, the casting agent, was angered, as were many prosecution witnesses, that her honesty would be challenged by defense attorneys. Even before the trial had begun, the defense attorneys knew it was important for them to discredit her testimony, potentially damaging because of its implication that Landis, Folsey, and Allingham had disregarded warnings of danger.

Liroff recalled with a confident memory the incident 4½ years before when "Mr. Landis asked myself and Mike Fenton to hire two actors to fill these parts in this scene he described to us. I explained that to hire children for this scene would be illegal due to the hours that they were planning on shooting.

"I also mentioned it sounded kind of dangerous to me." Landis and Folsey did not respond to that comment. Afterward Allingham entered the room and discussed the hiring issue with Landis and Folsey. Liroff quoted Landis as having remarked, "We'll take care of it. We'll hire the kids." Liroff recalled that Folsey had said, "We won't tell anyone what we're doing."

"They discussed not hiring a welfare worker and paying with petty cash," Liroff said.

In fact, in a conversation with Tom Budds a year after the tragedy, Liroff had discussed the incident in even harsher terms. Pressed by D'Agostino, who refreshed Liroff's memory with a transcript, Liroff continued her testimony with a description of Landis's demeanor at the end of the late-afternoon meeting: "He was a little gruff, I believe, because we wouldn't be involved in this, and said, 'The hell with you guys. We don't need you. We'll get them off the street ourselves.'"

Jim Sanders was looking for a flaw in Liroff's story as he cross-examined her, and noted that when she talked to investigators in 1983, she had specifically referred to Vic Morrow in connection with the June 16, 1982, casting session. How could she do that, Sanders wondered, if Morrow had not yet been hired? Wasn't it true that other actors were still under consideration?

"Isn't it a fact," Sanders asked, "that in recounting to the sheriff's department a year later what went on in this meeting, you have included in that certain things that you simply read in the paper and heard from other conversations?"

"No, that's not true!" Liroff snapped. "I might have used Vic Morrow's name, because that is who played the part. I didn't remember his character's name at the time I explained that," Liroff replied.

At this stage of the case, Liroff's reference to Morrow instead of his character's name in the script was an honest substitution. Landis also did so.

Court ended for the day with Liroff upset at the grilling she had undergone. She was then further antagonized by an incident, apparently unnoticed by most in the courtroom, that was all the more surprising in light of the secret bench conference that morning about the finger-pointing incident.

The only path for witnesses to leave the courtroom was between the counsel table and a row of chairs in which several defendants sat a few feet behind the lawyers. As Liroff stepped down from the witness stand, Landis was seated behind Jim Neal, his legs outstretched in front of him, blocking the path. The director was hunched over, looking down at his notepad, on which he was writing.

I watched Liroff stop when she saw that Landis impeded her exit. "Excuse me," she said, standing inches away and looking down at the director. Landis continued writing and did not look up. Liroff hesitated only a few seconds before awkwardly stepping over his legs. Her annoyance was apparent as she concentrated on keeping her balance. She walked briskly out of the courtroom, shaking her head angrily, followed by a glaring stare from Landis, who had looked up as soon as she had passed him. When Neal stood up a few seconds later, Landis quickly pulled his legs back to let him pass.

Neal, who hadn't seen the incident but learned of it later, said he discussed it with Landis. "I gave him unshirted holy hell about that," Neal told me. "He says he didn't do it." Soon afterward, though, Landis moved to a seat just to Neal's left at the counsel table, where he remained for the rest of the trial.

Harland Braun elicited the testimony from Liroff that Spielberg executive producer Frank Marshall had known about the plans to hire the children illegally. From the defense lawyers' viewpoint this was important because they believed that the more people who had known about the illegal hiring, the less blame could be levied on their clients.

"He said, 'I will check it out,' " Liroff quoted Marshall as having said when she talked to him a few days after the June 16, 1982, casting session.

"Did he ever raise [the issue] again with you?" Braun asked.

"That was the end of the conversation on that subject," Liroff replied.

The defense was also successful in diminishing the importance of Liroff's warnings of danger by showing that after her conversation with Frank Marshall about the illegal hiring, she had not pursued the matter herself.

D'Agostino tried to recover the point in her redirect examination, asking, "Why didn't you report the illegal hiring to the California Labor Board?"

"I told the director it was illegal," Liroff answered, "I told the producer, the production manager. I didn't know it was my job to be a policeman. In hindsight, I wish I had."

D'Agostino didn't have to worry about proving that the children had been hired illegally—the three defendants involved admitted that readily. The prosecutor's difficulty was to demonstrate that the production team members had also violated the law because they knew the scene was too dangerous to obtain a permit, not just that it was planned for filming late at night.

The prosecutor drew deputy state labor commissioner Coleen Logan through detailed testimony in an attempt to show that it was possible for moviemakers to obtain waivers of the late-hour regulations but that the prevailing standards prohibited the use of children in proximity to helicopters and special-effects explosives.

Logan had been in the job for twenty years and, in 1982, had been the government official with final authority over theatrical permits for children. California had long ago instituted regulations for working children —the first set of rules had been established in 1929. Usually the state required that a child be fourteen years old before being allowed to work. The exception was in the entertainment industry, and there the rules allowed babies at least fifteen days old to "work" onscreen and were in effect for children up to age eighteen.

According to the written regulations, no child under eight years old could work past 6:30 P.M. An unwritten policy, however, allowed exceptions. "The labor commissioner allowed me to do that because they felt the industry was leaving the state," Logan explained, "and they wanted to accommodate the production companies in the best way that they could."

The rules were published in a document known as the "Blue Book" and titled *Rules and Regulations Governing the Employment of Minors in the Entertainment Industry.* The most recent revision had been in 1981. The producers' guild paid for twenty thousand copies, which were distributed throughout the movie and television industry. The Blue Book contained no specific regulations about children and special-effects explosions.

Prior to Logan's testimony, D'Agostino had lost one important point when Boren ruled that the jury could not hear the deputy commissioner's speculative conclusion of what she would have done had the *Twilight Zone* producers come to her for a permit to use children in the 11:30 P.M. and 2:20 A.M. scenes, the ones with the helicopter and explosions.

Importantly for the prosecution, though, Logan was able to say that she believes helicopters are hazardous if children are nearby and that special-effects explosions near children are "absolutely" hazardous.

The employers of children, including studios and independent producers, must obtain a permit, valid indefinitely. Each child hired must also have a permit, effective for six months and granted after a physician affirms that the child is healthy and a school official certifies that the child's grades meet minimum standards. It is the duty of the producer or the casting office to advise parents that permits are necessary, Logan explained. Once permits are granted, producers are required to hire state-credentialed teacher-welfare workers, who must be on the set whenever a child is working.

"The teacher on the set really has the final say about whether a child can work under certain circumstances. If they think it is an unsafe condition, they stop the movie," Logan told the jury. As a matter of course the teacher-welfare worker receives the script ahead of time to enable him or her to determine if something seems dangerous to the child.

Neal attempted to show that the Landis production company had been unaware of the unwritten, informal waiver procedure and that Landis, Folsey, and Allingham had assumed the Blue Book hours as inviolate.

"I think everybody in the industry knew about [waivers], but we didn't want too many people asking for an exception for babies that young," Logan said. Other testimony, in fact, confirmed indisputably that the availability of waivers was common knowledge in the movie industry.

Even Boren, at a bench conference, told Neal it was apparent many movie people knew about waivers.

The testimony of the parents offered D'Agostino the opportunity to make her most emotionally compelling presentation. Cross-examination of the parents could be difficult for the defense attorneys, who did not want to appear callous by harshly questioning the still-grieving immigrant families. Still, they could not let the testimony go unchallenged, knowing beforehand that the parents would accuse the producers of not adequately advising them of the potential danger of the scene, nor the legal requirement for permits.

Neal attempted to mitigate the potential sentiment with a request to the judge: "I would hope that the prosecutor has worked with these witnesses enough so we would have no emotional outbursts, and if she hasn't, I would ask the court to instruct her to."

Boren allowed the use of leading questions—queries that guide the witness. The judge added, however, "As to the emotional aspect, if we stick with the relevant matters, that should be a diminished problem. However, it seems to me, instructing someone not to get emotional may have just the opposite effect. I don't know how you could tell somebody not to get emotional if certain questions were asked."

Neal accepted that reasoning.

Even though the parents were immigrants without a full command of the English language, they were, nonetheless, well-educated, professional people of obvious intelligence. The defense wanted to show that the parents stood to gain by the defendants' criminal convictions, which would aid their multimillion-dollar civil lawsuits still pending against the moviemakers.

The first of the children's relatives to testify was Peter Chen, Renee's uncle, whom Dr. Harold Schuman had recruited in his search for children. Chen held a Ph.D. in social work from the University of Southern California and worked in the Los Angeles County jail system.

He denied that Dr. Schuman had told him anything about a helicopter, special-effects explosions, or a permit when he called on George Folsey, Jr.'s, behalf in 1982.

"You know that Dr. Schuman testified under oath he did tell you?" Jim Neal asked.

"Well, I'm supposed to tell the truth, nothing but the truth. I'm doing just that," Peter Chen answered.

Hoa-Kim Le, My-Ca's mother, a social worker dealing with abused and neglected children, was the first of the four parents to answer in the negative to three important questions posed by D'Agostino. She and Mark Chen, Renee's father, neither of whom had been at Indian Dunes on Thursday night, preceded the testimony of their spouses, whose eyewitness accounts of their children's deaths would undoubtedly be the most emotional time of the trial.

"Did you know that your children were not supposed to be working there at night unless they had a permit?" D'Agostino asked Hoa-Kim Le.

"No," the mother answered.

"Did George Folsey ever tell you that My-Ca was going to be filmed anywhere near explosives?"

"No."

"Did he tell you that My-Ca was going to be filmed anywhere near a helicopter?"

"No."

Both she and Mark Chen testified about Folsey's comment that the parents did not have to return with the children on Thursday night, repeating for the jury that he had said, "You don't have to come back. I will treat your children as my own."

On cross-examination, Braun suggested that the parents had misunderstood Folsey.

"Did not Mr. Folsey say that one parent would have to come back with each child?"

"He didn't say that."

Mark Chen said that no one told him about a permit, or that Renee would be filmed in proximity to explosives and a helicopter.

Neal, who recognized the potentially treacherous ground of cross-examining the parents, asked Chen about a statement he had made to state labor board investigators in 1982, in which the father indicated that Folsey had intended to have the parents return with the children Thursday night.

"Sir, it has been, the time when I took that interview was ten days right after they killed my daughter, and it has been four years. How do you expect me to remember everything that I said?"

Boren asked Chen to avoid reading inferences in questions.

Braun pursued the same point as Neal: "Isn't it a fact that what Mr. Folsey said was, 'You don't have to come back, but one parent for each child has to be here'?"

"No, he didn't say that."

* * *

Prior to the testimony of the two parents who had witnessed the crash, the jurors were first shown the horrifying film of the events at Indian Dunes.

The defense had fought the theater-screen viewing of the twenty-minute sheriff's department compilation of confiscated film (from all the cameras used during the 9:30 P.M., 11:30 P.M., and 2:20 A.M. scenes, plus the 2:00 A.M. rehearsal), arguing that Landis had been all too successful in using film's illusion to create more of a sense of danger than had actually existed. Boren was not swayed by the suggestion that the film would unfairly bias the jurors against the defendants.

"My concern is this, we're going to get into almost a theatrical production here," Allingham's attorney, Leonard Levine, said.

"Well, it was one," Boren commented drily.

Not only would the jurors see the film in a movie theater, but in the most symbolic of places: the Samuel Goldwyn Theater at the Academy of Motion Picture Arts and Sciences on Wilshire Boulevard in Beverly Hills. The Academy Theater, as it is commonly called, is considered to be the most technically advanced in Southern California in both its projection and sound facilities. Here, Oscar-nominated films are shown to the voting members of the Academy, and other special screenings take place throughout the year.

On Wednesday, October 1, court was convened in the theater. There were no spectators allowed, apart from the defendants' wives. I joined about twenty reporters who were authorized to attend. Television news cameras were allowed in the soundproofed control booth, from which there was a glassed-off view of the theater.

One debate, conducted prior to the arrival of the jury, concerned the sound level to be used. Of course, the defense attorneys wanted the lowest level the judge would allow, and D'Agostino the highest. In the center of the eleven-hundred-seat theater a console containing a number of controls, as well as a telephone to the control booth, served informally as the judge's bench. District attorney investigator Jerry Loeb told me that before the jurors and reporters were brought in, as the sound tests were being conducted, Landis picked up the phone and yelled at the technician in the booth: "Keep it low! Don't you know these guys are trying to put me in prison?"

Boren, who had not seen the film before, selected a moderate volume, midway between those suggested by the two sides.

Two eight-foot-tall replicas of the Oscar trophy, which normally stand on either side of the stage flanking the big screen, had been placed in a telephone alcove away from the theater.

In the lobby was a display of historical Hollywood photographs. Before the screening, Harland Braun talked to a group of reporters and gestured with his hands and arms to make a point about the helicopter's fatal flight. Just behind him was a large photograph of Alfred Hitchcock instructing the crew during the filming of a motion picture, his arms held in just about the same position as Braun's.

Three canisters of film—People's Exhibits 15, 16, and 17—were under the watchful care of district attorney investigators.

While everyone waited for the jury, *Los Angeles Herald Examiner* reporter Andy Furillo noted that the screen was twenty-four feet high, exactly the distance from the helicopter skids to the ground when the tail rotor was damaged by the explosions.

The jurors, who had been brought from the downtown courthouse in a sheriff's department bus, were led into the theater by the bailiff and seated in a single row about a third of the way back from the screen and several rows in front of the judge, defendants, and lawyers. Court was officially in session, and Boren wore his black judge's robe.

There was silence in the auditorium as the lights were dimmed. The first image on the screen was a close-up of a movie marker—the chalk-board clapper containing information about the scene for later use in the editing.

The movie began with scenes from the nine-thirty shot, close-ups of Morrow running to the hut where the children were huddling, and carrying them away just before two mortars explode.

The film had not been edited, just spliced together in the chronological order it had been exposed at Indian Dunes. Each separate camera angle of the various scenes lasted only a few minutes at most.

In the 9:30 P.M. scenes, the helicopter's engines were heard from off-camera. Filling the screen was the ramshackle bamboo hut, the children barely discernible inside, the rotor wash straining the hut's supports. With the call of "Action!" Vic Morrow entered the scene from the left in his rehearsed half-running, half-limping gait.

After picking up the children in his arms and getting a good grip, the actor spun around and quickly moved toward the camera. Just as his left foot was about to hit the ground, only four steps away from the hut, the bomb in the mortar behind the hut exploded, sending a bright-yellow gasoline fireball skyward. Almost instantaneously, a smaller mortar on the side of the hut detonated to complete the effect of a rocket attack.

The brightness of the blast washed out the images to whiteness for a second, just as Morrow and the children left the camera frame. Just a second after they were no longer visible on camera, Landis yelled "Cut!"

and walked in front of the camera. He looked up at the helicopter and with his hand signaled for Wingo to fly away. Then the film quickly cut to a shot of a special-effects man using a hose to extinguish the fire on the hut.

Two segments from other cameras, both with about the same perspective, were shown. "Be ready, you guys!" someone was heard to yell to the children as the camera began to roll.

The effect of the hurricanelike rotor wash is clearly visible as dirt and bits of matter fly about. My-Ca's hair is forcefully blown flat against his head.

The fourth and final segment from the nine-thirty scene was an eerily silent, distant view looking through the windshield of the helicopter from just behind Wingo.

The 11:30 P.M. scene was an experience that should have provided the moviemakers with an unavoidable warning of the danger of using special-effects explosions near a helicopter, according to the prosecution. The film is dramatic support for that argument.

The first view, soundless and from the helicopter, showed the water and huts below buffeted by the rotor wash. Flashes of light are seen from the machine-gun muzzle just before a plume of water from the mortar in the river below obliterates vision. Cameraman Roger Smith's unsteady movements as he stands on the skid and then jumps back into the helicopter are quite apparent, since the film is being shot from his perspective, with the camera on his shoulder. Fireballs can be seen rising up the cliff, and their glow illuminates the cliffside as the helicopter quickly lifts away.

The fourth and final view of the eleven-thirty scene, a wide-angle shot from across the river, depicted most clearly the frightening effects of the explosions on the helicopter hovering above the village.

The helicopter lowers into place above Morrow and the huts. A mortar in the Santa Clarita River explodes, driving a column of water forcefully against the front and right side of helicopter. Just as that dissipates, large fireballs erupt against the cliff. As the third explodes, the helicopter lifts up and away from the village—just before the fourth fireball bursts and hurtles upward. Landis then excitedly splashes through the water toward Morrow, where he makes congratulatory gestures to the actor. Cheers and applause from spectators are heard.

The brief film segment depicting the 2:00 A.M. rehearsal is a silent prelude to what was a chilling time for everyone in the theater. The rehearsal segment shows Landis from the rear, standing in the river, well away from shore and megaphone in hand. In the final seconds of the sequence, Landis sidesteps toward the shore by the village, apparently moving to the spot over which he will position the helicopter for the two-twenty shot. The rehearsal view, intended only for a proposed "behind the scenes" documentary, ended before the rehearsal flight was complete.

By this stage of the trial, the jurors had heard enough testimony to know the fatal sequence of events at 2:20 A.M. An uneasiness was palpable in the theater as the final segment of the film began. Everyone, of course, knew what they would be seeing. Any novelty of being in a movie theater for a court session had long since worn away. The reality of what was about to be shown—from six camera angles—was horrific.

The sheriff's office had made only one addition to the raw film taken from the moviemakers: white, block-letter titles on a black background to introduce each sequence. The final title is stunning in its simplicity:

Twilight Zone, Landis Segment

(Friday)
—July 23, 1982—

2:20 A.M.

The first shot was filmed by a camera not far from Landis's position on the peninsula, looking west toward the dam. First Landis is seen, bullhorn in hand, sloshing through the river on his return to the spit of land fifty feet from the village. Then Morrow is seen on the river's edge, holding the children under his arms. Light from the first explosion flashes from the left of the screen just as the actor reaches the bow of the sampan. Sprays of water from the squibs and marble gun, simulating machine-gun fire, kick up near Morrow. As he passes the stick in the water, the large mortars at the dam explode in the distant background, forming two gigantic, brilliant flashes of light.

Then Morrow stumbles forward in the water, which rises to his waist. Suddenly there is only a large spray of white water filling the screen, accompanied by the splashing sound of a large object on the river's surface. The wall of water quickly falls and reveals the helicopter's fuselage, lying at an awkward angle on the ground.

The sound ends, creating a silently fearsome scene. Each of us in the audience knew what could not be seen on the screen. Branches of a bush, apparently held back during the filming, snap into the camera's view and partially block the sight of people running toward the helicopter. Landis runs desperately to the far side of the helicopter as a red landing light on the aircraft flashes on and off in a steady beat, reflecting off the water.

As the camera pans left, the village huts are engulfed in billowing flames.

The second view is from the camera on top of the cliff, looking almost directly down at the village. A fireball rushes up the cliff toward the camera. The concussive force and the fireball's heat obviously send the cameraman reeling backward. The camera is left to point skyward and film burning embers and black smoke. The crash is heard in the distance as the camera rolls on for another thirty seconds, filming only black sky and a flurry of still-glowing bits of burned sawdust.

The third shot is a close-up of Morrow, apparently taken from directly across the river, looking into the village. He is seen tightening his grip on the children as the rotor wash pushes at him. Here, his struggle—whether exaggerated by his acting or made real by an unexpected combination of wind, water, and the children's weight—is obvious. The children's feet drag in the river, and Renee is immersed to her knees. Just after Morrow stumbles, the flash of a fireball washes out the images. When the three are seen again, My-Ca is held high above the water, but Renee is in water up to her neck. She appears to slip in Morrow's arms as he tries to stand upright.

Just as Morrow strengthens his grip on the children, the sound of a rotor blade hitting the water is heard. A massive spray of water hides from view the terrible moment of death. The bodies of Morrow, Renee, and My-Ca are never discernible on film. The main rotor blade makes one revolution before the tip of one blade sticks in the mud of the riverbed.

The soundless fourth view from the helicopter contains only a few seconds of steady filming before the cameraman obviously recognizes trouble and jumps back into the helicopter, leaving much of the segment, shot as the helicopter spun and crashed, a view only of blackness.

The fifth segment is another view looking downriver to the west, showing Morrow crossing from left to right and the helicopter crashing directly in front of the camera.

The most terrifying vision of the crash was filmed by the master camera on the crane across the river from the village. It is the last scene segment.

The helicopter is seen in the upper right of the frame above the village. The aircraft hovers and then descends. Three explosions detonate in sequence at the base of the cliff, shooting up large fireballs. The first explosion on the shore silhouettes Morrow and the children in midriver. Thick, black smoke is vacuumed back down into the village by the helicopter's rotor wash. The aircraft appears unsteady during a left turn away from the village.

There is an obvious delay of a few seconds before a second shoreline explosion detonates, immediately followed by another explosion just adjacent. The air above the village is filled with fire and smoke. The helicopter glides completely out of the picture frame, to the upper left of the screen. A noticeable change in motor noise is heard. When the helicopter appears on screen again, from the left, it is lower over the water and beginning an obviously uncontrolled spin. Morrow stumbles, then he and the children are obliterated from view by the water spray as the helicopter crashes.

That the three victims are not seen does not make the moment any less appalling or horrible to watch.

There is a full view of the chaos on the set as people run toward the helicopter from all directions. The shock of the crew and spectators is evident as survivors are pulled from the aircraft. The camera crane lowers, and the view slowly becomes that of ground level. A second, unmanned movie camera is silhouetted just in the foreground, resting on its tripod with the helicopter beyond. The view is a tableau of tragedy on a movie set: a portrait of bewildered people milling around the downed aircraft as the village burns in the background.

When the theater lights were turned on, the stone-faced jurors were led out. The theater was solemnly quiet. As the jurors departed, Belinda Folsey sobbed and rested her head on her husband's shoulder. Dorcey Wingo hugged his pregnant wife consolingly. Tom Budds had long before developed a sense of personal loss over My-Ca and Renee, and the trial constantly reminded him of the drowning death of his own little boy. He, too, was crying. Dan Allingham had not seen the film before this day, and still had averted his eyes most of the time. "Why do I want to remind myself of that?" he said to me later. "For what reason do I want to see three people get killed? I did not want to see that."

On the sidewalk in front of the theater afterward, D'Agostino said she, too, had cried, but now her voice was filled with indignant outrage: "Mr. Landis's quest for realism exceeded all bounds of safety. And he got his effect. But at what cost?"

The next morning—Thursday, October 2—Shyan Huei Chen took the witness stand. She sat limply, weary with emotion. Although she spoke English, she had requested that she testify through a Mandarin interpreter, who stood nearby.

"We decided to let our daughter to go make the movie. Let her have good experience, a very good memory," she answered to an opening question by D'Agostino.

She remembered being reassured by George Folsey after the 9:30 P.M.

shot; he told her it "not dangerous. Just the sound, very loud sound." Later that night, she told the jurors, Folsey came to the trailer and said to her, "If the fire department people come over and if they ask what you are doing here, just tell them you are friends helping us. Don't mention anything about money."

The defense attorneys asked for a bench conference in which they complained about D'Agostino's tactic of having Mrs. Chen repeat in English certain quotes—such as Folsey's. They argued that such repetition overemphasized the evidence for the jury. Boren, however, allowed D'Agostino to continue.

Mrs. Chen remembered that the children were taken to the makeup trailer at about 1:30 A.M.: "I saw my child and the actor. He carried her across the river. John Landis was right behind us. Then he went over to a hill. Then I saw him with this speaker, a big speaker. Then I saw the helicopter in the sky above the three people. Then the producer [Landis] was yelling, he's yelling, 'lower lower.' Then I heard loud explosions, and then the sparks and the wind. Very windy and dusty.

"Then I saw the helicopter fall, fall on top of three people. At that moment I was so scared. I felt something happened to my daughter. They were running, also yelling, asking to run. I was yelling for my daughter."

The mother then began to sob, and Sanders interjected, asking the judge to call a recess, but Shyan Chen kept talking and crying: "They wrapped me, tell me not to go. They told me to run," she said, referring to the moment when Folsey protectively pushed her into the bushes, away from the helicopter's path.

She dabbed at her eyes with tissue and rocked back and forth in her chair, her head down and her eyes closed. The interpreter, a woman, knelt at Mrs. Chen's side and consolingly stroked her arm. The witness was obviously overcome by the frightening memories, and Boren called the noon recess.

Mrs. Chen had regained her composure when the afternoon session began, and her testimony ended soon after. On cross-examination by Braun, she admitted that she had not listened carefully to Folsey at the Franklin Canyon audition a week before the crash, leaving open the possibility that he had informed her of the various elements that the production team was planning for the scene at Indian Dunes.

Daniel Le sat in the witness chair wearing a white shirt and dark blue suit. His rimless glasses gave him an academic look.

He said he had had one worry when he and his wife decided to let My-Ca be in the movie: "The only concern I had was that if the actor Vic Morrow was strong enough to carry the two children on his arms across the river. Because I knew [My-Ca] was quite heavy. And then I ask my wife and then she told me that she was told Vic Morrow is a strong man and that this is not going to be a problem. That is all we are concerned."

He testified that he had been paid My-Ca's $500 in cash early Wednesday morning, and Folsey promised that work the following evening would be short: "He would take the picture of the children the first thing, right after we get there, and it won't take very long, about half an hour to one hour. And then we can go home. He told me there is no danger, it is safe."

At first Le had thought that the work was over after the nine-thirty shot and asked if he and his son could go home, but Folsey said, "It's not quite ready yet. We have some other things to do. You need to stay behind. We have some other minor things to do."

So he and My-Ca went back to the trailer and fell asleep. "I was told to stay in the trailer, not to get out, but to stay there. By Mr. Folsey." He recounted Folsey's request that he not tell any firemen that the children were working.

Daniel Le's account of the two-twenty scene was sad and upsetting.

"I heard the voice, loud voice, bullhorn, saying, 'lower, lower.' Then explosion went off. When I saw and heard the first explosion I was horrified. I was shaking. And then I fell on the ground. Because I was so horrified. The next thing I saw chaos, people running, pushing, shoving, running for their life, and then, finally, I saw the body of my son."

He told the jurors that no one had warned him about explosions or a low-flying helicopter.

"I wish someone told me that," he said.

Under cross-examination by Braun, Le said that the explosions at the nine-thirty shot did not adequately warn him about what was to come in the later scenes. "[That] was much much smaller than the explosion I saw at two-o'clock filming, before my son was killed. That's why, to me, is not danger. If I know it is danger, I would take my son right away to leave this place right at this moment."

Le had seen explosions in Vietnam: "I live in the city and sometime the Communists, the enemy, they shell the city and I observe from my house where I live. We see the blast, we hide ourselves either underground, tunnel, inside the house."

When court had ended for the day, Le told a KCBS television reporter: "If I ever knew that my son would be involved in something dangerous, close explosion, under low-flying helicopter, I would never allow my son to be there. We come here to live, to enjoy the freedom and justice of this country. Not to be killed in such a way. It is tragic."

The defense, trying not to alienate the jury by being overly harsh, did suggest that the parents had selective memories about their dealings with the production team and the two nights at Indian Dunes and were sometimes wrong in their recollections. The defense lawyers hinted that the parents' civil lawsuit still pending against the defendants was motivation for the families to tailor testimony.

The emotional struggle Le had had since My-Ca's death was evident in his answers to questions about his memory: "I remember sometime. I couldn't remember that time, and even right now sometime my mind just go blank. So I tell whatever I can remember, anything. Even right now I still grieving my son. I am right now in very deep grief for my son. For the whole week I were crying a lot."

The questioning of Le ended just before noon on Monday, October 6, with his recounting of the horrible discovery he had made seconds after the crash. Le's voice was filled with sadness and anger: "I saw my son's body without a head."

TWELVE

LEA D'AGOSTINO announced at a conference with the judge and other lawyers at the sidebar that she had discovered the driving motive behind Landis's use of spectacular action scenes.

"At least a dozen witnesses whom I have interviewed, I don't know who because I did not write it in any of the reports, when queried as to why they thought Landis did what he did in the manner which he did, they have all responded by saying the same thing in different words. And that is, they believed he was in direct competition with Steven Spielberg and he wanted to show Spielberg that he could do bigger and better than Spielberg."

The defense attorneys were upset by this unsubstantiated allegation, inadmissible as evidence, and, they speculated, presented in court solely as a sensationally quotable tidbit for reporters, who would see the statement the next day when the day's transcript was released. (D'Agostino later admitted that she well knew the material was inadmissible. "It's people's opinions," she said, refusing to discuss the matter further.)

"Why don't you make a list," Boren said to the prosecutor.

"Oh, God," she replied with frustration.

"As long as you are going to lay something like that out, I think you should. So [the defense] doesn't walk into the lion's den," Boren said.

A few days later, D'Agostino produced a list of thirteen names, which Boren ordered sealed. As the defense expected, the prosecutor's sources of information were low-level crew members and others who had little if any direct knowledge of Landis's creative thinking. Also as expected, D'Agostino did not attempt to offer this speculation to the jury. Even if Landis had felt competitive, comparisons between the filmmakers was difficult. Landis's dramatic Vietnamese rescue episode, for example, was of a style quite different from the masterful mixture of subtle mood and creative effects employed by Spielberg in his popular movies.

Two Warner Brothers executives testified in D'Agostino's effort to demonstrate that even though the movie had been a Warner Brothers film nominally, the studio's relationship with the John Landis production company was at arm's length. Landis was largely an independent contractor.

D'Agostino thought that the executives would counter the defense allegation that high-ranking studio managers had known all along that the children were being used illegally. "They had the script, but they had no way of knowing how the scene was to be shot," she said. "And it never occurred to anybody that the children were going to be shot at the same time as the special effects and the helicopter."

James Henderling, a man well into his seventies who had been a liaison between the studio and the Landis production office, took the stand on September 23. His authority included cosigning all *Twilight Zone* production checks.

Henderling, who had been in the movie business for close to fifty years, said that he had been suspicious in the days before the deaths that children were being used illegally but had not acted upon those suspicions. He recalled that Bonnie Radford in the Spielberg office had asked how to hire children without going through the Screen Extras' Guild. He told her that under any circumstances a permit was needed. Later that day, he said, she called to say children would not be used after all.

Within hours of the telephone call, however, Henderling said, he received a request for a $2,000 check, to be made out in the name of George Folsey, Jr. He did not sign it initially because "the whole method seemed unorthodox. I didn't feel like signing it."

Henderling was ambiguous about whether he had specifically related his suspicions to his supervisor, Edward Morey, who advised him that a request for money from a producer cannot be refused during production, and the check was delivered to the Spielberg production office, where it was cosigned by Frank Marshall before being sent on to Folsey.

Morey, in the movie business for forty years, did offer damaging testimony against the defendants by describing Landis's independence from his Warner Brothers financiers. He also told the jury about his phone call to Allingham the afternoon before the crash, when he had asked why there were no children listed on the call sheets and Allingham had told him that he didn't know anything about children working because he had been up in the helicopter during filming.

During lunch, Morey had told D'Agostino that he "absolutely" had not ever heard of children working near special-effects explosives during all his years in the movie business. D'Agostino wanted him to say that in front of the jury, but also now asked that the jury be told the statement could be used as evidence against Paul Stewart. Previously she had agreed to an instruction from Boren that Morey's testimony could only be used against Landis, Folsey, and Allingham in relation to the illegal hiring charges. Klein objected to her proposal, and in a sidebar debate issued a backhanded compliment to the prosecutor that irreparably intensified their bad feelings toward each other.

As Klein was talking, he referred to her as "Ms.," and she angrily told him to use the appellation "Mrs." Then Klein retorted that D'Agostino's argument about Morey's testimony "shows that she's not the boob that she appears to be."

Boren quickly admonished Klein, saying, "I don't think that kind of remark is called for."

"I apologize, Your Honor," the defense attorney responded. "It was done under the heat of the moment."

Boren's more significant rebuke, however, was delivered to the prosecutor, whom he instructed to inform the defense before trying to present important testimony to the jury that had not previously been turned over in discovery.

Insults were hurled frequently throughout the trial, the result of an increasingly sour mood between prosecution and defense.

Landis—unwisely, his lawyers thought—was particularly bold in his verbal challenges to D'Agostino in the early stages of the trial. Neal wondered whether he would be able to control Landis and avoid a damaging encounter. Landis, during a recess once, unwisely teased the prosecutor: "The press is outside, Lea, run quick."

As soon as the break was over, D'Agostino had the lawyers gathered at the sidebar in front of Boren:

"First of all, he has no right calling me by my first name. I don't even want him addressing me. Secondly, I find it particularly offensive, and thirdly, and I refrained from ever bringing it to the court's attention, but ever since this trial has started Mrs. Landis has the habit of making the most grimacing gestures to me. I can take it. I am a big girl, and I realize she is concerned her husband is on trial for killing three people, but if she cannot behave in a professional manner then maybe she has no business being in the courtroom."

D'Agostino later told me that she had singled out Deborah Landis for criticism because of her fear that others sitting with her might also make facial expressions, thus giving jurors the impression that the spectators collectively agree that the prosecutor's questions are "stupid or something."

Boren agreed that he had seen Deborah Landis grimace on a few occasions during D'Agostino's presentation, but he had not noticed any facial gestures for a few weeks, which he attributed to his own intervention. "I happened to look at her right after she did it, and she seemed not to do anything like that again after that. And it's just not a good idea," the judge said.

Boren instructed Neal to tell Landis that there should be no more repartee with the prosecutor.

"Judge," Neal said, "he told me that he did that and I said, 'John, you must be crazy. Don't you know she is going to go up and bring that up and this is just one more argument? I have to talk to her, you don't. So, will you stop that?' And he has already apologized to me for doing that, but this is a tense matter for him."

Several weeks after the trial had begun, the prosecution team learned that Gloria Landis, John's aunt and widow of his Uncle Benjamin, the former Superior Court judge who had died the previous August, was still using her late husband's passkey to park in the building's underground garage. She had also been seen in the corridor that runs past Boren's chambers and the jury room, after riding up to the fifteenth floor in the courts' private elevator reserved for judges. No one presumed that Gloria Landis was intentionally trying to misuse the privileges, but Boren concluded that the woman's special access could appear improper and taint jurors' opinions of the court's judicial neutrality. He worried what jurors might infer from seeing a close relative of a defendant in restricted areas. On the direction of Arturio Muñoz, who was now presiding judge of the Superior Court, Boren directed his bailiff to confiscate the passkey.

D'Agostino questioned various members of the production crew to expose the details of the illegal hiring and its cover-up and to demonstrate that planning for the important scenes with the helicopter and explosives had been haphazard and reckless.

From Hilary Leach, the production assistant, the jurors learned that the permit requirement for children was well known, and even had been taught in her Directors' Guild training program. She also confirmed that the children in the European scene had been legally hired and that a teacher-welfare worker had been on the set during their performances.

Anderson House testified about his repeated calls to Allingham in late June before filming had begun: "My first concern was that [the script] indicated the children would be working at night. I called back within a day or so. I had been concerned about the mention of the helicopter and the explosives in relation to the children. And I asked [Allingham] if there had been consideration made of using doubles for the children to avoid breaking the law, in respect to working the children at night. It seemed to me that he indicated that there had been considerations made of that before, and that they were going to go on and do it as he had told me previously."

Then there had been a third and final telephone call: "I had done a little bit of research on doubles and he indicated that it was ground that had already been covered and that it had been rejected. He indicated that he had spoken to the director about it, and that the dummies look like dummies and they would not look real. And would not satisfy the demands of the script in the shot the director wanted."

Important to the defense cross-examination was to show that in 1982 House had not mentioned to anyone that he thought the scene was dangerous but only discussed the illegality of the late hours.

"I had concerns about a lot of things that were unknowns to me," House testified. "There were explosives, there was a helicopter, water, gas fumes. I was a bit concerned with Vic Morrow out in the middle of the river with them. If he had tripped or something and lost his grasp on one of the children, they might go underwater, and other people may not be able to get their footing out there."

But defense attorneys showed that that worry had not been relayed to Allingham.

House recalled how tongue-tied he had become during filming at Franklin Canyon when he had the opportunity to confront Landis on the hiring issue. "I just wasn't up to questioning John Landis on the subject. I was intimidated."

The impact of House's testimony was mitigated by his admissions that he, too, had participated in the cover-up of the illegal hiring. His involvement proved, defense attorneys argued, that his concern about danger had been minimal. House did testify: "If I had believed the helicopter was going to fall down and kill somebody, I wouldn't have been a part of it. No."

House talked about his written warning to Allingham that Jack Tice was a teacher-welfare worker; his request to location manager Richard Vane to determine where Tice would be positioned during the Thursday night filming; his direction to Hilary Leach that she cloak her radio transmissions about the children; and Allingham's instruction, with which he had complied, that the children's names be eliminated from any production reports.

First assistant director Elie Cohn implied that Landis had been the singular, strong proponent of illegally hiring the children: "Dan [Allingham] came to me and said he'd rather we did not have to use the children. He said he would rather use midgets or dummies, and John Landis said he had to use real children."

Anderson House was the first of several witnesses to recount Wingo's confrontation with Landis after the 11:30 P.M. shot, when the director retorted by promising bigger explosions at 2:20 A.M. He was also the first of several witnesses who recalled overhearing Landis and Stewart discuss the placement of a mortar under hut number four after the eleven-thirty shot.

This was the heart of D'Agostino's involuntary-manslaughter case: that despite the eleven-thirty buffeting of the helicopter by special effects and the instructions of Wingo that there could be no debris anywhere near the helicopter, Landis and Stewart nonetheless decided at the last minute to add another special-effects explosive to the 2:20 A.M. scene—the explosive that was responsible for disabling the helicopter.

The witnesses, however, had various recollections about whether the discussion between Landis and Stewart concerned placing a bomb under the hut or in the sampan.

"I don't want to embarrass anybody, but I must stop this," Jim Neal said at a bench conference that soon evolved into a secret session in the judge's chambers. Neal was outraged by a comment D'Agostino had made after House had speculated that Landis could have been killed had the crashing helicopter merely tipped in the opposite direction when it struck the ground.

"Too bad," D'Agostino had muttered.

"It certainly behooves everyone to observe some decorum here," Boren added.

D'Agostino didn't deny the comment. Instead, she accused Landis of having "made a snort" during the testimony of another witness.

D'Agostino wanted desperately for the jury to understand that the fear of blackballing was causing a number of witnesses to temper their testimony. Initially, Boren had ruled such testimony inadmissible. He changed his mind after hearing witnesses refer to their job fears: "My previous ruling was in error, and there is a right to ask witnesses about whether or not they have feelings of trepidation because of industry pressure, things like that."

Richard Sawyer, the production designer who had fashioned the Vietnamese village and has worked on other Landis movies since (the most recent was *Three Amigos*), was one person who softened his testimony because of his continuing professional relationship with Landis, D'Agostino suggested. She showed that Sawyer's grand jury testimony had been harsher than his trial testimony.

When asked what damage the helicopter had caused the set during the eleven-thirty shot, Sawyer testified: "The only thing I had to rearrange was some of the foliage." Unsatisfied with that answer, D'Agostino read to him, in the jury's presence, his 1983 grand jury testimony when he had said, in answer to the same question: "I remember in my head saying, 'Boy this place has been so torn apart, it's hardly what it really looked like when I first started out this evening.' "

"This man is fudging," D'Agostino said at the sidebar. "There is a tremendous fear on the part of these people to come forward and really tell the complete truth. These people are scared. They have this threat hanging over them and it is a known fact. Everyone knows what happened to Cliff Robertson. That man didn't work for five years." (Her reference was to the David Begelman scandal in which the Columbia Pictures executive forged company checks, including one for $10,000 using Robertson's name. The actor exposed the scheme after discovering a discrepancy in his financial records, and later asserted that afterward his job offers had declined dramatically.)

The investigators frequently heard from witnesses about their fear of blackballing, although ultimately little of that perceived concern reached the jury. At least one witness told investigators of threats. Landis's *Twilight Zone* secretary Alpha Campbell told D'Agostino that a year after the crash she had received anonymous telephone calls during which a male voice warned her that if she said anything unfavorable to Landis, "You are aware you would lose your job."

* * *

D'Agostino demonstrated that prior to the two-twenty shot, crew members had varying impressions of what Landis actually was planning for the upcoming scene.

Richard Sawyer said that Landis had told him: "The scene would carry forth with a continuation of the explosions inside the village [and] after Vic Morrow was out of range in the middle of the river. We would start to have the village blown up."

Elie Cohn believed that there were to be no explosions within the village, just water mortars and the two large explosions in the distance at the dam.

D'Agostino believed that the disparity in recollections among high-ranking members of the production team proved that Landis's communication system was inept and had compromised safety.

The prosecutor knew that Elie Cohn's testimony, which supported her contention that there had been no detailed planning meetings with all of the principals present, would be contested by the defense. Cohn, technically the second-ranking authority on the set after Landis, said that he didn't specifically remember meeting with Landis, Stewart, and Wingo about the two-twenty shot, adding, "I am sure there was one." But even in statements closer to the time of the crash, Cohn had not recalled such planning sessions.

That Landis had been aware of the risk involved in the two-twenty shot was implied in his warning to all the spectators to stand. "I asked him why he said that," Cohn testified. "He said that 'people standing up can take the explosion better,' the effect of the explosion."

"You mean the magnitude of it?" D'Agostino asked.

"Yes," Cohn said.

D'Agostino thought that Landis's final order to the helicopter to fly "lower, lower, lower," which he consistently denied having said, was indisputable proof of recklessness.

The evidence was overwhelming that Landis had yelled those orders, and that they had been relayed to the helicopter by Elie Cohn, who testified that he was "ninety-five percent sure" he had relayed the "lower, lower" command at Landis's direction.

Jim Neal countered such presentations with his fundamental trial tactic of continual reference to what he called "The Plan": Landis's purported vision that in the rescue scene, before the shoreline explosions were detonated, the helicopter would be "a safe distance away," on its way to becoming a hovering camera platform on the shore opposite the village.

Neal believed that if he could convince the jurors that a reasonable plan had been communicated to others on the set, he could then easily demonstrate how the plan went awry beyond the control of Landis and the other four defendants.

Neal was aware that the argument had its weaknesses, the greatest of which was that no one, including Landis, could truthfully testify that there ever had been a discussion of precisely what a safe distance was.

In cross-examination, Neal asked Elie Cohn about the plan, and although he received an ambiguous answer, it was the sort of response that created the impression Neal wanted to offer to the jurors.

"And then was the plan for the helicopter to turn north, go across the river, and then raise up in the air and film what was purporting to be the burning of the village?" Neal asked.

"Yeah, but before the helicopter made the turn, the plan was, and it did happen, for the machine guns to fire, and the special effects to go off, or the special effects to start to go off," the first assistant director responded.

"Was there any part of a plan to set off special-effects explosions under a helicopter?" Neal asked.

"Not that I know of," Cohn said. "It was a well-rehearsed plan."

As a group, the camera crew, of all those employed on *Twilight Zone: The Movie,* offered the most consistently negative testimony against Landis.

Lee Redmond, the assistant to cameraman John Connor, related his story of Landis's sharp remarks to Connor when the cameraman had questioned safety at Indian Dunes and Landis angrily said that Connor could go home and he would film the scene himself.

Michael Scott, the cameraman positioned on top of the cliff with the bird's-eye view of the village, was first questioned out of the presence of the jury, so Boren could determine if his testimony was admissible. He had told investigators before the trial that he thought the 2:00 A.M. rehearsal had been rushed and inadequate.

"The things that were described to me that were going to happen did not happen. The helicopter, actors, were not in the scene at the same time, which was one of the purposes of my shot," he told Boren.

His appraisal of the production team's safety consciousness was harsh: "I got no sense whatsoever that the people who were running the operation had any sense or care, or sense of responsibility for anyone involved, whether it be actors, crew, bystanders, or whatever."

He said that he had not expressed those reservations at Indian Dunes because he had been hired only for one night's work, and as "the new kid on the block, you don't rock the boat. You try not to get a reputation for always asking questions that people don't want to hear. So you try to avoid that, so you can get future employment. You do your shot and you go home. I felt it was very dangerous, but I have to admit, I, like everyone else, had no thoughts that the machine would actually crash."

The defendants apparently found Scott's testimony especially preposterous. Boren warned Landis not to shake his head, and Allingham not to laugh. At the end, Boren decided to let Scott testify in front of the jury.

Randy Robinson and Steven Lydecker were particularly critical of Landis, whom they found to be arrogant and mean-spirited. Robinson told the jury about Landis's screaming over the walkie-talkies, and Lydecker related his conversation with Landis in which the director had said, "We may lose the helicopter."

D'Agostino exploited that comment to the fullest in her attack on the director, although there was always ambiguity about whether Landis was joking in his dark manner or was referring to the aircraft not being in the camera frame.

Robinson and Lydecker testified about a challenging rebuke Landis had made to the electricians at Indian Dunes. Part of the illumination for the set came from lights on thirty-foot-high stands which moved when buffeted by the helicopter rotor wash. The fragility of the platforms apparently frightened the workers who didn't want to risk climbing the structure to secure the lights. Lydecker quoted Landis as having yelled, "Is there someone on this electrical crew that is not chickenshit enough to run the light up on the parallel?"

By October, the television camera crews had tired of their tedious daily task of laying cable and wire for the in-court pool camera, and then picking it up again at night. Early in the month, Boren granted a request from KCBS to lay camera and sound cables that would remain until the conclusion of the trial.

It was to be expected that among Landis's friends at the trial there would be some famous faces from the movies. One of the most widely recognized supporters was Ralph Bellamy, an elegant, white-haired gentleman who, even many years after the movie *Sunrise at Campobello,* was still Franklin D. Roosevelt to many Americans. Bellamy, along with Don Ameche, who had visited court on another day, had found some new fans in a younger generation when they starred in *Trading Places,* Landis's first film after *Twilight Zone: The Movie.*

Bellamy was obviously fond of Landis, telling reporters in the courthouse hallway that the prosecution of Landis amounted to persecution, and the director's oppressor was "the district attorney's office. This thing smacks of personal ambition and there's a question of legal manipulation. There is a theatricality to this."

D'Agostino saw opportunity in the actor's outrage and immediately issued a subpoena for him to testify the following week. When defense attorneys immediately criticized her, she responded with cloying innocence: "It's information I'm not aware of and I would like to hear what he has to say on the witness stand. He is a well-respected actor. His opinions will be carried on television and in the newspapers, and I have a right to know on what he bases them."

Few could see any constructive point to D'Agostino's challenge to Bellamy. District attorney investigator Gerald Loeb was so outraged at what he thought was a publicity grab and a waste of time that he refused to serve the court summons. An assistant was instructed to serve the papers, though, and Bellamy received them as he stood in the hallway with Landis waiting for court to resume.

"It's Mrs. D'Agostino, she wants your autograph," Associated Press reporter Linda Deutsch heard Landis say to Bellamy. Landis later said the subpoena amounted to nothing more than harassment. Jim Neal called the subpoena "a bush-league effort to discourage any of Mr. Landis's friends from attending the trial."

Harland Braun called the subpoena an outrageous abuse of power and then angrily unleashed an invective that became the nadir of the constant name-calling. "She's scum," Braun said bitterly. Later he told *Los Angeles Times* reporter Paul Feldman: "It was like the KGB moving into Los Angeles and working for the district attorney's office. You say what you think in the hallway and then you get hauled away."

After the subpoena had been handed to Bellamy, he, Landis, and Braun went back into the courtroom to talk to the prosecutor, but she refused to discuss the matter.

If the defense attorneys were angry that afternoon, they were furious the next morning when they saw that Chief Deputy District Attorney Gilbert Garcetti was publicly supporting the prosecutor's action against Bellamy. "You don't mess around with Lea," Garcetti had been quoted in the morning edition of the *Los Angeles Times.* "If you make light of the case, or make out that you knew something about the case, we're going to dig and find out what you actually know."

Boren, however, wasn't inclined to give the district attorney's office any time to dig in this area, quickly quashing the subpoena on a motion by Harland Braun. D'Agostino told the judge: "The prosecution has a great deal of respect and admiration for Mr. Bellamy's illustrious career. There was no attempt to intimidate him." The judge called the subpoena "a fishing expedition. I will not permit that."

Boren was reaching his fill of all the squabbling among the lawyers. On another occasion, Neal was the object of Boren's pique. As D'Agostino was questioning a witness, Boren heard Neal say, "I am dumbfounded." When the judge admonished him for the comment, Neal said, "I just can't make any sense of it, Judge. I said it. I didn't mean to say it so the jury could hear it."

A few days after the Bellamy subpoena, Boren issued an order by which he intended to harness the lawyers' behavior. First he wanted them to address each other in the third person—"no more 'you.' I do not want any further use of epithets or descriptive names for other counsel, or reputation-type descriptions obtained from other attorneys in other cases. These do not help the court at all. I don't want people interrupted during arguments to the court. No speaking objections in front of the jury."

Other well-known friends of Landis attended the trial without incident after the Bellamy affair, among them actresses Jenny Agutter and Carrie Fisher, and comedian Dan Aykroyd, the late John Belushi's best friend and costar of Landis's hit *The Blues Brothers.* This was a serious Aykroyd in court, dressed in a conservative light blue suit, button-down shirt, and striped tie, and accompanied by his wife. His words were tempered.

"I love John," Aykroyd told KABC reporter Paul Dandridge. "He's a good friend and a superior human being in my estimation, and one who is involved in tragic circumstances, like everybody else in this thing, and he just, I felt, needed our support and our love. And we really think a lot of him, and I'd back him up to the wall on anything he was going through."

D'Agostino's next witnesses, the fire safety officers, should have provided D'Agostino with brief, damaging evidence against the defendants. But she was unprepared for all they had to say. Dewitt Morgan was the first fire official to testify, appearing before the jury on October 9. That morning D'Agostino revealed in court that she had met for the first time just that morning with four of the five firemen who had worked on the set.

Morgan, who had issued the movie company their special-effects permit, testified as expected, explaining to jurors that it is dangerous to detonate special effects under a structure with a helicopter flying overhead.

"Were you told those things were going to happen on this set?" D'Agostino asked.

"No."

"Was there compliance by this motion picture company with the conditions of the permit which you did issue?"

"No, ma'am."

"No further questions," the prosecutor said.

Harland Braun suggested that the fire safety officers had had an obligation to check carefully the special effects for safety, an argument Morgan rebuffed.

"Wouldn't it be the responsibility of some of the firemen on the set Wednesday night, while the special effects were being set up, to go look at them?" Braun asked.

"We were relying on the expertise of the special-effects man to properly place those explosives. There was a plan in operation and we expected to see that plan carried out."

The testimony of the fire safety officers continued in anticipated fashion. Then, on October 15, D'Agostino's case fell off its tracks, in a fashion similar to the debacle over the Donna Schuman testimony.

The problem for D'Agostino arose when Los Angeles County fire safety officer Richard Ebentheuer revealed that earlier in the evening he had warned the fire safety office supervisor that the helicopter could crash because of the conditions under which it was being flown. Ebentheuer's testimony gave the appearance that not only had some fire department officials covered up his August 1982 report about the incident, but also, once again, the prosecutor was accused of proceeding in a less than forthright manner.

Ebentheuer's revelations were first made out of the jury's presence.

The retired fireman had worked for Los Angeles County for thirty-four years, and since his departure from active duty had worked on more than one hundred television shows and movies.

He had been at Indian Dunes both Wednesday and Thursday nights, assigned to a spot atop the cliff, watching for fires ignited by burning debris from the fireballs. Ebentheuer knew about explosions and helicopters. After seeing the buffeting of the aircraft during the eleven-thirty shot, he worried that the helicopter could actually crash if it were subjected to the same forces again at two-twenty. Ebentheuer was particularly worried about the concussive effect of the explosions reflecting off the cliff face. For much of the meal break, he had stood on the mesa with the squad supervisor, George Hull, arguing about his worries.

Even more astounding than the fact that less than two hours before the crash a fire safety officer had worried about lethal danger was Hull's reaction to Ebentheuer's prophetic worry: apparently believing that Ebentheuer didn't know what he was talking about, Hull had refused to alert the moviemakers and angrily told Ebentheuer to tell them himself.

The argument ended as Ebentheuer walked away and said, "Goddamn it! The helicopter will be on the ground."

During Neal's cross-examination, the defense learned that shortly after the deaths, Ebentheuer had written a memo containing details of the incident and turned it over to Dewitt Morgan. Morgan's subsequent report to a battalion chief of the Los Angeles County Fire Department, however, never mentioned Ebentheuer's misgivings. On the contrary, that report spoke glowingly of the actions of all the fire safety officers on the night of the crash and concluded that all had acted in exemplary fashion.

Furthermore, Neal elicited from Ebentheuer, D'Agostino had been told all of this in her meeting with the firemen several days before. (The prosecutor later wrote "no way" in her copy of the trial transcript.)

During Neal's questioning of Ebentheuer, he had several conferences with his Nashville law partner James Sanders, whom he referred to as "my brains." (Other defense attorneys, disappointed in Neal's lackluster trial performance, agreed with that assessment and were impressed with Sanders's deft display of legal intellect.)

When Ebentheuer left the witness stand, the jurors were still in their waiting room, unaware of the turmoil in the court. Sanders presented the defense's analysis of the controversy: The jurors had been told by Dewitt Morgan that no fire safety officer had expressed any concerns to him about safety on the set, and now Ebentheuer has testified that he had expressed precisely those sentiments in writing in 1982.

"It appears to be so," Boren said, privately dismayed at D'Agostino's handling of the issue.

Sanders continued: "It seems to me that now we have a second example of information of a significant nature, going to the truthfulness of testimony, to the very heart of the discovery process."

D'Agostino responded: "I am getting to the point of being quite dismayed with the consistency and persistency with which counsel keeps accusing me, at least inferentially, of withholding things deliberately from them."

"That was the testimony of the witness, in essence, I suppose," Boren reminded her, then added: "I do feel there are certain indications here that suggest that the prosecutor was less than candid in the examination. But I also feel that on the other side that some of what she said does make sense, in that she has been handling a number of witnesses over a period of time who come in together and some of it could have gotten lost in the shuffle."

Boren told D'Agostino the next day that there could come a time where the cumulative effect of her lack of candidness could lead to sanctions against her—or even a mistrial. The judge said she had used poor judgment in not assessing the importance of the allegation that Ebentheuer's memorandum had been suppressed by county fire officials.

On the following Monday, Ebentheuer returned to the witness chair, this time to tell his story to the jury. He is a thin man with white hair, a sliver of a white mustache, and wire-rimmed glasses. One of the spoils garnered by the defense in this little war was that D'Agostino was not allowed to elicit in her direct examination the testimony about Ebentheuer's postcrash conversation with Dewitt Morgan or that his incriminating memorandum had mysteriously disappeared. Instead, the defense would be able to use the information to its fullest impact by bringing it forth in their cross-examination.

"The cliff acts like a wall and the explosions cannot expand in three-hundred-sixty-degree pattern," Ebentheuer had explained to Hull. "I told him that I felt that the concussion from the explosions would put the helicopter on the ground. He felt that there wouldn't be any problem."

The defense had the opportunity to make the fire safety officers look bad on several levels, and even Ebentheuer was subject to criticism.

If he thought the two-twenty scene was going to be so dangerous, Neal asked, why hadn't Ebentheuer taken Hull's suggestion and gone to warn the movie people himself?

"That's not the way the chain of command works in the fire department," Ebentheuer replied. "I am not stating I could assure that the helicopter would go on the ground. It was my sincere belief."

Dewitt Morgan returned to the witness stand, where he endured some tough cross-examination. He had previously testified that no one had voiced any complaint to him. He now said that he didn't recall Ebentheuer's report: "As far as I know, our guys did an outstanding job," he said in reference to the six-man Indian Dunes fire safety squad. That was the same opinion Morgan had written in his 1983 report to superiors.

"Your report was a cover-up of what occurred on that set that night, in terms of Mr. Ebentheuer's conversation, isn't that correct?" Braun asked.

"That is absolutely not true," Morgan replied.

"Where did you bury the reports, Mr. Morgan?" Neal shouted.

Boren sustained D'Agostino's objection, so Morgan didn't have to answer.

A new twist in the controversy developed when battalion chief Gary Nelson called Jerry Loeb to say that he had located the missing memorandums from the fire safety officers. He said they had been in his files all along. It was Thursday and Boren sent the jurors home for a long weekend so the lawyers could study the documents before any more questions were posed to the firemen.

"Sometimes you get to a stage in the proceeding where the gremlins get loose, and they're loose," Boren said to the jurors. "We're not going to be able to proceed today."

The next Monday D'Agostino regained some of the drama of her case when fire safety officer Jack Rimmer described the crash, saying that he had been surprised at how low the helicopter had been flying, and ended by saying that he first knew children were involved when he found body parts.

The fire safety officers' reports, which the defense lawyers now had in their possession, were double-edged swords, because they also included allegations of drinking and carelessness on the part of the moviemakers. Those were issues Neal and the others didn't want to have brought before the jury. Therefore, they decided not to pursue the fire department cover-up issue, to avoid having the memorandums entered as evidence.

For several days, the news coverage of the trial had been negative for the prosecution because of the fire department controversy. Levine told reporters: "The fire safety officers who thought the scene was dangerous and did nothing are not being prosecuted, while the defendants, who thought it was safe, are being prosecuted."

With the questionable actions of fire department officials certain to dominate the news coverage again on television that night and the next morning, D'Agostino provided one television news reporter with a document that led to at least some anti-Landis coverage that night. Elizabeth Anderson of KNBC, using a photograph of a National Transportation Safety Board transcript (it was D'Agostino's copy), reported what was essentially an old story: that after the crash, when asked whether the helicopter came to a different spot above the village at two-twenty than it had been placed in the rehearsal, Landis had responded: "Basically it wasn't where it was supposed to be, but I figured that I didn't care."

The NTSB transcripts had been made public years before.

After the Landis quote had appeared in large letters on the screen, the news report cut to a videotape of D'Agostino in her office, radiant in a bright red dress. Smiling, D'Agostino looked into the camera and said, "I think, Elizabeth, that that says it all."

The next morning the defense attorneys were livid when D'Agostino confirmed that she had been the source of the "exclusive" news story.

Anderson, of course, had the right to air any story she and her station managers chose to present. The defense attorneys, though, believed that D'Agostino had tried to influence the jury through the television news. At that stage of the trial, because John Landis had not taken the stand, his previous statements were inadmissible as evidence. And D'Agostino could not know then whether he would eventually become a witness, allowing her to present that statement to the jury.

Eugene Trope said to Boren: "I am too old, and I can't be that naive to believe that if we keep doing this, that it will not eventually filter down to the jurors."

Although the jurors had been told to avoid all news coverage of the trial, everyone understood that even the most conscientious jurors could not help hearing something about the case unless they avoided television altogether.

Boren issued a limited gag order, prohibiting the attorneys from discussing with reporters any evidence that had not yet been presented to the jury. That order was later extended to defendants as well, after George Folsey gave an exclusive on-air interview to Paul Dandridge of KABC.

To the dismay of the prosecution, George Hull took the witness stand on November 5, after returning from a hunting trip, to undergo four days of questioning, a great deal of it relating to Ebentheuer's warning that he refused to heed.

Before his retirement, one of Hull's duties had been captain in charge of the county fire department's helicopter operations, and that, he told the jury, was the basis of his judgment that Ebentheuer was wrong: "I told him that predicated upon my experience with our helicopter pilots that [Wingo] would not endanger himself by flying into a hazardous area, and I felt that he wouldn't do anything foolish."

Hull admitted that after his argument with Ebentheuer he learned from Jack Tice that Wingo's face had been singed during the eleven-thirty flight. He believed then, however, that the plan to move the helicopter farther away from the cliff for the two-twenty shot would solve any potential problems. He later had to concede that he did not even talk to Tice until after he had already rejected Ebentheuer's warning.

Levine asked why Hull decided not to pass on the warning to the film crew.

"It is not my responsibility," Hull said. "We do not deal in aircraft traveling."

The questioning of the fire safety officers had been favorable to the defense until Trope enraged his colleagues by eliciting from Hull in front of the jury the NTSB conclusion that debris had caused the helicopter crash. The jurors had not before been told that a federal agency had come to some conclusion about the cause of the crash, particularly a conclusion that contradicted the defense's theory that the cause had been heat delamination, purportedly an unforeseeable event.

"Do you know of your own knowledge if debris brought down the helicopter?" Trope asked.

"I've been told that was the findings," Hull said.

"You were told?"

"By the NTSB."

"Were you also told that heat also affected the helicopter?"

"No."

D'Agostino thought that Trope's slip would now allow her to enter the entire NTSB report as evidence, but Boren ruled that she was still precluded from doing so under the rules of evidence. (Abdon Llorente, the NTSB investigator, under congressionally approved regulations was not allowed to testify about his conclusions concerning the causes of crashes. The purpose was to protect NTSB investigators from getting bogged down in courtroom testimony that could hinder their primary purpose of ensuring safety for air travelers.)

The examination of Hull ended in a fashion typical of the proceedings: not with revealing testimony from the witness but at a bench conference over a trivial matter.

D'Agostino had said that during his cross-examination of Hull, Klein had walked behind her and "deliberately thumped my chair. I have a very bad back to begin with. If he could be requested by the court not to thump my chair."

"I didn't see him thump on your chair," Boren replied, drawing laughs from the defense attorneys by adding: "I will ask all counsel to leave her chair alone. If anybody is doing it, leave other counsel's chairs alone."

The fire safety officers had consumed fourteen days of trial time over a period of a month.

Both Budds and Loeb had had arguments with D'Agostino about her trial strategy, particularly during her seemingly endless parade of fire safety officers who, on each successive day, were chipping away at her

credibility, and embarrassingly distracting the jury from what these investigators thought were the crucial issues of the case.

Budds, particularly, was offended by the prosecutor's curt dismissal of
his advice. "One shake of the head for the things I have to say, I don't
think is enough reflection," Budds angrily told me.

The detective believes that D'Agostino had made a mistake by trying
to protect the credibility of the firemen, just because they were nominally
prosecution witnesses: "If somebody does something wrong [referring to
the controversy over Ebentheuer's report], then shame on them, don't sit
there and say, 'That's not wrong.' You do that for enough witnesses, what
happens? The ones that really need protecting, you don't believe her
anymore."

THIRTEEN

JOHN LANDIS, in his exuberant manner, once told his lawyers that the *Twilight Zone* special-effects crew members were "very funny-looking guys. They're huge! They're like, you know, six-foot-five, three hundred pounds, big beards. They look like, you know, hillbillies."

Lea D'Agostino, who chose to present all four members of the special-effects crew as prosecution witnesses, although their sympathies were certainly not with her cause, may not have had any better appreciation of these men than did Landis.

Paul Stewart's lawyer, Arnold Klein, was the one attorney in the courtroom who had the trust of the special-effects technicians, and he knew that their testimony would almost certainly help Paul Stewart.

The special-effects crew were prosecution witnesses more by default than commitment to the state's cause. Harry Stewart, Jerry Williams, Kevin Quibell, and James Camomile had been given immunity from prosecution based on the assumption that their grand jury testimony would prove that a mortar had been switched after the crash in an attempt to hide incriminating evidence from investigators. Instead, the testimony had indicated that there had been no switch after all, an assertion proven by the sheriff's department's scientific analysis.

The most important of the special-effects crew to testify would be James Camomile, who, the defense argued, bore responsibility for the damage to the helicopter because he had controlled the firing board.

The testimony of the three other special-effects crewmen, as well as the two stuntmen who had been in the helicopter firing the machine guns, was an inconclusive preamble to Camomile, whose appearance before the jury was anxiously awaited by both sides.

Harry Stewart, who had detonated the two large explosions at the dam in the two-twenty shot, said he did not think that even a bomb underneath the food-drying shack (designated hut number four for the trial) would result in dangerous debris: "It takes a great deal more than [a six-ounce black powder bomb] to blow anything heavy up into the air."

D'Agostino challenged the witness with the observation that this answer was different from his grand jury testimony in which he had said: "It is common knowledge to any powder man that you don't place mortars under huts, because debris can fly around."

Throughout the trial, both sides made extensive use of past testimony (from the grand jury, preliminary hearing, NTSB hearings, sheriff's interviews, and other state inquiries) when the statements of witnesses before the jury conflicted with what they had said in the past. The technique was often used with effective and dramatic results. Many times the prior testimony of defense-biased witnesses was shown to have been harsher against the defendants than their trial testimony, and in other instances prosecution-oriented witnesses appeared to be more accusatory than they had been before.

D'Agostino won a point important to her when Boren reversed an earlier ruling and agreed to allow her to tell the jury about the use of live ammunition in the banana plant scene filmed at Indian Dunes two days before the crash. The prosecutor argued that the incident demonstrated the recklessness of Landis and Paul Stewart.

The point was mitigated by Harry Stewart, who testified that the shotgun shells fired in the scene had actually been filled with "red jets," hard plastic pellets that might sting but that would not be lethal if they struck a person positioned twenty feet away (the distance between the crewman with the guns and the banana plants where Morrow had been just before they fired). The use of red jets had not been mentioned to investigators who, in the months after the deaths, had questioned Paul Stewart and others about the use of shotguns. D'Agostino, though, did not have a strong witness who could testify that more lethal ammunition had been fired in July of 1982. Kevin Quibell supported D'Agostino's thesis with his testimony that Paul Stewart had decided to use the shotguns following Landis's complaint that it would take too long to implant small explosive squibs all over the plant leaves to simulate the effect of bullets.

Stuntman Gary McLarty, who had been hired as Vic Morrow's double but had been in the helicopter firing a machine gun for the Thursday night shots, testified that even before filming began, Morrow had said he wanted to do a good number of his stunts himself.

"All the time during the filming, anytime I was even in his clothes I believe he was intimidated by it. He told people for years he did all his own stunts in *Combat,* and he wanted to do that stunt there, too."

McLarty seemed to contradict himself when he once referred to the 2:20 A.M. scene as a "stunt" for Morrow. At other times both he and Landis had denied that they considered the scene a stunt. This distinction is important because in the movie business, labeling an activity a stunt denotes recognition that it carries an added risk to the participants, and generally has a more rigid planning procedure involving the movie's stunt coordinator—in the case of *Twilight Zone,* McLarty, who at the time was instead working in the helicopter. (Even Landis's attorney, Jim Neal, who continually professed his client's innocence of criminal negligence, told me that he believes there should have been one person coordinating the overall safety at Indian Dunes.)

Jerry Williams, who had placed the mortar under hut four at Paul Stewart's direction, testified that earlier in the evening before the crash, he and Stewart had discussed putting mortars in the cliffside huts and decided against it because "we didn't want any debris coming up." Williams, however, said he did not question Stewart's later instruction—made while Landis stood only a few feet away, although he wasn't sure Landis heard—to place a mortar under the number four hut.

James Camomile, the special-effects technician who fired the fatal explosions, is a husky man, but not extraordinarily so, with thick, broad facial features. He took the witness stand on Monday, December 1.

The lawyers for both sides recognized that his testimony would be pivotal. D'Agostino's trial investigator, Gerald Loeb, told me that Camomile felt tremendous guilt about the deaths and the prosecution team worried that he would take the witness stand and say, "I did it!"

Klein, the only defense lawyer ever to have interviewed Camomile, told the *Los Angeles Times,* "I'd say James Camomile is either going to make Mrs. D'Agostino a talk show guest or a deputy district attorney adjudicating juvenile cases for the rest of her life."

Klein was also the only defense attorney not arguing "The Plan" in its fullest form: that the helicopter was supposed to be well across the river before the shoreline explosions were detonated in the two-twenty filming. Klein knew from his conversations with the special-effects personnel that their only prearrangement had been that they would fire the mortar explosions in a close, "chasing" pattern adjacent to the aircraft—a practice that at the time they presumed to be safe.

The special-effects crew defined a safe distance not in specific measurement but as one that did not result in the helicopter being engulfed by flame. That standard allowed for fireballs to pass only feet, or even inches, from the aircraft.

Sending billowing fireballs close to helicopters is a common special-effects practice. The difference here was that the helicopter was hovering, not moving forward, a distinction not made to the jury.

Potentially, Camomile could contradict a number of critical defense arguments, but he could also, in the perception of jurors, shoulder the blame as well. In fact, when Kesselman was in charge of the case he had worried that Camomile, who felt he shared a deep moral responsibility for what had happened, might accept sole guilt for the events. The lawyers for both sides, through their examination of the witness, would have a great deal to do with shaping the perception of his testimony, much more so than other witnesses.

Camomile, who began movie work in 1965, carried the highest special-effects classification, a California-issued, number one powder card, as does Paul Stewart. Camomile is a Navy veteran whose ship had sailed off the coast of Vietnam during the war. He had worked with special effects for ten years and had received his number one powder card from the state of California in 1981.

Through Camomile, Lea D'Agostino gave the jurors a lesson in mortar construction, having him describe the procedure for packing the heavy steel pots with black powder bombs, gasoline, and sawdust.

Importantly for the prosecution, Camomile said he had not been told that the eleven-thirty explosions, which he had ignited from his firing board, had endangered the helicopter and its occupants. D'Agostino, however, did not continue with more questions to establish firmly the importance to her argument of that lapse in communication: that had Camomile been advised, he would have been put on notice of potential danger.

Instead, the prosecutor followed quickly with questions about a different facet of her criminal negligence theory—that Landis had ordered the bomb placed under hut four in order to enhance the visual effects in the two-twenty scene.

Camomile was a central witness to the conversation between Landis and Stewart in which, D'Agostino alleged, the director, despite previous warnings about the danger of debris, unwisely ordered Paul Stewart to destroy the hut with a special-effects bomb during the scene.

Camomile testified, "I overheard a question regarding the feasibility of being able to do something regarding [the hut], a fireball, somewhere in the vicinity of this hut. Landis wanted to see an explosion of some sort in the vicinity of that structure. He wanted to see something happen."

His recounting, however, was vague, so D'Agostino showed him a transcript of his 1982 National Transportation Safety Board interview in which he had been more definitive about what he had heard. Then Camomile revised his answer for the *Twilight Zone* jurors: "Landis said he would like to see the shack go up."

Camomile said that he had been running electrical connecting wires to other mortars when he overheard the conversation between Landis and Stewart. Soon afterward, Stewart directed Camomile to arm the square mortar that had just been placed under the hut by Jerry Williams. (As a matter of industry standard, the man on the board himself arms the special effects that he will detonate.)

Camomile was specific about the structure Landis and Stewart had referred to in their conversation, describing it as the open, four-legged shack with the raised platform floor, now called hut number four. (Other witnesses testified that Stewart and Landis had been discussing the sampan, in which no bomb was placed.)

Williams testified that when he imbedded the mortar in the mud under the hut he had tilted it toward the cliff, to direct the concussive effect away from where the actors and others would be. Camomile was shown a photograph taken by sheriff's deputies the morning after the crash that showed the mortar standing upright. He testified that the picture seemed to show the position the mortar had been in when he armed it, suggesting that the explosion had fired straight up, not at an angle toward the cliff.

D'Agostino made no attempt to explain to the jury why Camomile had been granted immunity from prosecution. Instead she portrayed the witness as a solid ally.

The result was that defense attorneys were able to argue that Camomile was solely culpable in the tragedy but was being protected by D'Agostino, free from liability for what he had done, just to bolster her case against the defendants.

Budds, for one, thought that D'Agostino's presentation of Camomile had been ineffective. He thought it better to let the jury decide whether Camomile, too, might have made mistakes, and instead emphasize that whatever Camomile may have done, his actions did not detract from the liability of the defendants.

Budds also held a harsh view toward the actions of Morrow, who himself had been killed. The detective said that the actor, who was experienced in the use of special effects, also should have recognized the potential danger. (Budds did not know that Morrow had made ambiguous complaints to his attorney about safety, although the actor apparently did not express them to Landis or other high-ranking production team members.) Budds told me, "Had Morrow lived, he should have been charged. He knew about the problems they had at eleven-thirty and what they were doing about it. He's an adult, he can make a choice."

D'Agostino was successful in eliciting from Camomile that the use of special-effects explosives is inherently risky. He did, however, represent the risk as minimal when movie explosives are used correctly. One constant worry, though, was the premature ignition of dangerously flammable materials used to increase the visual effect: "The rubber cement [used as a fire enhancer on the huts] is very volatile, as is the gasoline. You always have a lot of vapors hanging around in the area. And if anyone should wander through or even come close to it with a cigarette or another incendiary device, you could have a premature explosion."

Camomile didn't remember any meetings with Landis and the special-effects crew in which planning for the final scene was discussed. He did say that Stewart himself had given a briefing to the special-effects crew.

Camomile's position for the two-twenty shot had been on a mound of dirt about five feet high, just west of the village on the cliff side of the river. The helicopter was above and to his left, and he watched Morrow and the children leave the village and cross the river from his right to his left. John Landis stood on the peninsula directly across the river from Camomile's view, watching the action from the opposite angle.

"When the machine gun [in the helicopter] began firing, I was then going to focus my attention on Vic and the children as they were exiting the village. And at that point I would begin firing my mortars," Camomile said.

"Was there ever a discussion with you that you should not or could not fire your bombs until the helicopter left the scene?" D'Agostino asked.

"No, there was not," Camomile replied firmly.

Inherent in Camomile's answers, but only obliquely referred to by D'Agostino in a few questions, was that Camomile assumed the helicopter would not move from a hovering position while the explosions were going off.

Camomile's incorrect assumption was a key target of Klein's cross-examination, which, in concert with other defense attorneys, would last for two more days.

It was critical to the defense that the lawyers focus responsibility for the mistiming during the two-twenty shot on Camomile. They wanted to show that, ultimately, he had been the final and sole determinant of whether a special-effects explosion should be fired or not.

"At two-twenty you were the one who had the final duty to abort the firing if you thought it was unsafe?" Klein asked.

"That's correct," Camomile answered.

Klein and the others were unquestionably successful in raising the notion that Camomile had acted contrary to the standards of special-effects technicians. Most important, the defense lawyers emphasized his mandate to be aware visually of the movements of all the elements in a scene, including people and aircraft.

D'Agostino's counterploy was to demonstrate that, given the information and instructions Camomile had been provided concerning the two-twenty scene, all of his actions had been appropriate.

The defense had a concise response to that argument: It had been Camomile's job to look up and see where the helicopter was positioned before firing. He made a mistake and did not do that.

There seemed little doubt that Camomile had not expected that the tail of the helicopter would swing back over land, placing the entire rear rotor assembly directly in the trajectory of the fireballs.

Central to the defense's cross-examination were repetitive questions suggesting that Camomile was required to look up at the location of the helicopter, as well as down to the location of the actors, before he fired each of the eight special-effects explosions on his firing board.

D'Agostino countered with the argument that Camomile's responsibility had been to watch the movements of Morrow and the children carefully.

The prosecutor asked Camomile why he did not look up before firing mortars two, three, four, five, and six. (He had checked the location of the helicopter before firing the first mortar.)

"My attention was primarily focused on Vic and the children," Camomile said.

"Why?"

"Because of the possibility that the children may have tried to break free or run and get back into the village, where the mortars were."

Camomile had been told to space the explosions about one second apart. Jurors were aware that a scientific analysis of the film showed that there was a three-second gap between the third and fatal fourth explosions and less than half a second of time between the fourth and fifth explosions.

In marked contrast to the scientific analysis, Camomile continued to insist that, according to his memory, he had spaced the shots according to instructions.

Klein believed that his single most compelling argument regarding Camomile was based on the state regulation that required a powderman to be able to see the special effect—and presumably any of the area it might impact. Camomile agreed that "the man on the board must have a direct line of vision to his special effect."

"And did you look at the helicopter to make sure that the helicopter was a safe enough distance away from the special effects?" Klein asked.

"Prior to firing my boards, I did, yes," Camomile said.

Jim Neal, as well as the others, knew that in a long trial the subtlety and nuance of individual questions and answers would not be remembered by jurors. More important was the overall perception.

Neal was able to obtain an answer that he and other defense attorneys exploited to D'Agostino's great disadvantage, because it suggested carelessness on Camomile's part.

Referring to the special-effects meeting prior to the two-twenty scene, Klein asked: "And at that time Paul Stewart told you not to set off any of the explosives under or near the helicopter?"

"I believe so, yes," Camomile said.

That answer marked the first time Camomile had ever made public reference to a warning from Stewart about the position of the helicopter. The answer also contradicted his earlier answer to D'Agostino in which he had said he had been given no instructions regarding location of the helicopter.

Camomile confirmed that after the crash he had been dejected, with a sense of responsibility for the deaths. But while he accepted causal responsibility for setting off the bombs—he obviously could not deny that —he did not now accept blame for any wrongdoing.

While he confirmed that he had looked up only once to check the position of the helicopter—and the defense said that he should have looked up before firing each of the six mortars—Camomile insisted that he had followed instructions and had maintained a proper standard of safety.

"And your conduct in not looking [up to the helicopter] fell below the standard of care required of a number one cardholder?" Braun asked.

"I don't believe so, sir," Camomile said.

"You think it was okay not to look at the helicopter before setting off number four and five?" (the explosions that led to the damage to the aircraft).

"Given the situation, considering having to keep an eye out for the actors and fire the board and being told that the helicopter would not change, I acted on the best interests of all parties concerned. I believed it was in a safe position," Camomile said.

"Did you check after you set off number three, that four and five would not be within the airspace of the helicopter?"

"I don't believe so, no, sir. I don't believe four and five were in the airspace."

"And then you were supposed to make sure that the helicopter was a safe distance from the special effects before you set them off?" Neal asked.

"That's correct. The helicopter was, as far as I know, not going to change position. The helicopter was at a safe distance from the special effects as far as I was concerned at the time."

When Camomile finished his testimony, there was widespread agreement that he had been more damaging to D'Agostino's case than any other witness.

FOURTEEN

BY DECEMBER, with close to four months of testimony completed and no end to the prosecution's presentation in sight, Lea D'Agostino was under increasing criticism that she was overtrying the case. She was warned that she was wasting time on unimportant skirmishes, and even losing those without making headway into the trial's core issue of culpability.

Budds and others tried to convince D'Agostino to alter her approach, urging a course similar to what he and Gary Kesselman had planned. Budds told me: "We were going to keep it short and sweet, thirty-five witnesses [D'Agostino would present more than double that], show the film, and get out of there."

D'Agostino was being hurt by many of her own witnesses who offered testimony that was either hostile to her case or inconclusive. Still, she insisted to all who asked—including her bosses in the district attorney's office—that her all-encompassing method was the only way the jury would get the information it needed.

Typical of the problems the prosecutor encountered was the testimony of Virginia Kearns, the movie's hair stylist, who was completely contradicted on a significant point by a subsequent prosecution witness. Kearns testified that after the eleven-thirty shot she heard Katherine Wooten, the script supervisor, tell Landis that the next scene with the helicopter and the children should not be attempted because it was obviously too dangerous. "John told her to shut up," Kearns said.

Wooten was not friendly to the prosecution, but D'Agostino called her to the stand anyway. Although it is not unusual for prosecutors to call witnesses hostile to the government's position, it is usually done when the witness has compelling, helpful testimony. Wooten's value to the prosecution's case was debatable. She firmly denied that the conversation with Landis happened as Kearns had described. Wooten was an old friend of Landis's—she had been responsible for bringing his work on *Kentucky Fried Movie* to Sean Daniels, the Universal Studios executive who then offered Landis the chance to direct *National Lampoon's Animal House.*

On cross-examination, Wooten told her version of the conversation with Landis at Indian Dunes: "I went up to John [after the 11:30 P.M. shot] and said, 'This might be a stupid question but it just occurs to me in a logical continuity if they are firing machine guns out of the helicopter how come there are big explosions on the ground?' And he said, 'Don't worry it works, it will work for the logic of the movie.' "

While defense attorneys worried about Landis's courtroom antics, Budds was bothered by D'Agostino's noticeable gesturing, which seemed intended to influence the jury. Sometimes D'Agostino showed her displeasure by rolling her eyes skyward or mincing her mouth. Budds told me: "She would lean toward me or tap me on the arm and then it was my turn to assume a role for a jury that I'm in agreement with her. And I don't want to play those damn games. She started assuming a John Landis attitude that 'I'm the director here. It's my case.' "

Unlike Donna Schuman, whose testimony had erupted in controversy that did not go away, Allingham's former fiancée, Cynthia Nigh, talked about "going-to-jail" statements without arousing an attack from the defense. The difference in the testimony of the two women was that Nigh attributed only one joking comment to Folsey and did not suggest that Folsey was concerned about danger. (Folsey later told me that he no doubt had joked about going to jail but didn't remember specifically. He did say that he had always viewed the illegal hiring as a minor, technical violation of state law governing working hours for children and did not believe at all that he was endangering My-Ca and Renee.)

Landis's newest movie, *Three Amigos,* was released nationwide in early December and met with moderate reviews and ticket sales. The comic story is set in the silent film era and stars Steve Martin, Chevy Chase, and Martin Short. The three portray studio-created celebrities who go to Mexico to save a town besieged by bandits. The film won Landis some positive reviews that were generally more approving than those he had received for other movies in the past.

In light of the issues at trial, though, the review by *New York Times* writer Janet Maslin was noteworthy for its skeptical observations about the techniques still employed by Landis. She did not mention *Twilight Zone* in the review, but the comments had to be read in the context of the trial:

> As directed by John Landis, "Three Amigos" visibly radiates the conviction that bigger and costlier are better, even when the actors and the material seem cannier than that. But Mr. Landis consistently uses more extras, more props, and more fireworks than the film really needs. There also are a number of dangerous-looking stunts that are irrelevant to the action at hand.

Three Amigos had been filmed in Arizona earlier in the year and had been one of Landis's six major projects since the deaths. After *Twilight Zone*, Landis directed *Trading Places, Into the Night, Spies Like Us,* and the phenomenal music video *Thriller* with Michael Jackson, which included a companion documentary video titled *The Making of 'Thriller.'* Even as the trial was under way, Landis was involved in the production of a comedy anthology called *Amazon Women on the Moon,* which was released the following summer.

The testimony of fire safety officer Jack Tice, who was also licensed as a studio teacher-welfare worker, was crucial for the establishment of one important point: whether he had seen My-Ca Le and Renee Chen on the set before the fatal crash. The indications were convincing that he had not, but the defense tried to prove that he had. If the defense could show that Tice knew the children were working, they could then argue that he overlooked the late-hour regulations because even he assumed the special effects would be safe.

But Tice was adamant that he first learned about the children when he saw their bodies. In fact, in the summer of 1982, after the deaths, he had contacted a lawyer to discuss the possibility of suing the moviemakers for deceiving him and putting him through the mental anguish wrought by his experiences at Indian Dunes. Tice had been one of the men who collected body parts. He did not, however, follow through with a lawsuit.

Tice had been a studio teacher-welfare worker for over eight years, a combat air crewman in Korea, and a fireman with the U.S. Forest Service for six years.

Out of the presence of the jury, Tice said he would not have allowed the children to work under those circumstance at any time of the day. He said he used a different standard for children than for adults when assessing danger on a set: "Because the child cannot make those decisions. I have to make those decisions for him. You take into account the frailty of the child, height and athletic ability of a child. In a situation like that we would make the judgments for the child."

In front of the jury, Tice recounted his movements on the set and what he now recognized as the efforts of the production team to hide the children from him. Tice was also one of many witnesses who recalled Landis's expressions of ill temper.

The final day of testimony before a long holiday break was Thursday, December 18, which turned out to be a good day for the prosecutor.

Harry Ferguson, the helicopter mechanic, undermined the defense's delamination theory when he said he had long been aware that such heat damage was possible and, in fact, had checked for evidence of delamination damage to the aircraft after the eleven-thirty shot: "I saw fireballs going up beyond the level of the main rotor blades and coming back down through the blades. The main rotor blades are susceptible to heat damage at high temperatures. What can occur is known as delamination. Heat is initially used to cure the adhesive but also high heat can debond that adhesive. And that was a concern to me."

Neal was eager to discredit the testimony of cameraman Steve Lydecker, who was one of the first witnesses when the trial resumed in January after a two-week recess.

Lydecker gave the most detailed recital of the banana plant sequence, recalling that Landis became angered when marble guns did not properly mutilate the plants, and that Stewart then used shotguns after Landis complained about the time it would take to implant small explosive squibs to simulate bullet hits.

The element of Lydecker's testimony that worried Neal the most was the cameraman's recounting of his conversation with Landis about safety, a few days before the children's scenes were filmed. Lydecker told the jurors that after he expressed concern about the concussive effect of the explosions, Landis said, "We may lose the helicopter."

"Did you respond?" D'Agostino asked.

"No, I didn't. I was a bit shocked. At that point John was walking away from me and I went about my own business."

By the time Neal's cross-examination began, Lydecker had already told reporters in the hallway—and had been quoted in newspaper articles—that Landis had been joking when he made the statement. Lydecker did not serve the prosecution well when he answered Neal's question about his hallway remarks and apparently contradicted himself.

"Mr. Landis was joking about that, isn't that true?" Neal asked.

"I didn't say joking," Lydecker responded.

"You did not tell Mr. Andy Furillo that Landis was joking when he made that remark about the helicopter?

"No."

Later, when the defense put on its case, Neal subpoenaed Furillo, and the newspaper reporter confirmed that his published quotes of Lydecker were accurate.

D'Agostino was frustrated in her attempts to have the NTSB report introduced as evidence. The report established that debris had been one source of the damage to the helicopter. The prosecutor argued the absurdity of not allowing the jury to know that the federal agency charged with investigating aircraft mishaps had come to a conclusion that was published in an already publicly available report.

When NTSB investigator Abdon Llorente came to court under subpoena by D'Agostino, he was accompanied by an NTSB attorney and an assistant U.S. attorney from Los Angeles, both of whom were intent on limiting Llorente's testimony. The agency opposed testimony by its investigators in order to keep them free to conduct quick, thorough, unencumbered investigations of aircraft crashes.

In a preliminary questioning session out of the presence of the jury, D'Agostino learned just how difficult it would be for her to obtain substantive commentary from Llorente.

After showing him two pieces of the broken tail rotor, she asked if he could tell by looking at the separation whether it could be termed a fracture.

Both federal attorneys objected, saying the answer called for a conclusion Llorente was not allowed to give.

"When does it require you to be an expert to say the word 'fracture' means it's broken in two?" D'Agostino asked in frustration.

Boren shared D'Agostino's opinion that justice would be better served with the introduction of the NTSB report as evidence, but concluded that he could not overturn what was the obvious intent of Congress to protect NTSB investigators having to testify in a myriad of trials, whether civil or criminal, every time there was an aircraft crash.

Finally, Llorente was allowed to testify only to a few obvious facts about what he had observed, such as the size of the dent on the broken rotor blade.

As D'Agostino approached the end of her case, the district attorney's office made one final effort to snare a surprise witness, one who no doubt had the potential of being a devastating accusor of John Landis: his codefendant Dorcey Wingo.

(Budds had previously gone to Klein and suggested that if Paul Stewart would testify that Landis had ordered the bomb under hut four—which Budds believed to be the truth—the charges against the special-effects foreman could be dismissed. Stewart declined. "I'll take immunity, but I'm not gonna lie on the stand for her [D'Agostino]," Stewart told me one day at lunch during the trial.)

Of the five defendants, Wingo was the most easily separated from the others according to the prosecution's theory. He had had nothing to do with the hiring of the children, nor did he even know that My-Ca and Renee were working illegally. He also had had nothing to do with the placement of the mortars. He was a defendant because the grand jurors who indicted him accepted prosecutor Gary Kesselman's argument that the helicopter pilot should have taken more definitive action to ensure safety at 2:20 A.M. because of the 11:30 P.M. episode when the explosions rocked the helicopter.

Ideally, D'Agostino hoped, Wingo would testify that he had been deceived by Landis and the others.

Determining the cooperativeness of Wingo and his lawyer, Eugene Trope, was tricky. District Attorney investigator Jerry Loeb was chosen to make the contact. On the morning of February 4, Loeb told Trope that the district attorney was considering dropping the charges against Wingo in exchange for the pilot's testimony. Would he like to discuss it? Trope enthusiastically accepted and during the lunch hour he was brought to District Attorney Ira Reiner's office. Ground rules were set for an interview of Wingo to be conducted later in the day. If, after the interrogation, the officials decided Wingo would remain a defendant, nothing he said could be used against him in court by D'Agostino.

None of the other defendants, nor their attorneys, knew about the negotiations. Late in the afternoon a district attorney's office team composed of Garcetti, the chief deputy; Richard Hecht, the director of central operations; Harry Sondheim, chief of the appeals division; Tom Budds; and Loeb went to Trope's West Los Angeles office.

D'Agostino did not attend, Loeb told me later, primarily because the antagonism which existed between her and Trope and Wingo would have made her a disruptive influence on the delicate negotiations.

Wingo was interviewed for nearly three hours, primarily by Budds who was the most familiar with the details of the case of those present. The investigators had hoped that Wingo would accuse Landis and the others, more directly than he had in the past, of changing the plans at the last minute. For the most part, Wingo's testimony corresponded with what he had told authorities earlier.

Even though the pilot's answers were tempered, there was general agreement afterward that he could be an important prosecution witness. Importantly, the move would alter the balance of the defense team and give jurors a new perspective on the remaining four defendants. Reiner was called at home late that night and the next morning the interview team met with him. Still, D'Agostino was excluded from the discussions.

Loeb played for Reiner some excerpts from the interview that had been tape-recorded. Reiner was convinced and said he would hold a press conference the next day announcing that the charges against Wingo had been dropped and the pilot would testify for the prosecution.

Loeb walked down the corridor and told D'Agostino that "it's all set." Her plan to "flip" Wingo had succeeded. The prosecutor's reaction, however, astounded Loeb. "She exploded," he told me. "She was ranting and raving about Reiner: 'How dare he interfere in my case without consulting me! I'll quit!' It was a violent outburst."

Loeb went to Garcetti and said, "The reason she is killing the deal is because of ego."

In a meeting with Reiner, D'Agostino, who by now had listened to the entire tape of the Wingo interview, offered an extended and forceful argument why the pilot's answers conflicted with his past testimony and that of other witnesses and why he should remain a defendant. Loeb, who attended the meeting, recalled that Reiner yelled at D'Agostino to "Do your homework!" Loeb returned to D'Agostino's office with the prosecutor who began to cry.

D'Agostino remained adamant that she would not go along with the deal. Loeb informed Trope that there would be no immunity from prosecution offer. "That entire week was an absolute strain for me," Loeb told me. He, Budds, and others recognized that D'Agostino's presentation to the jury had been so wide-ranging and complex—and the defense attack so skilled—that guilty verdicts might now only be won through some dramatic change of direction. But D'Agostino was unwavering. Loeb had heard several times from her that she would not allow others to "dictate" how she ran her case—including Ira Reiner.

D'Agostino and Trope then secretly went to Boren to advise him of the now-abandoned negotiations. They asked him to rule that the evidence discovery code did affect this situation and therefore that the transcript of Wingo's interview did not have to be turned over to other members of the defense team. Boren agreed, a decision that other defense attorneys would criticize as mistaken when they learned of the negotiations after the trial.

D'Agostino believed that her last witness, actor and director Jackie Cooper, would be a powerful conclusion to her presentation. She anticipated that the defense would call famous directors and other Hollywood celebrities as defense witnesses to testify that what Landis and others had done on the set was common practice and acceptable professional behavior.

(D'Agostino later told me: "How do I dispute that? And I already had questions ready in advance to ask these big-shot directors." The defense had initially planned to call some directors to testify on behalf of John Landis. For example, John Huston had told Neal and Sanders, "My job as a director is to tell them to ride the horses harder. That's my job. Their job is to tell me when they can't ride them any harder." In 1984, a group of prominent Hollywood directors bought space in an issue of *Rolling Stone* magazine in a show of support for Landis to express the sentiment that blame was being misdirected in the case. Neal told me: "We had a number of directors prepared to testify that what John Landis did in the scene was really safe. But then we thought we'd direct the damn thing back to the children and they would have to say [if cross-examined by D'Agostino] that they wouldn't [have used] the children [illegally].")

One way for D'Agostino to counter the defense she expected was to offer to the jury a witness of stature who would say that what Landis and the others did was reprehensible. Cooper had been a member of the Directors' Guild Safety committee that had done a study of movie set safety following the deaths. And he was a vocal critic of the *Twilight Zone* production team.

Budds, during his investigation, and D'Agostino more recently, had had a difficult time finding movie industry people willing to publicly criticize Landis and the others. The prosecutor told me, "There aren't that many people in Hollywood who were willing to come forward. It took someone with an inordinate amount of courage and I think this man [Cooper] is a hero."

Cooper began his career in 1925 at the age of three as a featured player in two-reelers, four years later became a member of the *Our Gang* comedy series, and since then had appeared in hundreds of movies and television shows. He had run a production company and directed hundreds of television programs. He was a member of the Directors' Guild of America safety committee which, after the deaths in 1982, instituted a program of safety bulletins to codify acceptable practices for stunts, the use of special effects, and other on-set activities.

Cooper, who had been outraged by the film shot on the night of the crash, placed responsibility with Landis: "The director is, in the opinion of the directors that I respect, a great many of them to which I have spoken—the captain of the ship, responsible for just about everybody's deportment, conduct, performance, and has an obligation to discharge his duties in such a manner that it is within the amount of money that he's got to spend. In my opinion, he is responsible for the work being done on schedule and in the safest possible manner," Cooper said.

Cooper had been incensed at the idea that at the nine-thirty scene My-Ca and Renee had been left alone in the hut with a bomb in a mortar three feet away: "Had it gone off accidentally, those children had a very good chance, in my opinion, of being injured if not fatally."

He went on to explain why he believes children need special attention on a movie set: "If [the children] have never suffered the feelings of the buffeting from the helicopter's rotor and the noise it makes and the debris that is flying around, dust and water and so forth, who is to say which way the children are liable to run? They are liable to run right in the direction of the explosion, one. Two, yes, Morrow picked them up and took them supposedly some distance away from the explosion, not safely far enough away for me. But in the meantime, suppose he fell and dropped one of the children, who is to say that at six years old they would not run right back to where they would feel safer because the helicopter has now moved and is not over the hut? No, I don't feel the children or the actor were safe in that situation."

"What would you do after eleven-thirty?" D'Agostino asked hypothetically.

"I would have sent the company home. There is a lack of communication here. Somebody is going to get hurt. Somebody was already slightly injured. I had a warning and I would have shut down the company."

The cross-examination of Cooper was not extensive—defense attorneys believed Cooper's responses to D'Agostino's hypothetical questions would be contradicted by defense testimony. The effect of Cooper's testimony was weakened even further after he made some hallway comments to reporters questioning Paul Stewart's skills. Pressured by Stewart's lawyers, Cooper issued a public statement several days later saying he retracted any such comments he had made because he had no basis on which to judge Stewart's professionalism.

There was not a trace of the Vietnamese village to be found in the shadow of the cliff at Indian Dunes on February 10, 1987, the day the jury was brought there to view the site of the crash. This exhibit required that they use their imaginations.

D'Agostino had argued for and won approval to take the jurors to the *Twilight Zone* location so they could see for themselves the dimensions: how a helicopter must have filled the space in the air above the village, how powerful the explosions must have been to send fireballs well above the one-hundred-foot-high cliff, and the distances Morrow and the children, and the helicopter, had been from the mortars when they were detonated.

Boren had been understandably reluctant to grant D'Agostino's request to show the jurors a demonstration of gasoline and black powder special effects. In refusing, Boren explained his dilemma: "If the court orders something like that, what am I supposed to do? Decide what is a safe distance? And then is somebody going to interpret that what the court says is a safe distance as meaning that anything closer is not a safe distance?"

Boren had reserved his decision on whether to allow a Los Angeles County Fire Department helicopter to hover over the area where the village had been. The lawyers were still arguing the point until just before the jurors were brought to the site by bus.

D'Agostino said that even without special effects detonating nearby, seeing the size of the helicopter above and feeling the force of its rotor wash would demonstrate to the jurors that it had unquestionably been a wantonly reckless act to allow Morrow to carry the two children in his arms with the aircraft above.

Boren was persuaded to allow the demonstration but was careful to separate the legal argument from the emotional: "As callous as it sounds, what the victims actually felt is not relevant to the issue of law," he told the lawyers in their makeshift court on the riverbank.

Prior to the jury's arrival, Boren watched the helicopter fly through in the same pattern that D'Agostino proposed would be done for the jury.

I stood with other reporters and watched the aircraft move slowly past the cliff wall, flying at a height approximately that at which Wingo's aircraft had been at 2:20 A.M. on July 23, 1982. The rotor blades whipped through the air with a fierce power. The sight, evoking memories of the film of the crash, was undeniably compelling.

After the helicopter had traveled through twice, once at twenty-five feet and once at two hundred feet, the defense lawyers continued their arguments against allowing the jurors to view the aircraft in flight. Eugene Trope pointed out that a water tank on the sheriff's helicopter made it much heavier than the *Twilight Zone* aircraft and thus created a more turbulent rotor wash, which whipped dust and debris through the valley. Trope argued that that might create an unfairly negative impression on the jurors trying to protect their eyes.

D'Agostino herself provided the defense with an argument: They noted that she had made fearful grimaces and hid behind Budds during the fly-by demonstration, and they worried about her prejudicially reacting the same way in front of the jury. D'Agostino later told me that she had, indeed, been terrified. She had never been that close to a helicopter before.

The prosecutor lost the point by arguing the intrinsic safety of helicopters rather than emphasizing the movie set conditions. (She also is fearful of driving on the freeways—she cowered in the back seat of Budd's car on the drive back downtown.)

Braun took a different approach to the argument than his colleagues. He said he and George Folsey would be happy to stand under the helicopter while it hovered at twenty-four feet.

Without comment, Boren announced: "I am going to disallow the helicopter." (He later told me that he had almost decided to allow the demonstration but that the deciding factor had been the amount of dust and debris forcefully circulated by the prop wash during the demonstration. Had the prosecution dammed the river—as had been done by the moviemakers in 1982—thus covering a larger ground area with water, he probably would have allowed the flights in front of the jury.)

The jurors, viewing neither a low-flying helicopter nor explosions, spent about forty-five minutes wandering the area, using charts to visualize where people and things would have been on that July night in 1982. (A county fire department helicopter did pass at high altitude, generating interest among jurors who wondered whether that was the demonstration.)

D'Agostino caused a furor among defense attorneys when she remarked to reporters after the demonstration flight for the judge: "If I was a member of the jury I'd take the defendants out and hang them."

D'Agostino also told reporters that she was chagrined by the joviality of the defendants "in the sacred spot where they killed three people. To see them standing there smiling as though this is a trip to the fair is distasteful." The lawyers and the defendants, the judge and the court staff, reporters and investigators had spent about two hours at the location, and conversation had understandably varied from the solemn to time-passing chatter. In contrast to her rebuke, I watched the prosecutor accept the invitation of a female deputy sheriff—who had been patrolling on horseback to keep unauthorized spectators away—to ride the deputy's horse. Most of the other reporters and all of the television cameramen had gone ahead, as D'Agostino rode the horse the quarter mile to the parking lot—joking as she went.

Back in the downtown Los Angeles courtroom the next day, Boren asked the prosecutor: "Do the people now rest?"

"Yes, Your Honor," Lea D'Agostino said.

FIFTEEN

AFTER D'AGOSTINO had rested her
case, the defense lawyers spent a day
presenting motions that Boren dismiss
the charges. Neal upset the others when
he casually told the judge that he hadn't
had one of these motions granted in
twenty-five years and was ready to move
on with the defense side of the case. Neal was right that it was unlikely
that Boren would dismiss the charges against Landis based on the testimony thus far.

But what the lawyers didn't know is that Boren was almost swayed to
drop Dan Allingham and George Folsey from the case. (The two, of
course, had been dropped from the case once before, after the preliminary hearing, but had been reinstated on the district attorney's appeal to
a higher court.) The judge later told me that he had been dissuaded from
dismissal by D'Agostino's argument, which he considered one of her best
presentations during the trial.

Neal ended the day's debate with an announcement that sought to rest
speculation about how the moviemakers would defend themselves: "If it
please the court, the witness being put on tomorrow would be on behalf
of Mr. Landis."

Neal paused and then said: "It will be Mr. Landis."

In the hallway, Neal told reporters: "It's about time that the jury heard
the truth, and we decided to start with the truth."

At ten-thirty on a Wednesday morning in mid-February 1987, John and
Deborah Landis walked hand in hand through a jostling crowd of report-

ers, cameramen, and spectators. From the elevator to the courtroom door, the director's expression was studied by everyone. People searched for a hint of his mood, whether there was fright or defiance in him, whether his spirit was guilt-ridden or clear of conscience. There was, though, only a look of bemused self-control.

Cameras and tape recorders were thrust toward Landis, and an assortment of microphones on booms dangled overhead. Requests for comment were voiced as the couple squeezed through a narrow path where the assembly had parted. For someone as publicly reticent as Landis had been at the courthouse thus far, this was the unlikeliest of times for him to indulge the press with remarks.

Inside, John Landis stood in front of the witness chair and swore to tell the truth. Then he sat down facing the courtroom. Directly in front of him at the counsel table, fifteen feet away, was Lea D'Agostino.

His clothes were subdued in color and texture: a brown paisley tie, dull yellow button-down shirt, light brown shoes, and a tweedy coat. He wore his wire-rim glasses.

Jim Neal stood and asked his first question.

"You are John Landis and you were the director of the Landis segment of the *Twilight Zone?*"

"Yes," Landis responded crisply.

"How old are you, Mr. Landis?"

"I am thirty-six," Landis answered.

Neal and Landis were commanding the attention of everyone in the room, as well as a crowd gathered around the television monitors the media crews had set up in the hallway. Smoothly, gently, Neal led his client through a biography: born in Chicago, his parents moved to Los Angeles before he was a year old. He went to public schools through the ninth grade and attended a private school for the tenth. "That was the end of my formal education." He followed his ten-month job as a mail boy at Twentieth Century Fox by working as a "gofer" (a lackeying assistant who "goes for" things) on the 1969 production of the film *Kelly's Heroes,* being made in Yugoslavia.

After working on "many movies" in Spain with a friend, he returned to the United States at age twenty-one and made his low-budget gorilla feature, *Schlock.* Success was not immediate. He became a busboy at Hamburger Hamlet, a restaurant in the Los Angeles neighborhood of Westwood, near UCLA, and worked as a parking lot attendant, among other odd jobs. "I had a job engraving little signs that go in lobbies of buildings that say where the doctors are."

The jurors were not given a lengthy explanation of his years between films. Success began in 1977, six years after *Schlock,* when he directed *Kentucky Fried Movie* and his first big-budget studio film, *National Lampoon's Animal House.*

Neal, to establish his client's sense of responsibility, asked about family: wife Deborah (whom the jurors had long ago come to recognize as Landis's constant, and demonstratively affectionate, courthouse companion), four-and-a-half-year-old daughter Rachael, and eighteen-month-old son Max.

Neal had speedily brought Landis to the meat of his testimony: his creative thinking for *Twilight Zone.* He asked the director to explain the screenplay's story. Landis, though, first had an introduction of his own.

"If I can preface that a little bit," Landis replied. "The thing that attracted me most about the *Twilight Zone*—I'm a big fan of Rod Serling's, and he used the fantasy element of his [1960s television] program to deal with social issues. And I felt that especially with Steven Spielberg, we would be making an entertaining movie. And the story I made up, trying to use the magic, the idea of the *Twilight Zone,* was to deal with racism."

Moving on to describe the character of William Connor, and his travels through time and space, Neal and Landis began to offer their explanations of the allegations, questions, contradictions, and charges that D'Agostino had previously brought forth. For one, she had suggested that the only reason Landis had ordered secrecy for his script was to limit knowledge about the new and dangerous scenes that he had written in.

Landis told the jury that scripts are closely guarded because "in the last ten years movies for television are very prominent, and a movie for television takes from inception to airtime less than five months. A feature always takes about a year before it gets to the screen, and you're concerned about being ripped off. This has happened quite a bit." (In fact, Spielberg has a reputation for the secrecy with which he envelops his works in progress.)

It was important for Landis to show the jurors that the addition of the children in the rescue scene with special-effect explosives had artistic merit.

"Through dialogue with these children, [Connor] comes to not just an intellectual but an emotional realization that these children are in the same position he's in. That they are victims, too, and he understands that," the director explained. Furthermore, the helicopter attack offers the opportunity for moral salvation: "This is where Bill, instead of just running away and hiding, does something heroic. He redeems himself and rescues the children."

Yes, Landis said, he had told his casting agents the story of the new scene a few days after he had written it in June 1982. Then Neal asked if Marci Liroff had said that the proposed scene sounded dangerous.

"Absolutely not," Landis replied. He also denied asking the two casting agents to hire two Asian children for the new Vietnamese scenes.

The challenge to Liroff's credibility was the first of many times that Landis would firmly contradict the statements of prosecution witnesses.

The decision to hire the children illegally, he said, was not made until early July, after Spielberg associate Frank Marshall had confirmed that the producers could not get a waiver for children to work beyond 8:30 P.M.

Without explaining why he had insisted that the scenes be shot at night (he later said that explosions then are more effective on film), Landis explained that eight-thirty in the evening "to our state of mind, wouldn't accomplish what we needed, because it was still light at eight-thirty. We decided to break the law. We decided wrongly to violate the labor code. We thought that we would . . . honor, not the letter of the law, but the spirit of the law, and I thought, and we discussed, that we would find children to whose parents we would explain that we were doing a technical violation."

For the remainder of the trial, there would be no other admissions of wrongdoing of any sort by the director.

D'Agostino wasn't impressed with this confession. Undeniably the violation of state law had been committed, and she saw this minimal confession a classic defense ploy to add credibility to denials of the more serious and complicated charges.

Neal's consistent premise to the jury was that the moviemakers never thought the scenes were dangerous. In continuing questions and responses, Neal and Landis emphasized that the moviemakers worked in a blameless state of mind.

To find the defendants guilty of criminal negligence, however, the law did not require that it be proven that they specifically knew of and defied the risk—the jury could determine that any "reasonable person" would or should have recognized the danger. D'Agostino, though, had stressed that Landis and the others were well aware of the potential for death. Even if the logical sequence of events suggested that they had been aware, it was not easily proven beyond a reasonable doubt. Neal's legal theory here, as it had been in the Ford Motor Company criminal negligence trial, was that acts without evil intent should be subject only to civil liability.

To that point, Landis was asked about conversations concerning the use of dummies instead of children.

"I recall the conversation. I think it was with Dan. It was suggested, to get around the lateness of the hour, if we could use dummies or puppets to replace the children, because we had a scene in *American Werewolf* where a puppet replaced an actor. And I decided no, that even in the *Twilight Zone,* I didn't think that would work."

"Was there any suggestion of danger in this conversation?"

"No."

"Did anybody at any time suggest to you that those scenes as planned were dangerous?"

"Never."

To the same point, Landis told the jurors that his wife, Deborah; George Folsey's wife, Belinda; and the Folseys' two children were present on Wednesday night, July 21, when it had been planned the rescue scenes would be filmed. "It was [to be] the last night of shooting, and besides having a party when you finish, we were also doing big pyrotechnics. And everybody wanted to see it. There were lots of visitors, yes."

The rapport between lawyer and client was apparent throughout Neal's direct examination. Sometimes Neal referred to Landis as "Mr. Landis" and sometimes he called him "John," elongating the pronunciation in his southern drawl to "Jawn-n-n." Landis concentrated as he listened to each of his lawyer's questions.

Neal was not hesitant to elicit statements from his witness that contradicted other testimony, including that of the parents of the dead children.

"Did you tell [the parents] about the helicopter?" Neal asked.

"Yes."

"Did you tell them about the special-effect explosions?"

"Yes."

He did not, though, inform the parents that their children would be working illegally. He had asked Folsey to do that, Landis said, and he understood that his longtime associate had done so.

Landis indicated that the hiring of two important experts—the special-effects foreman and the pilot—had been made with care and deliberation.

"I met with Paul [Stewart] and I chose Paul. He had very impressive credits. I liked his manner. He was very professional and low-key, no-nonsense. Dan approached me and told me that he had located a Huey helicopter from a company called Western Helicopters, and the pilot was named Dorcey Wingo. He showed me Dorcey's credits. He gave me the paper from Western Helicopters that had Dorcey's background on it." (Landis was mistaken; there had been no printed résumé for Wingo.)

Landis was presenting himself well, at least partially the result of the trust and affection that had grown between him and Neal.

There had been a small, revealing moment between the two a few days earlier. As Neal was reading a document, Landis leaned closer and intently read along. Neal playfully reached up and tugged on Landis's earlobe. The serious look of concentration on Landis's face transformed into a broad smile as he pushed Neal's hand away and said "Stop it" in an amused tone of voice.

The friendship, Neal maintained, was genuine. He had grown fond of the man he had once viewed as dislikably arrogant. But the bond was also necessary. Neal recognized that if Landis was to avoid a prison sentence he would have to accept Neal's advice completely and unhesitatingly, not an easy task for someone as independent-minded as John Landis. Toward the end of the trial, Landis wrote a note while sitting at the counsel table and passed it to Neal. It read: "Dear Jim, I've done many things I regret in my lifetime. Getting you to represent me is one I will never regret. John Landis."

Sanders had also quickly grown fond of Landis. The previous August, during jury selection, Sanders's wife was visiting from Nashville and required some emergency surgery. At the hospital, Sanders waited through the night for word from doctors, accompanied by John and Deborah Landis who sat with him, having brought flowers and food.

Neal talked to me about the efforts he and Jim Sanders made to help Landis become a presentable witness: "We had him come over to the hotel suite and have breakfast. We calmed him down. We said, 'John, you're doing fine. Speak slower. Look at the jury more.' John was exhausted at the end of every day."

Facing the television cameras and reporters in the hallway during the lunch break on Landis's first day on the stand, D'Agostino coyly said, "I believe he is totally conforming to what I anticipated so far."

Neal was asked if any more admissions of guilt, besides that of the illegal hiring, would be forthcoming.

"No, that's the only thing that we did wrong, and we've admitted that from the very beginning."

"Are you worried about what's going to happen on cross-examination?" someone asked.

Slowly drawing out his words, Neal replied: "No. No. I think if you're telling the truth, you don't have to worry about anything."

He then went on to challenge some of D'Agostino's comments that had been repeated to him: "It's incredible to me, coming from Mrs. D'Agostino, that anything is too theatrical."

"Was he rehearsed?" a reporter asked.

"Absolutely not. What's a prosecutor going to do, say this man is telling the truth? She ought to keep her mouth shut. But she doesn't. She's going to call anybody who doesn't agree with her theory a liar."

The afternoon session began with an in-chambers conference with Roger Boren in which Harland Braun chastised the judge: "What we are here about is Your Honor's demeanor while Mr. Landis is testifying. I think the contrast of your countenance, the way you are handling yourself with respect to Mr. Landis, than with respect to Mr. Cooper and other witnesses when I felt you were gracious and concerned. I think your face is such that it indicates a certain skepticism."

"I frankly disagree entirely with you on that," Boren said.

Leonard Levine also contended that other witnesses had been treated more courteously.

"There is a difference," Boren responded. "Mr. Landis has been here for long periods of time and he knows the rules of the game, and I may not have been as solicitous as other people. I'm not going to orchestrate my behavior to what everybody else thinks is the proper mode."

Neal then interjected: "It's probably a tense time and we all might be overly sensitive."

"I think that is what it is," Boren said as the session ended amicably. "I am not tense about this and I am rather interested in what he has to say. And I was enjoying listening to the testimony this morning. I am not holding it against anybody that you brought it up."

Neal found it necessary not only to counter D'Agostino's argument that the helicopter scenes were dangerous, but also that Landis had pursued a risky course throughout the making of the movie. Landis said that the banana plant scene had been shot without incident or argument, in contrast to the confrontation that cameraman Steve Lydecker had related.

Neal asked Landis about the cameraman's allegation that Landis had joked at Indian Dunes about losing the helicopter.

"Did any such conversation take place?" Neal asked Landis.

"No."

"At any time?"

"No."

"With anybody?"

"No."

(In his cross-examination of Lydecker, even Neal had suggested that Landis had made the statement, although jokingly.)

D'Agostino had argued that the moviemakers did little serious planning and that communication on the set in preparation for the scenes was virtually nonexistent. Throughout his testimony, Landis made reference to continual meetings between himself and various crew members, including Paul Stewart and Dorcey Wingo. Some of the gatherings he referred to were corroborated by others, some were not. That the director had talked to the crew more than D'Agostino suggested he had seemed likely.

Referring to his planning for the eleven-thirty shot, Landis said:

"Actually you see it on film, we had many meetings. We were going to have water mortars in the water that were very close to where the actor was going to be. So that is why Vic and Paul [Stewart] and I walked all around this area."

"Did this discussion, and the placement of the mortars and the helicopter take place there with Wingo, Allingham, Stewart, Cohn, and you?"

"Yes. There was no dissent. There was no disagreement."

Landis confirmed that he hadn't been aware, initially, that the helicopter and its occupants had encountered problems during the eleven-thirty filming. Before Wingo complained to him, Landis said, he had planned to begin the 2:20 A.M. shot—in which Morrow carries the children across the river—with the helicopter in the same position over the village, and close to the cliff, as it had been at 11:30 P.M.

Basic to any analysis of the crash was a determination of whether the moviemakers had properly coordinated the placement of the airborne helicopter with the timing and location of the explosions on the ground. To this point, there had been no firm answer. No one had ever said before, with certainty, exactly where the helicopter was supposed to be during the two-twenty scene when the fireballs erupted from the shoreline mortars.

Landis's first explanation of his plan for the two-twenty shot differed from other testimony on a striking, crucial element: The director's testimony placed the proposed position of the helicopter during the shoreline explosions farther from the detonations than had anyone else. And that testimony raised some dispute among defense team lawyers.

Illustrating with a chart of the set, Landis traced what he said had been the proposed 2:20 A.M. flight plan of the helicopter across the river, away from the village. On the opposite shore, he said, the helicopter would then have hovered, serving as a camera platform to photograph the shoreline explosions more than one hundred feet away. Landis had not mentioned this plan to either the NTSB or the grand jury.

In his opening argument the previous September, and in his questioning of witnesses since, Neal had not suggested that the helicopter was to be as far away as over the north shore when the bombs detonated on the south shore.

Klein sat quietly dismayed as he listened to Landis's testimony on this point: He recognized that it was blatantly contradictory to a great deal of other testimony and evidence. He was silently furious at Landis and Neal, because he believed he had been given assurances that all defense testimony would confirm only that the shoreline explosions would not go off until the helicopter was an undefined "safe distance away."

Landis's testimony jeopardized Stewart, Klein believed. If it had been the case that the helicopter was supposed to be over the opposite shore during the explosions, then that would indicate that Stewart, and only Stewart of all the defendants, had been derelict by not specifically directing James Camomile to wait for the helicopter to be so positioned when he closed the electrical circuits on his firing board. Klein assumed that D'Agostino would now ferociously attack Landis on this point in her cross-examination.

If Neal recognized the dilemma his client's testimony was creating, he was not overt in his attempts to give Landis an opportunity to alter his response. Landis, however, did not waver from his statement.

"What would the camera in the helicopter film?" Neal asked.

"The village supposedly blowing up," Landis said.

"When it becomes a camera platform, do you mean the blowing up of the village?"

Landis explained that the fireballs would only create the illusion of destruction: "Explosions in the front of the village would give the appearance of the village blowing up which I could then [edit into the film with] specific shots [of huts exploding] we were going to do at the end of the night, after the actors and the helicopter left."

Neal continued: "So when the helicopter became a camera platform, it was to film these explosions in the front of the village that were going to go off, to make it appear the village was being blown up?"

"Yes."

Landis ended the day by testifying that he had quickly acceded to two safety suggestions by his colleagues in the hours before the crash. He said that he had readily accepted Stewart's advice not to blow up the sampan during the two-twenty shot. The director had also agreed with Elie Cohn that the special-effects crew be given extra time during the midnight meal hour to complete their preparations for the rescue scene.

As usual, Neal was unruffled and confident in his remarks to reporters afterward: "He's doing a first-rate job. We don't know what the jury senses."

(Klein told me that he informed Neal that evening, with angry profanities, that he had not viewed Landis's testimony as first-rate, and confronted Neal over the potential cross-examination problems posed by

Landis's camera platform statements. Neal also told me later that he did not recall a discussion with Klein about the matter, nor was Landis coached on the issue.)

When Lea D'Agostino approached the microphones for her afternoon press conference, a reporter sarcastically yelled, "Action!" With a smile, the prosecutor said, "That sounds like John Landis. It's a little premature."

D'Agostino was enthusiastic about Landis's first day on the stand: She believed that his testimony provided her with much opportunity to attack him in cross-examination. She said: "The testimony of [my witnesses] is so devastating that right now, just in his testimony today—I started counting—if he's telling the truth at least nineteen other people are lying. And for what reason? The whole world is lying according to John Landis, except John Landis. I find that somewhat incredible. I'm assuming that the jurors will too. I think he's operating within a very-well-rehearsed and -choreographed script."

Riding down in the elevator, Jim Neal turned to Leonard Levine and suggested that it would be beneficial to spend a couple of hours that night with Landis, to prepare him for D'Agostino's cross-examination. "Oh, great!" Landis said with a weary smile.

One person sympathetic to Landis's plight was his codefendant George Folsey, Jr. It was generally agreed among the trial participants that he displayed the deepest emotional pain of any of the defendants. His emotions were mirrored in his wife, Belinda's, endurance of the trial. Each afternoon they made the ten-minute uphill walk to the garage at the Los Angeles Music Center, where their car was parked. Following Landis's first day on the stand, George Folsey expressed anger his anger to me about what was happening to his friend John Landis: "He's been persecuted for four years for something he didn't do." It was typical of Folsey's loyalty that he referred only to Landis's plight and not his own, even though he, too, was a defendant in the same courtroom.

On Thursday morning, Landis answered the district attorney's allegation that he had not adequately reacted to the warning of danger that the eleven-thirty shot had presented.

"Dan came to me during lunch [the midnight meal] and told me that he had felt heat, that they had felt heat in the helicopter, from the explosion, and that the pilot, Dorcey, was upset. That was the first I learned that anything was wrong. So I said, 'Okay, we'll fix it. Let's have a meeting with Dorcey. Bring Dorcey to me and we'll talk.'"

Landis admitted that when confronted by Wingo he, at first, joked about the incident. "I said something like: 'The way I shot is nothing' or 'You ain't seen nothing yet.' " He said that Dorcey then complained that the fireball had been too close: "So I said, 'Okay, we'll fix it. I'll meet you in the village.' "

The director said that he then joined Allingham, Stewart, Wingo, and Cohn for a meeting: "Dorcey said, 'I want to be out over the river more.' And I said, 'How much more?' And he said, 'About fifteen feet.' I said, 'Okay, fine. We'll do that.' "

When Neal led Landis into another series of questions about plans to use the helicopter as a camera platform, the director's response was markedly different from what he had stated the previous day.

Landis now repeated several times that the shoreline explosions were to go off only when the helicopter was "a safe distance away."

"The explosions would go off one—two—three. Dorcey would turn, start to go this way. When he was a safe distance away—by that time, actually, Vic and the children would be well out—then these explosions in the front of the village would go off, and the children would have reached the other shore and Dorcey would become a camera platform to film the burning village."

In less than twenty-four hours the explanation of the plan had changed from a hovering helicopter filming the explosions across the river to merely filming an already burning village.

Refuting other aspects of D'Agostino's case, Landis said that he didn't know until after the crash that a mortar had been placed under the number four hut. He also said that his script supervisor, Katherine Wooten, had never suggested to him that the two-thirty scene was dangerous, nor had he told her to "shut up."

Neal's direct examination had elicited a chronological narrative, and as Landis neared his description of the accident, tension was palpable in the courtroom.

There was one statement Neal didn't want Landis to make, but he couldn't convince his client to do otherwise. Landis insisted on testifying that he and Morrow had discussed ahead of time that halfway across the river, Morrow would appear to stumble.

The stumble was a singularly frightening occurrence onscreen, and Neal recognized it appeared painfully real and unplanned on film—particularly when Morrow's grip on Renee loosens and the little girl is almost submerged. Landis was the only witness who testified that he had prior knowledge that Morrow would pretend to slip for dramatic effect.

Still, Neal asked the question of his client: "Did you suggest to Vic Morrow that he stumble during the shot?"

"Yes, during the rehearsal we talked about where he would fall," Landis said.

Neal, of course, was anticipating D'Agostino's cross-examination, and he tried to soften its impact by being the first to ask Landis potentially embarrassing questions about his trial testimony that was inconsistent with the statements of others, or even his own prior statements.

D'Agostino thought that one of Landis's most damaging previous statements had been made to the National Transportation Safety Board in August 1982 when he had said that he "didn't care" that the helicopter was hovering at 2:20 A.M. in a place different from where it had been at the rehearsal. The answer implied carelessness—since safety mandates precision in the use of volatile special effects.

"What did you mean when you told the National Transportation Safety Board that you didn't care?" Neal asked.

"I meant I didn't care in that it was not any closer to the shore, it was not in any place that impacted my shot, and it was where Dorcey wanted it to be, and I didn't care if Dorcey was hovering."

"Did you say, 'lower, lower'?"

"I don't recall saying that. I don't know if I said it or not, but I have no recollection of saying that."

Almost stoic throughout his testimony, Landis finally showed emotion as he talked about the crash itself.

"Did you see the helicopter start to turn?" Neal asked.

"I think so. I'm not certain. I was watching Vic and the children. I watched them struggling across the river, and I saw Vic fall where we discussed he would fall. And then the helicopter crashed in front of me. The helicopter really just startled me. I go, 'What?' And then, yes, I became aware. I said, 'Oh, my God! Where is Vic, and My-Ca, and Renee?' I ran to them, yes."

Landis's voice quavered. After Neal asked him to show on a chart exactly where the helicopter had crashed, there was a long, silent pause before another question was posed.

As he recalled the crash, Landis removed his glasses and rubbed his eyes with his fingers. He hung his head and shielded his eyes from the view of others for a few seconds. Then he put his glasses back on and looked up at Neal once again.

"Before the shot, did any fire safety officer or special-effects man say they thought the scene was unsafe?"

"No."

"Did anyone tell you that he or she thought the scene as planned was unsafe?"

"No."

"Did you think the scene was safe?"

"Yes."

With that, Neal ended his direct examination.

The other defense counsels' questioning of Landis was brief. When Leonard Levine stood, tears welled up in Landis's eyes and he looked away from the jury. He rubbed his temples with his index fingers. Responding to Levine's first question, Landis's voice was shaky. While answering, he cried more openly, finally regaining his composure and wiping the tears away.

The questions of the other defense attorneys were designed primarily to vindicate their own clients. Landis said that Allingham had had no responsibility in positioning the helicopter, actors, or explosions, that Folsey did not have a role in adding children to the script or running the set the night of the crash, and that Wingo was not informed the children were working illegally.

Harland Braun was stopped by Jim Sanders from asking a question whose answer Braun thought would be the most compelling vindication of Folsey. Braun wanted Landis to confirm that Folsey had recommended substituting his own two children instead of illegally hiring two Vietnamese children. If Folsey was willing to use his own children, he could not possibly have thought the scene was dangerous, Braun reasoned.

"Don't ask him that question right now," Jim Sanders asked of Braun, explaining that he knew Landis would smile at hearing it. Braun held off and at lunch asked Landis if he remembered that Folsey had made such an offer. Landis smiled at the question, just as Sanders had predicted, and Braun became enraged at the director.

"What do you think is so funny about that?" Braun asked Landis. "These two kids get killed and George Folsey was suggesting his own kids?"

"Oh no, it was so silly, the idea of using two larger Caucasians that I think is ridiculous," Landis replied.

Incredulous, Braun continued, "Don't you understand the moral distinction between you as a director thinking it was cinematically silly and George Folsey as a father instinctively using his own children?" When Braun finally asked Landis the question in front the jury, the director answered without a smile.

Klein asked no questions on behalf of Paul Stewart.

At about 11:00 A.M. the defense finished, and Landis was left to

D'Agostino's cross-examination. The test for both defendant and prose-cutor was to maintain emotional equilibrium, to block anger and resent-ment that might taint the jury's perception of either person. Both needed to keep negative personality attributes in check. Jim Neal, not necessarily prone to athletic metaphors, believed that the team that made the fewer mistakes would win.

D'Agostino reached for a box of tissues on the table in front of her.

"Mr. Landis, would you like some Kleenex, sir?" she asked, holding the box, yellow and decorated with birds and flowers, in her right hand. She pushed back in her chair, as if about to approach Landis, as she spoke. Only those who had not observed her for the past months could have interpreted her question as anything but cuttingly derisive.

"No, thank you, I have some," Landis replied sharply.

The prosecutor remained seated for her opening questions, the jacket of her purple suit draped over her shoulders.

Her opening gambit was not to attack Landis's testimony by question-ing its substance and candor, but to challenge the tone and emotion of his responses—which she believed to have been an actor's sham intended to create a false image of sincerity.

D'Agostino asked Landis about techniques a director might urge an actor to employ in order to engender sympathy from an audience.

"One of those techniques would possibly be to have the character cry. Correct?"

"Depends on the scene."

"Another might be to make the character sort of hesitate in his words?"

"Depends on the scene."

She referred to different directing methods and mentioned the "Elia Kazan method."

"I don't know what you mean by the Elia Kazan method."

"Well, there are various schools on how you direct. There is a modern school, that Marlon Brando and certain people espouse. Old-fashioned type of school of what directors did or actors did. Am I correct so far, or are you too young?"

"I can't speak for your knowledge. I really don't know what you are talking about. There are many different directors. Each directs differ-ently."

"Does it come easily to you, Mr. Landis?" D'Agostino asked unspecifi-cally.

"Crying?" he asked back.

"Yes," D'Agostino replied.

"No," Landis said, pausing first. His tone was incredulous and he shook his head slightly, as if to indicate no.

D'Agostino asked a series of questions about techniques used to make actors cry and whether he had employed any such methods in his movies.

"I can't recall a scene where an actor was crying, except for *Schlock,* at the end. The monster is shot and he cries. That was glycerin. That was me. Rick Baker put it in my face."

"You had to have glycerin?"

"I was in ape makeup."

There was a snippy petulance infusing D'Agostino's approach, which seemed ineffective to her purpose of exposing Landis's skill as a manipulator of emotions.

Talking to reporters during the lunch break, D'Agostino insisted that Landis had been acting when he had cried on the stand that morning. She based her judgment on his demeanor during other sensitive moments of the trial: "If you're not crying when the parents of the children are sobbing their heart out on the witness stand, then I don't know what other time you would cry. I doubted his sincerity because I was here the day Mrs. Chen, Renee's mother, testified. There was one particular recess in the afternoon, where this woman was literally giving anguished, heart-rending sobs. I had to leave because I started to cry. I walked out in the hallway and there's Mr. Landis shaking people's hands with a huge smile, thanking them for being here, as though this were some kind of premiere. You've got to keep in mind that he knew Mrs. Chen was going to be testifying. Why was he inviting people to come and watch this poor, bereaved mother cry her heart out? Do I doubt his sincerity? Yes, I do. I frankly wish I had an Oscar I could give him for his performance."

"If it was real emotion," a reporter asked, "is there any possibility you could alienate the jury by making fun of him?"

"I didn't think I was making fun of him. Well, he was dabbing his eyes, he had already used his one piece of Kleenex. I didn't know he had any in reserve."

"That was totally out of your goodwill?"

"No comment on that," she said with a big smile and laugh.

Asked whether she might have overplayed her attack on Landis's courtroom emotions, she said with a loud snap of her fingers, "Did I? It seemed like it just whizzed by, because I was definitely having fun."

Harland Braun stood nearby, smiling as he listened. "I love her," he bellowed. "She's a character right out of the *Twilight Zone.*"

As the afternoon session began, D'Agostino dealt with matters more objectively factual than she had done in the morning.

"If you didn't know you were going to do the scene because you hadn't gotten the okay from Warner Brothers, then why did you even ask [the casting agents] about hiring the two children for you?"

"I did not ask them about hiring two children."

"Is it your testimony, Mr. Landis, you never discussed with either Marci Liroff or Mike Fenton hiring children?"

"Yes, that's my testimony."

D'Agostino then showed him Liroff's original schedule sheet from the July 16, 1982, casting session, on which she had written the note about two Asian children being needed for two nights of work.

"Can you explain why this is written?"

"I don't know. I assume that is Marci Liroff's and I have no explanation for her writing. No."

"You never said, 'We'll get them off the streets ourselves'?"

"Absolutely never said."

Landis also denied making other incriminating statements attributed to him, including the joke about going to jail. He also said that he never heard George Folsey, Jr., make such a statement.

"Did you believe that having immigrant parents totally untrained in filmmaking was an adequate substitute for trained, teacher-welfare workers?" the prosecutor asked.

"If you are referring to my state of mind, yes," the director answered.

Landis conceded that he wanted the explosions in the final scene to be big.

"You wanted to wipe this village off the face of the earth?"

"No."

"You never made that comment in the office?"

"I don't recall that."

Landis, of course, was contradicting many previous witnesses. To emphasize that, D'Agostino periodically asked whether he thought another witness was lying or not. Boren consistently sustained defense objections to these opinion questions and finally ordered D'Agostino to stop asking them.

D'Agostino did not expect Landis to admit that he had been aware the scene was dangerous, but by her questions, she tried to imply to the jury that the risk involved should have been quite evident beforehand.

"Did you, Mr. Landis, need anyone to tell you that this was a dangerous scene?"

"Yes. If my own common sense was allowing something to take place that I have no expertise in, I would expect someone to tell me, 'No, that's dangerous, John, don't do that.'"

D'Agostino was thorough in pointing out to the jury contradictions between Landis's trial testimony and his statements four years before at the grand jury. For example, Landis had just testified about several conversations among himself, Wingo, and Stewart in preparation for the eleven-thirty shot.

D'Agostino read the following grand jury excerpt:

> Q: Before the 11:30 shot, did you get together with Paul Stewart and the pilot to go over in detail precisely what was going to take place?
>
> A: The pilot in his helicopter in the air—in fact I stood exactly where I wanted Vic to be positioned, and positioned the helicopter. Paul Stewart was standing next to me. I don't know if Paul and Dorcey actually spoke. On the ground I'm unaware that Paul and Dorcey actually [had] a specific conversation about that specific shot.

"Was that true at the time you testified?" the prosecutor asked.

Landis answered, "Yes," but was interrupted by D'Agostino when he tried to explain. Boren told Neal, who objected to the prosecutor's interruption of the witness, that he could ask Landis to explain during the defense's redirect examination. In her copy of the trial transcript, D'Agostino later wrote a note to herself: "They never did, did they?"

Landis returned to the witness stand the following Monday, when the trial resumed after its usual three-day weekend. The volatility about which Neal worried had not surfaced in front of the jury. For much of his cross-examination, Landis sat cross-legged in the witness chair, his hands clasped in his lap, his answers usually delivered in a calm and deliberate fashion.

The only maneuver Landis conceded had had an element of risk was firing the machine guns in the helicopter. The director explained that he had asked stuntmen Gary McLarty and Kenneth Endoso to perform that task. "I thought there was an element of danger, because they were hanging outside a helicopter firing a fifty-caliber machine gun, and I wanted someone with experience doing that."

D'Agostino contended that as stunt coordinator, McLarty would have been of far greater service on the ground supervising the safety aspects of the scenes.

"He's being very cool and slippery. He's certainly being caught in quite a few inconsistencies," D'Agostino told reporters during the lunch break, claiming the most important was the contradiction between his grand jury testimony that there had been no meeting after the eleven-thirty shot and his statements here that all of the principals had discussed the matter.

It was true, curiously, that Landis denied a number of statements attributed to him, comments that had been heard by several witnesses. For example, he was asked about his conversation with Wingo after the eleven-thirty shot.

"Did Dorcey Wingo ever tell you at any point, 'How would you like a fireball under you?'?" D'Agostino asked.

"No," Landis replied.

"And did you say to him at that time, 'Well, don't be so squeamish'?"

"I don't think so, no. I . . . no. I made a joke with Dorcey because he was upset. It's a method I've used to calm people down."

D'Agostino did not question Landis with specificity about his differing statements concerning the use of the helicopter as a camera platform, nor did she probe extensively the matter of just how the moviemakers had determined a "safe distance" for the helicopter to be from the fireballs. The longest exchange on the subject ended without resolution of the issue.

"So, in other words, the front explosions were set to go off before the helicopter reached the other shore. Is that accurate?"

"Not exactly. I can't tell you precisely where the helicopter was supposed to be. It was supposed to be a safe distance away."

"Now, did Paul Stewart tell you, or did you discuss with Paul Stewart, what would be the safe distance for the helicopter to be in when the rest of the explosions went off?"

"Yes, it was somewhere in the middle of the river. I don't . . . I couldn't tell you exactly where now."

"Well, when did you have that discussion?"

"Prior to filming."

"And how was that particular distance determined?"

"Paul told us."

"Paul told who?"

"Myself and Dorcey and Dan Allingham and Elie Cohn."

"Did he tell you the helicopter is going to be at a certain spot before the other explosions will go off? Is that correct?"

"He told us the helicopter . . . well, I told him, and he agreed, that the helicopter had to be a safe distance away."

"I understand that. But who determined what the safe distance away was?"

"Paul."

One of D'Agostino's more effective lines of questioning concerned Vic Morrow's stumble in the river during the final scene.

"It was planned that Vic should stumble," Landis said. "I think you are having a problem with the fact that what makes this so especially terrible, which is that they are acting, that Vic is acting, and it looks horrendous. Because it's supposed to look horrendous. And the tragedy makes it that much harder to watch."

The prosecutor asked Landis if it was also planned that Morrow would almost drop Renee in the water.

"We did not discuss dropping Renee, and I don't believe he did."

He said it was first decided during the 2:00 A.M. rehearsal that Morrow would stumble, but also conceded that Morrow did not practice carrying either the children or other weights through the water first.

"How did you rehearse it then if they [Morrow or his stand-in, Robert Liddle] weren't carrying the children?"

"I don't know how . . . That is such an odd question. What do you mean? Could you explain?"

"Mr. Landis, isn't it true, sir, that you have seen the film and you saw how horrendous, in fact, it did look to have Vic Morrow struggling in the water? And that he did almost, in fact, drop Renee? And that you manufactured this story about how it was all planned for Vic to stumble, because of how terrible it did look on the film? Isn't that true, sir?"

"No, it is not true."

Landis said that he had seen the film only twice before seeing it again when it was shown to the jury.

"You only watched it twice?"

"It's very hard for me to watch," he said with a quick snap to his voice, sweeping his right hand through the air in front of him, as if to brush away the question. His tone quickly changed, though, and with tears in his eyes, he apologized for his burst of temper: "I'm sorry."

"Would you like some Kleenex, sir?" D'Agostino said in a stale gesture.

"No, thank you," he said with disdain.

D'Agostino was not always precise in her technical terminology, as was the case when she questioned Landis about the danger of placing the children in the hut at the nine-thirty shot with armed mortars very close by. Landis corrected her when she interchanged terms and alleged that the children had been two or three feet from an "explosion" when she should have said "mortar." D'Agostino may have been well aware that the word "explosion" would have a stronger effect on the jurors than "mortar."

Some defense attorneys believed that the moviemakers were vulnerable on that point because the scene had posed a risk to the children who had been left alone in the hut with armed, black powder bombs nearby.

"Did you have any way of knowing when they were in that hut by themselves, unattended, whether they would listen to instruction and stay there rather than running out?" D'Agostino asked.

"Yes. They were very bright children. We had rehearsed it and they understood what to do. They did it."

The courtroom was filled to capacity for each day of Landis's testimony. On Tuesday, the director's fourth day on the witness stand, D'Agostino continued with the same approach with which she had begun the previous Thursday, suggesting that the director's testimony was largely fabricated.

"Did you decide what type of image you wanted to project in this courtroom to the jury?"

"I hope they understand I'm telling the truth."

Coming close to the end of her cross-examination, the prosecutor asked questions touching on her thesis that Landis had always followed a pattern, as a moviemaker, of taking unnecessary risks.

"Have you ever compromised safety for the sake of realism?"

"No," he answered with unusual firmness.

"Do you want to be known for big stunts?"

"No."

"You were not in competition with Steven Spielberg?"

"We were coproducers of the film. We were not in competition."

Sometimes during her questioning, D'Agostino rested her glasses low on her nose and peered at Landis over the tops of the rims, her hands folded in front of her.

"Why did you feel you had to use real children?"

"It was not a question . . . you're making it seem like it was a choice."

When D'Agostino asked that his answer be stricken because it was not responsive to her question, Landis turned to Boren, explaining that the prosecutor's question implied there was a choice between something dangerous and not dangerous, which he did not feel was the case.

"Isn't that what Hollywood is built on? Illusions to create the illusion of danger?" the prosecutor asked.

"Sometimes. You would never do a scene where you think you are putting people in danger."

"Did you, or did you not, know it was dangerous and quite risky to film those children at two-twenty in the morning without a permit?"

"To their safety, absolutely not. If you're talking about did I feel it worth the risk to have the children there, the risk that someone could shut us down, I would have to say yes. That must have been my state of mind, because that's what we did. If you're asking me did I take any sort of risk endangering their lives, absolutely not, not to my knowledge then."

"If you believe that was a perfectly safe scene to film, you would have no hesitation in filming it again?"

"I would . . . I would not film it again. I'm sorry. Three people died closer to me than you are. And absolutely not. I am not emotionally prepared. Regardless of who told me it was safe. No, I haven't shot with a helicopter since then."

Landis, upset by the question, waved his hands in front of him in a negative gesture. His voice cracked, on the edge of emotion, the next time he spoke.

Before asking her last question on cross-examination, D'Agostino read aloud his previous answers, when he said he had never discussed hiring the children with Liroff and Fenton.

"And my question to you today, sir, is, are the answers to those two questions as truthful as the rest of the answers you've given during your testimony here?"

"Absolutely."

"Thank you, sir. Nothing further."

Jim Neal saw no need to allow D'Agostino to emphasize again the contradictory or hazy parts of Landis's testimony—which she could have done had Neal chosen to conduct a lengthy redirect examination of his client. He believed that Landis was in a better position with the jury now than he had been before he took the stand. He chose not to ask any more questions. The other defense lawyers asked only a few more questions of their own, and D'Agostino was quickly allowed to begin her recross-examination, necessarily short by court rules because of the limited defense redirect examination.

"Does it sound like with you it's got to be the real thing or nothing?" she asked.

"No. I've had people turn into werewolves in movies," Landis replied.

SIXTEEN

THE UNRESOLVED dispute between Lea D'Agostino's first witness, Donna Schuman, and former prosecutor Gary Kesselman was the cancer of D'Agostino's case.

Six months had passed since the days of Schuman's September cross-examination and her testimony that Kesselman had told her in 1983 that he would willfully commit a felony by hiding from the defense his knowledge of her incriminating recitation of jail statements made by Landis and Folsey— so that he could surprise the opposition at trial.

The jurors in September had been secluded in their waiting room when both D'Agostino and Kesselman had taken the stand, when Kesselman vigorously denied that he would ever have been so unprofessional and D'Agostino supported Schuman. That testimony had been for Boren's benefit, so that he could rule on legal motions of both sides. Both deputy district attorneys were intent on protecting their integrity and wanted the jury to hear their testimony. The defense lawyers had wanted the panel to hear Kesselman while Schuman's testimony was fresh in their minds.

But Boren would not allow jury testimony then by either government lawyer. The defense would have to wait until it was their turn to put on their case, when the prosecution's presentation was over. Finally, in March, the jurors heard some more on the matter.

What the jurors had been told by Schuman in September had been enough to raise doubt in their minds about who was telling the truth.

Kesselman was subpoenaed by the defense, and on March 10 he arrived in court, bitter about the controversy but eager to assert his prosecutorial honesty and ethics. Kesselman later told me that he felt his district attorney supervisors had abandoned him in favor of D'Agostino, relegating him to unimportant office work and ordering him not to talk to the press. D'Agostino was not happy with her supervisors either. Although they publicly supported her, she felt there should have been a formal, internal investigation and more forceful action taken against Kesselman.

Chief Deputy District Attorney Gilbert Garcetti later told me that the supervisors felt the office had a conflict of interest in the matter and would wait until any investigation by the California attorney general's office was complete before acting.

Harland Braun thought it unusual that Kesselman's supervisory nemesis, Richard Hecht, was making his first courtroom appearance of the trial, sitting quite noticeably in a chair against the back wall, notebook in hand, just as Kesselman was about to testify. Braun asked the judge to instruct Hecht to leave the room: "I am concerned that this will resemble the scene out of *The Godfather* where they bring in the brother from Sicily to be present in the courtroom."

"I will be greatly surprised if Mr. Kesselman is intimidated by that and I will deny that," Boren said, aware of Kesselman's tenacity and resolve.

For the jury, Braun drew Kesselman through the history of his dealings with Donna Schuman and later D'Agostino.

Of critical importance were Kesselman's original notes of his May 11, 1983, interview with Schuman, which D'Agostino said she had located in her files in a more thorough search after first insisting she had never seen the papers in the boxes of documents Kesselman had turned over to her in the fall of 1986.

(When asked later why she had not produced Kesselman's notes sooner, she told me and others, "I wasn't even aware that they existed until after this Donna Schuman thing arose, and I started looking high and low through every drawer in my office until I finally found the folder into which I had thrown all these things that I thought were outlines and unimportant things. That's why I do have to take the witness stand. Because, at this point, it becomes Mr. Kesselman's word versus mine. Not only mine, but versus Donna Schuman, versus Dr. Harold Schuman, versus Kendis Rochlen, versus Gail Wellens, versus Tom Budds.")

One reporter asked her if her boss Garcetti had said it was okay for her to testify.

"I don't know that I have to ask anyone to testify," she replied.

Kesselman maintained that had Donna Schuman told him about jail statements in his interviews of her prior to the grand jury, he would "absolutely" have put them in his notes. He questioned the wisdom and logic of not using such testimony then, as Schuman alleged was his strategy.

The prosecutor said that he, of course, couldn't have known then that the issue would even come to trial, and would not have jeopardized obtaining grand jury indictments first. In fact, that is what Tom Budds had told Leonard Levine was the truth when the detective had made his hallway plea to the defense attorney the previous September to be put on as a witness before the jury. Budds had then maintained that, undoubtedly, Kesselman would have used all significant incriminating evidence at the grand jury.

The defense pursued the point vigorously exploiting its implication that Schuman and D'Agostino had manufactured some of Schuman's testimony the previous September in an attempt to bolster the case against Landis and Folsey.

Although Kesselman made convincing points, he also sometimes displayed a questionable agressiveness in defending his honor. For example, he insisted that his departure from the case had not been a unilaterally decided removal by Ira Reiner, but acquiesence by supervisors to his long-standing request that he be taken off the demanding case. Still, on key points, available documentation seemed to confirm Kesselman's version of past events and were consistent with the lawyer's previous testimony.

Kesselman's September testimony, offered before the notes he had not reviewed in several years had been located by D'Agostino, was quite consistent with what the notes said.

There was, however, one curious sentence, in quotes but not attributed to a speaker, in the several pages of material that had been written in outline form: "get a little fine working past 6 P.M. having them on the set with explosives."

D'Agostino had argued that that sentence was a shorthand version of Schuman's "butt in jail" quote that the witness had attributed to George Folsey, Jr.

Asked by Braun about that sentence, Kesselman said, "That was Donna Schuman answering my question as to what she thought would happen, and generally what they thought would happen in the office if the production people got caught using children on the set after six P.M. with explosives."

"Had Donna Schuman attributed the remark to either Landis or Folsey, would you have put that in your notes?" Braun asked.

"I would have," Kesselman said.

The most sensational part of Kesselman's testimony came when he told the jury his interpretation of D'Agostino's remarks to him the previous September, when he had assumed she was asking him to lie on the witness stand in order to protect her case against the moviemakers: "And I am not going to use histrionics, but she was very agitated. She said to me, 'You are not important, I'm not important, the only thing that's important is this case.' I said, 'Lea, if you are even implying that I would commit perjury for this case, you've got the wrong guy.' "

Later, Braun asked Kesselman the question central to the dispute: "Is there any truth to the statement that you told Schuman you would withhold evidence from defense?"

"Absolutely not."

Because it would have created an obvious conflict of interest, D'Agostino was not allowed to cross-examine Kesselman. Instead, office supervisors had assigned Deputy District Attorney Peter Bozanich. (His brother had been the lead prosecutor in the "Alphabet Bomber" case, in which D'Agostino had assisted and been labeled "The Dragon Lady" by the defendant. During the *Twilight Zone* trial, defense attorneys, outside the courtroom, had used the nickname disparagingly.)

Defense attorneys argued against Bozanich's role. His presence, Klein said to Boren, "would then lend esteem and credibility to Mrs. D'Agostino that the record shows she does not deserve."

Braun said: "I think it is unethical for the district attorney's office to come in here and question the veracity of one of their own attorneys. They are in a pickle of their own making."

Boren allowed Bozanich to cross-examine Kesselman. Bozanich, who had a quiet, gracious manner, seemed the opposite in style of D'Agostino.

Kesselman said that he had met almost daily with D'Agostino for about four months after she became the *Twilight Zone* prosecutor to help her prepare. "I wouldn't categorize the relationship as cordial. I had a business relationship with her."

Bozanich was obviously at a loss for the lack of time he had had to study the voluminous record of the case. His search for flaws in Kesselman's story was attempted methodically, but the former *Twilight Zone* prosecutor was unwavering in his statements.

Kesselman related how he had learned that statements that they would go to jail had been made by Folsey and Landis during the production of the movie: "I had sent out Tom Budds to interview Cynthia Nigh [in 1983, prior to the grand jury]. I believe it was in a telephone conversation and I believe it was at my home. I remembered because it was one of the highlights at that point. Sergeant Budds was extremely excited. He said to me, 'I got something. Finally we have something.' Within a day or two of that, I went back with Budds to interview Cynthia Nigh because she had told him about that going-to-jail statement. And that's the first time I had ever heard anything like that."

D'Agostino was obviously upset by Kesselman's presentation, and her display of displeasure almost led to her ejection from the courtroom. At a sidebar conference, Klein complained about D'Agostino's facial gestures, made as she sat at her place near the jury while Kesselman testified.

Because Bozanich was, for the moment, representing the prosecution, D'Agostino was not at the sidebar when Boren said: "I did see her arch her eyebrows and lower her head in such a way where she looked over the top of her glasses. And I would say that to a certain degree, Mr. Klein would be right in saying that was a look of incredulity. Mr. Bozanich, I'm going to ask you at this time to inform her that it's the court order that she remain expressionless to the absolute best of her ability, and if she is unable to do that I may have to exclude her during the remainder of the testimony of Mr. Kesselman."

D'Agostino had previously asserted that during the transition of prosecutors, Kesselman had labeled Schuman the best witness he had. Asked about that by Bozanich, Kesselman replied, "That would not be the case. She was extremely emotional, especially at the preliminary hearing."

One of the continuing features of the case was the inability of the lawyers and others to sense the leaning of the jury. That, of course, was partially attributable to the complexity of the matter, but, also, members of this group were particularly unrevealing of clues to their thoughts from the expressions on their faces.

Many who watched Kesselman testify agreed that he appeared to have defended himself well. In his report that night, KABC newsman Paul Dandridge referred to Kesselman's "apparently credible testimony."

Whether he or others would have found D'Agostino's testimony on the issue equally credible was not put to the test. Boren told her in an off-the-record session that because of ethical conflicts if she chose to testify in front of the jury as a witness he would be forced either to call a mistrial or to order that a new prosecutor be named. D'Agostino did not testify.

D'Agostino told reporters, though, what she thought of Kesselman's testimony: "I think you're dealing with a situation where you have a disgruntled employee basically. I did not threaten him when he came up to my office. I indicated to him, 'Gary, forget your pride, forget that. What's important right now is [Donna Schuman] is telling the truth and that's it.' I looked at him straight in the eye. I did not yell. I did not scream. If [Kesselman] construes that as being a threat, that's all in his paranoid mind, not in mine."

When Kesselman's testimony had ended, the defense asked for a mistrial based on what they alleged was misconduct by D'Agostino. Boren denied the motion. The issue would be revived later.

By this time in the trial, defense attorneys Klein, Braun, and Levine were distracted by an ongoing pay dispute with Warner Brothers executives. Each had been given about $100,000 the previous summer as an advance payment for legal fees. But by now, their unpaid invoices had risen to well over $200,000 each, and Warner Brothers was refusing to pay any more money. (Neal and Trope, whose clients were paying by other means, were not involved.)

Warner Brothers vice-president and general counsel John Schulman made no public comment and was abstract in his letters to the defense lawyers about the refusal to pay. Certainly, Warner Brothers executives wanted to distance themselves from the *Twilight Zone* controversy. A few months earlier, D'Agostino had received a copy of what appeared to be a confidential Warner Brothers memorandum supposedly discovered by a man who had purchased surplus studio furniture. The unsigned document, which D'Agostino did not use at the trial, discussed Landis's potential legal liabilities and concluded that there had been "a complete break of any normal procedures" for supervision of the project by Warner Brothers executives.

Braun wrote to Schulman: "What kind of cooperation do you expect from us when the civil cases go to trial? What duty to cooperate do we have with respect to a company that has done everything it can to send defendants to jail? Is Warner Bros. attempting to strangle the defense so that we do not point our finger at executives in high positions who are trying to cover their asses?" (The lawyers were paid some months after the trial after bitter discussions.)

With the Schuman controversy aiding their cause, the defense also pursued the delamination issue.

The technical cause of the crash—whether the rotor blade had malfunctioned because it had been dented by debris, or heat had delaminated its thin outer skin of metal—was always a confounding, unresolved aspect of the *Twilight Zone* case. D'Agostino's job, however, was made easier when Boren ruled that in order to prove the defendants guilty of criminal negligence, she need not prove the precise technical chain of events:

"If there is recklessness in this case, the consequences need not be foreseen, other than that explosions took place and brought down the helicopter. It is enough that the defendant should have foreseen the possibility of some harm of the kind which might result from his act."

Still, the defense attorneys argued consistently that the helicopter had been damaged by delamination, which had been, in 1982 and in relation to helicopter tail rotors, an unknown and unforeseeable phenomenon, and therefore their clients bore no liability for its occurrence.

However, rather than ignore the issue, D'Agostino attacked that position, but without sufficient technical data from government witnesses to balance the defense's scientific analysis.

Gary Fowler, an expert in metallurgy and also familiar with aerodynamics, was an articulate and convincing defense witness—particularly in light of the fact that he was not seriously challenged. After recounting his study, apparently carried out with great methodology, he said: "My conclusion was that heat from the special effect caused a delamination of the skin on one of the tail rotors. And that delamination set up aerodynamic forces that led to the fracture and failure of the adjacent blade and the eventual loss of the tail rotor system."

His conclusion contradicted, in part, the National Transportation Safety Board, which had concluded that debris had also been a factor. Fowler told the jurors that scientists define risk by estimating the probability that an event will happen, based on past occurrences. "There is not a historical basis for associating risk with this event," he said.

The defense argument was essentially a statement that the production team had not planned to expose the tail of the aircraft to high heat, but even if they had, there was no way to have known that something would go wrong.

D'Agostino queried Fowler on only a few issues in her cross-examination.

"Your theory of delamination, does that, in fact, mean that the helicopter crashed or that the crash occurred as a result of that helicopter being too close to the fireball?"

"Yes."

Later she explained to reporters: "The defense is entitled to put on a defense no matter how ludicrous. My cross-examination was zilch because it's irrelevant. Delamination is a red herring."

Despite the fact that the law did not require the prosecutor to prove the exact cause of the crash, D'Agostino always appeared at a decided disadvantage in this issue because of the specificity of the defense arguments and the weak, almost nonexistent technical evidence the prosecutor offered. For example, she couldn't, because of Congressional prohibitions affecting NTSB investigators, point out to the jury the differences between Fowler's study and that of the federal agency, even though Fowler had specifically told the jury that, "I found no evidence that debris caused this accident."

However strong the prosecutor's logic—that it should have been painfully obvious that the proximity of a helicopter to special-effects explosions posed a number of dangers, including high heat, this position was not being backed up by technical experts testifying for her.

Dorcey Wingo and his lawyers were subjected to weeks of intense lobbying by others on the defense side who were desperately trying to keep him off the witness stand.

Wingo and his lawyer, Eugene Trope, were viewed by some of their defense colleagues as loose cannons in the courtroom: men who could easily wander into contradictions and unwittingly damage trial strategy.

They didn't know about the secret meeting Wingo and Trope had had with Richard Hecht and others to discuss the possibility that he become a prosecution witness in exchange for being dismissed from the case as a defendant.

D'Agostino had attempted to use Wingo's past statements to her advantage, because they were so obviously at variance with current defense testimony. But the judge had previously prohibited her from telling the jury about Wingo's pretrial comments. He based his action on the Aranda rule, which stems from a California Supreme Court decision regarding trials with multiple defendants. The rule prohibits the use of statements by one defendant that implicate another defendant—unless the person who had made the statement takes the witness stand in his own defense, thus allowing examination of him by other defense attorneys.

(Earlier in the trial, defense attorneys had ridiculed D'Agostino's legal competence when she told reporters she had forgotten about Aranda. Garcetti, who kept his embarrassment over D'Agostino's gaffes private, told me that the legal issue is "as basic as basic can be.")

But now that Wingo was taking the stand, everything he had said in the past could be admitted as evidence, and used to impeach his truthfulness if it was contradicted by his trial testimony.

Jim Neal had fought the hardest to convince Trope and Wingo to remain silent: Neal's client presumably had the most to lose. There had been gentle cajoling and angry argument. Trope was enraged when he learned that Neal had been having private conversations with Wingo, and he confronted the Tennessee lawyer about it. "Up yours, Neal," the usually gentlemanly Trope once said to Neal.

(Neal didn't know the story behind the antique gold ring Trope wore on the pinkie finger of his left hand. The design was of an Egyptian scarab, with a top that flipped open to reveal a message in hieroglyphics that translated means: "Beware those who challenge the bearer." Neal also didn't know that in the February meeting, Wingo had been asked on the record if any attorney had tried to persuade him to change his testimony. He answered "yes," but without identifying who the lawyer was. Hecht chose not to pursue the matter with more questions, suggesting it was an inappropriate issue under those circumstances. Several people later confirmed for me that Wingo had meant Neal. He had attempted no such thing, though, Neal later said to me.)

Other defendants tried to convince Wingo not to testify. Just a few weeks before, John and Deborah Landis invited their codefendants and wives to a Sunday morning brunch at their Brentwood home. The lawyers were not included and, Leonard Levine says, the men were told not to discuss the case. Wingo later told me that the brunch was "just a friendly gesture" and "the subject did not come up at all."

However, Paul Stewart, who turned down the invitation, told me: "They had that party to try and get Wingo to stay off the stand." Stewart thought that Wingo was "crazy" to testify, but he also thought it pointless to intercede in the man's decision. Beforehand, he encouraged Wingo to do what he felt was right. "You're gonna do what you're gonna do. Go do it," he said to the pilot.

If any lobbying of Wingo did take place it was ineffective, and on Thursday, March 19, Wingo, accompanied by his wife, arrived at the courthouse to tell his story to the jury.

Trope prefaced his client's appearance with brief testimony from Wingo's boss, Western Helicopters president Clair Merryweather, who told the jurors that he and Wingo had been firm in their warnings to Dan Allingham that they wanted great care taken to prevent debris from special-effects explosions from damaging their aircraft.

"I wanted to be assured that we had care taken that those kinds of things wouldn't happen," Merryweather said. "The most important thing that I remember, the most vividly, is when [Allingham] commented that the man in charge of special effects was the best in the industry."

Wingo walked to the witness stand shortly after 11:00 A.M., dressed in a dark blue, three-piece suit, white shirt, and striped tie. On his lapel he wore a small gold pin commemorating Americans missing in action or prisoners of war in Vietnam.

He conceded that *Twilight Zone: The Movie* had been the first time he had ever flown in a major Hollywood film with pyrotechnics. Trope went on to show, however, and D'Agostino agreed, that Wingo was a combat-experienced, highly qualified pilot.

After the Army, Wingo logged close to thirty-five hundred hours flying in all sorts of conditions: fighting forest fires, aiding crop control, moving heavy equipment, and ferrying television camera crews. He had transported oil workers and their equipment over South American jungle when barges couldn't travel any farther up the Amazon, and he had flown over vast stretches of rural Mexico on a government contract to eradicate opium poppy fields. He had also aided mountaintop rescues of injured hikers, one such rescue taking place after a Navy helicopter crew had failed to reach a teenage mountain climber trapped fourteen thousand feet up for two nights in cold, stormy weather. Wingo had dropped warm food and clothing to the boy so he could survive until a rescue party could reach him by foot.

When Trope asked Wingo if he had participated in a rescue mission in the past six weeks, D'Agostino objected that the question was irrelevant, and Wingo wasn't allowed to answer. (He had, in the mountains near Palm Springs, during a weekend trial recess.)

Wingo said he thought that the *Twilight Zone* work would be relatively easy for a pilot of his skill: "I was used to doing live performances before hundreds of thousands of people at a time. And I thought [in movie work] if there was a problem, the director would say, 'Do it again.' And in the live performance, you only had one shot at it."

After the lengthy introduction establishing Wingo's credentials as a pilot, Trope finally turned his questioning to the *Twilight Zone* production team.

"Did he say 'safety first'?" Trope asked Wingo about Allingham.

"Dan used that phraseology often," Wingo answered.

At the counsel table, Leonard Levine was silently fuming, because Trope and Wingo were now implying that Allingham bore some responsibility for safety on the set. Throughout D'Agostino's case, Allingham's liability had been discussed primarily in connection with the illegal hiring, not his on-set activity. Suddenly Allingham was being portrayed as influential in the planning of the special-effects scenes. Wingo recalled Allingham having explained to him that after Morrow crossed the river in the final scene, "the village would be destroyed behind him." Wingo said that Allingham became the liaison between himself and Landis.

(Levine, disheartened, and seeing his job of defending Allingham become harder, scribbled a sarcastic note to his friend and associate Klein: "I hope the next time you go to trial you represent a man who has totally forgotten the facts of the case, both those that hurt him and help him as well. Then have your entire defense destroyed by a crazy co-counsel who makes your client the 'big enchilada.' Hopefully you then will at least be left to argue the one thing I am left to argue—'Safety First.' ")

As he left the courtroom after his first day of what would be six on the witness stand, Wingo looked composed, although testifying had been unsettling for this shy, introspective man.

"Mr. Wingo, could you comment on how it feels to finally be able to tell your side of the story?" a television reporter asked. "I'd like to say hello to my mom in Ardmore, Oklahoma, and my dear Aunt Calley, who is in ill health, and I wish her the best," he said with a sardonic edge to his voice as he leaned toward the microphone.

D'Agostino, whose August 1986 attempt to have Trope removed from the case for alleged incompetence still was not publicly known, was asked by KABC reporter Paul Dandridge to assess Trope's questioning ability. I watched her first say she would rather not comment. Then she said, "He's going a little more slowly than I expected." She stopped in the middle of her next sentence, eyebrows raised and her lip turned up in a slight smile, which was now her familiar expression of ridicule. There were no words. Just laughter.

When Wingo returned to the stand on Thursday morning, Trope turned his client to the important matter of safety on the set.

"The helicopter and the special effects could not occupy the airspace at the same time," Wingo said he had told Stewart in their first conversation. "And what I was talking about was timing. And that if there is any debris involved, as there was in the *Blue Thunder* thing with intentional debris—for example, cork was used in that particular mortar—that I would approve it in advance. That they would not just stick it in there and blow it up. And Mr. Stewart understood that. I just concluded that he knew more about pyrotechnics and the way of the fireballs than I did. And I said, 'You're the professional. I'll look forward to working with you on the set.' "

Wingo's testimony was dotted with references to preparation meetings on the night of the accident, attended by Landis, Stewart, Cohn, and Allingham. Some were sessions about which he had not before testified; some were not corroborated by other testimony; and some contradicted not only the pilot's previous statements but also prior remarks of others, including Paul Stewart. (Because Stewart would not testify, under the Aranda rule the jury would not be informed of his prior statements to investigators.)

By now, all pretense of civility between D'Agostino and the defense lawyers had vanished, and once again, this time during the lunch break, spectators in the hallway were entertained by the repartee between both sides, this exchange appropriate to a Hollywood-connected trial.

Neal, who may have been thinking it wise to deflect press attention away from the testimony of Wingo, emerged from the courtroom and said, "I have one announcement. The academy has reconsidered and they've decided to nominate Lea for best supporting actress."

(The Academy Awards were held the following Monday night at the Dorothy Chandler Pavilion, just up the hill from the courthouse. Court recessed early that afternoon so jurors and others could avoid the traffic congestion caused by hundreds of limousines in the neighborhood. Ironically enough, in light of the subject of Landis's segment of *Twilight Zone: The Movie,* the award for best picture was given to writer-director Oliver Stone's *Platoon,* a masterfully executed drama of combat soldiers in Vietnam. Spielberg was given a Special Achievement award.)

"She's a wonderful actress," Neal continued.

"Today?" someone asked.

"Oh, nooooo," he said in his Nashville drawl, "throughout the last, how many—two years we've been in the case?"

The defense reaction to Wingo's testimony so far was reflected by Landis, who walked out of the courtroom and muttered: "Boy, what a relief. That's a pleasure," in apparent reference to the arrival of the noon-hour break.

In the afternoon the jury finally heard Wingo's account of the first of the two helicopter scenes in question.

The pilot recounted that he had hovered about thirty-five feet above the shoreline at the eleven-thirty shot. He recalled hearing two explosions but did not see any fireballs until the third: "As the fireball erupted, two things happened. Water came into the aircraft cabin area, a spray of water if you will, and startled me. And the other thing that happened was dirty water came down on the windscreen. The heat from one of those fireballs was pronounced, I could feel it. And I was agitated from this water, which I didn't expect."

Wingo's formal, monotonic manner of speech lacked the emotion that he must have felt that July night in 1982. "I uttered an expletive voicing my dissatisfaction to Dan Allingham as we left the scene. I was angry, I was surprised that we had water. The water [had not been] discussed. The heat was excessive, and [I said] that surprises would not be acceptable."

Allingham's response to his complaints, Wingo said, was to say: "You're right, you're absolutely right. Safety first. Safety first. I've got a vacation to go to in Hawaii. I've been working hard and I've earned that vacation. I am going to go, we're going to keep this safe."

Wingo testified that he then told Allingham that he wanted to talk to Landis. Allingham, however, convinced Wingo to let him assume responsibility for communicating the pilot's dissatisfaction to the director.

The jury then heard Wingo's account of his conversation with Landis following the midnight meal break: "He looked down [from the camera crane] and said, 'What do you think?' I said, 'Well, it will be all right as long as the fireballs don't get any larger.' Mr. Landis responded with, 'You ain't seen nothing yet.' I pointed to an area under him and I said, 'How would you like a fireball under you right now?' "

Then, contradicting Landis's testimony of just a few weeks before, Wingo quoted the director as having responded: " 'Don't be squeamish.' That was the end of our conversation."

The pilot said that he met Allingham later at the helicopter: "Dan Allingham said that he had met with John and that he had made the complaints known and not to worry about anything. There would be no surprises and that we would be further away from the cliff, away from the heat and that there would be another briefing prior to the final scene."

(The jury was not told about Allingham's 1983 grand jury testimony in which he said that he had no memory of communicating any complaints to anyone after the flight. Such prior statements could be used against him only if he testified.)

Wingo established that he had warned the others about the danger of fireballs and debris emanating from explosions, including his encounter with Morrow when the actor asked about throwing a piece of bamboo at the helicopter for dramatic effect. He also recounted one troubling exchange with Paul Stewart. The conversation seemed curious in light of other testimony. The pilot said that while walking through the village prior to the two-twenty shot, Stewart had pointed back over his shoulder and said: "They're thinking about setting off something in one of these huts." But if Wingo was correct about his placement of the conversation in time, the mortar under hut number four was already in place, armed with a bomb and gasoline.

Wingo said he was angered by the proposal and said to Stewart: "Paul, we talked about this from day one. What we are talking about here is timing. My helicopter cannot occupy the same airspace as the special effects. There can be absolutely nothing, no debris in the air around the helicopter."

Wingo testified that Stewart never expressed any disagreement and that in a meeting with Landis, Stewart, Cohn, and Allingham, the group discussed that the shoreline explosions would not go off until the helicopter was "a safe distance away."

As Landis had not, Wingo also did not specify exactly what the production team considered a safe distance.

The pilot's description of the fatal flight was detailed and dramatic.

He flew into the area at a height of fifty feet and heard Elie Cohn order him to descend (the "Lower! Lower! Lower!" order) until he was hovering at about twenty-five feet. (Analysis of the film determined the height had been twenty-four feet.)

Using a small plastic model of a Huey helicopter to describe his flight to the jury, Wingo said he felt the concussion from the first three explosions, as he had expected he would: "I initiated a left-hand turn, listening to Dan as he was describing 'Turn. Turn.' And then when I reached the approximate angle I wanted and started forward, the numbers four and five erupted at this point."

The sequence of explosions, the pilot said emphatically to jurors, was "absolutely not" what he had discussed in planning with others.

Trope's presentation of his witness was slow, and just as he was reaching the point in the testimony where the crash itself was to be discussed, the court's day ended. Since it was a Thursday afternoon, Wingo did not complete the recounting for four days. On Monday morning, he picked up just where he had left off:

"After the third explosion I looked up to ascertain that the fire from the third fireball had risen above the level of the helicopter. Then I initiated a slow, left-hand hovering turn. I think it was right at the last part of the turn, what felt like one large explosion at the time went off, almost directly underneath the helicopter. The aircraft was rocked to the left, as if a wave of water hit it, and pushed us out somewhere over the river.

"I leveled the aircraft immediately, and then I became aware that the aircraft was starting to turn left. I remember the aircraft turning left. The aircraft spun. I recall alternating fireballs and blackness. I could not see where we were. And then I recall two bushes were the first things I could associate with any place on the set. I saw two bushes coming up through the windshield. And we were rapidly descending for the ground. I couldn't figure out what was going on with the aircraft."

The steadiness in Wingo's voice, the type of calm associated with pilots, disappeared when he described his emotions after learning that Morrow and the children had been killed.

Trope's final point was to attempt to demonstrate that Wingo's testimony over the years, some of it contradictory, had been affected by lingering emotional distress that was a result of the crash and the deaths.

Wingo said that after suffering from sleeplessness and anxiety he had consulted a psychologist who diagnosed his condition as posttraumatic stress syndrome. Among the symptoms is a dulled memory of painful events. (The disorder is recognized in professional manuals and is common among Vietnam veterans.)

Wingo said that he had stopped psychological treatment in 1984: "I felt I had the key to relaxing. [The therapist] had taught me the various keys to relaxing where I could sleep better, where I could deal with what had happened to me, and also deal with the strife that it had brought my family. I began to recall some of the key conversations I had that were either at a briefing or were in the aircraft. Through the aid of the films, it triggered vividly some scenes I had forgotten completely about and brought to mind some of the care and concern that was taken into putting the production together."

D'Agostino, for one, was astonished at this last comment, particularly since she knew that Wingo had not withdrawn the old civil suit accusing the others on the movie set of recklessness. (D'Agostino wanted to tell the jury about the lawsuit, which seemed to conflict with Wingo's testimony, but Boren would not allow her to do so because Wingo, who was now discounting its validity, had never signed the document. When the *Twilight Zone* criminal trial was over, though, Trope and Wingo engaged an experienced civil attorney to pursue the matter.)

Wingo raised doubt about the quality of on-set communication when he testified that he had believed prior to 2:20 A.M. that Paul Stewart would control the firing board. This point was one in which Trope led him to answers that could only be damaging to the defense. The pilot was asked how he factors into his safety plan the possibility that the man on the board could make a mistake. "We talk to them," Wingo said. However, Wingo never spoke to James Camomile, the man on the board at Indian Dunes.

D'Agostino readied for her cross-examination with eagerness.

On the day that she was to begin, I happened to ride in the same elevator with her as she headed for the courtroom. There were no defense team members there, only office colleagues of hers and strangers. She was talking about Wingo and sang a verse of "Young at Heart," altering the lyrics in a reference to the pilot:

> *Fairy tales can come true*
> *It can happen to you*
> *If you take the stand*

Wingo realized that his confrontation with D'Agostino would not be easy. He entered the courtroom pretending to be on a tightrope. With his arms stretched out to the sides, he took careful steps along a piece of tape that the television crews had placed on the floor. "Walking the line," he said.

D'Agostino immediately began her questioning by referring to the transcripts of his interviews with the NTSB. These would provide her with a foundation for her argument that Wingo was now lying to protect himself and the other defendants.

"Most of what I said was absolutely correct," Wingo said of his remarks to investigators for the federal agency.

Trope had been unsuccessful in excluding the NTSB statements from the trial. When Wingo met with the NTSB panel for the first time in the summer of 1982, Abdon Llorente, the head of the NTSB's Los Angeles office, told Wingo that any statement he made to the NTSB could not be used against him in court. Llorente was wrong, and Trope now contended that Wingo should not have to forfeit his right against self-incrimination because of Llorente's error. Boren did not agree that Llorente's promise was sufficient to keep the evidence out of the trial: "It is quite clear Mr. Wingo knowingly and voluntarily allowed himself to be interviewed at that time. I believe beyond a reasonable doubt that had the statement of Mr. Llorente not been given, Mr. Wingo still would have participated in that interview."

D'Agostino quickly became combative with Wingo, jabbing at him with sarcasm:

"And the only things that you neglected to recall [to the NTSB] were a series of meetings that help your friend Mr. Landis?"

Neal angrily yelled his objection to the question, which Boren sustained.

"Since the trial have you become friendly with John Landis?" D'Agostino asked.

"We've found it—propinquity has set in, yes."

"You weren't friendly before the trial started?"

"No, no."

In a lengthy series of questions posed in a disparaging tone, D'Agostino attempted to show that Wingo's complaint of psychological problems were only a calculated excuse to explain the serious contradictions in his testimony. The questioning, however, served only to show more clearly the pilot's emotional turmoil. The therapy had not come easy for him, he said: "I am a very private person. I don't like to spill my guts to anybody. And if I was having this problem, I didn't want anyone interpreting that maybe I shouldn't be out flying helicopters."

D'Agostino suggested that Wingo had a number of motives to testify in a manner favorable to his codefendants.

"Did you expect future movie employment as a result of your testimony?"

"No."

"You would like more?"

"I have a large family. I could use the income."

On Tuesday, when the cross-examination of Wingo resumed, the prosecutor's limited technical knowledge seemed evident in a number of awkward questions. Throughout the questioning in the morning Wingo appeared to be suppressing a derisive grin when he looked at D'Agostino.

D'Agostino was unrelenting in her attack on his past statements.

In trial testimony Wingo had stated: "Dan wasn't giving any commands. He was giving me suggestions and keeping me informed of the position of the actors as they proceeded from right to left. I was the commander of the aircraft."

D'Agostino now read to the jury three earlier statements Wingo had made to the NTSB:

> I was following the directions of the unit director [Allingham]. We were also following commands from the ground [for] the framing.

> I'm a puppet. They pull the strings. They pull me where they want me.

> No one ever pointed out an explosive, a bomb, a firebomb as they were explaining them to me. No explanation really of where they were or really what they were going to do.

D'Agostino then asked: "However, you told this jury that you did know about the explosions for this flight because John Landis and Paul Stewart told you about them at this meeting?"

"Yes," the pilot answered.

"And when you made those statements at the NTSB, sir, yes or no, were you telling the truth?"

"Yes and no."

D'Agostino did not ask what he meant, to avoid giving Wingo another opportunity to reinforce his position that he had previously suffered from posttraumatic stress syndrome.

"Did you ever indicate that you were startled because you had never flown adjacent to a fireball going off, much less three of them?"

"No," Wingo said.

Then the prosecutor read from the NTSB transcript: "I use the word startled which best describes, because I had never flown adjacent to a fireball going off, much less three of them. So I was startled by this."

"Did you feel intimidated by Mr. Landis, did you feel afraid to confront him while you were angry?" D'Agostino asked.

"Yes."

"Didn't you believe that Mr. Landis was domineering?"

"Yes."

"Weren't you intimidated by that?"

"No, not in the least."

"You've been around domineering people a great deal?"

"Five years in the Army will put you in contact with plenty of domineering people."

"The truth of the matter was you wanted desperately to break into Hollywood and you did not want to leave that set because you didn't want to get a reputation for being a coward and not staying on a set no matter how dangerous it was?"

"That is not true."

"Is it dangerous to have someone under a helicopter that low?"

"No, not with me as the pilot."

The low point of Wingo's testimony came when D'Agostino then asked a series of questions that elicited a curious accusatory defiance in Wingo. Previously the pilot had talked about having given Morrow a warning about the dangers of a hovering helicopter: "I described to him that he should make himself like a chameleon and, that is, keep one eye on the helicopter at all times. I didn't want him to be ignoring where the helicopter was if something happened and I had to make an emergency landing."

D'Agostino wondered how Morrow could accomplish his work and meet Wingo's expectations. She asked: "How did you expect [Morrow] to keep one eye up on the helicopter making his way across the river with children and explosives?"

"It was not out of the ability of the man. I saw no problem in him looking up a few degrees to his left, to see if the helicopter was still there. I saw no problem in him keeping his ears tuned to any changes in the helicopter, because we were not that far away. And I am extremely distraught to this day that the man never looked up."

"Are you blaming him, sir?"

"I am saying it is extremely—it distresses me to the max that he never looked up after having that conversation with him."

"Excuse me, Mr. Wingo, are you blaming Mr. Morrow because with the helicopter twenty-four feet over his head and the prop wash and the noise and the explosions and carrying two children, he did not look up at the helicopter? Is that what you are telling us?"

D'Agostino wanted Wingo to answer only yes or no to that question, not to elaborate, but Boren said the witness did not have to be restricted in his response. The tension rose in the courtroom as D'Agostino pursued Wingo on this point.

"Where did you expect Mr. Morrow to run with these two children if he heard something was wrong with the engine?"

Other defense attorneys rushed to aid Trope, who was trying to deflect D'Agostino with objections.

Klein blurted out: "I object on the grounds of histrionics."

Boren allowed D'Agostino to continue along the same course.

"Where did you expect Mr. Morrow to run with these children if he heard a change in noise of the helicopter?"

"Away from the helicopter. He had over five seconds between the time that the sound of the helicopter changed and it impacted. I would hope to God that he could have used those five seconds to his advantage and the children's."

"And you are now assuming that Mr. Morrow had the ear that he would know precisely the split second when the pitch on that helicopter changed? Is that what you are telling us, sir?"

After Trope objected to the question, Boren, to the defense lawyer's relief, called for the afternoon recess. When court resumed, D'Agostino remained unwavering on the issue.

"Mr. Wingo, this five seconds that you indicated Mr. Morrow had, you had the same five seconds to bring the helicopter into one of those emergency areas, did you not?"

But Wingo didn't agree, because the helicopter was out of control and he could not do anything to maintain flight.

D'Agostino posed the question again: "Mr. Wingo, you had the same five seconds Mr. Morrow had, did you not?"

"No, I didn't have. I don't agree with that."

"How did you brief the children on what to do for this flight, sir?"

"I never talked to the children."

Wingo's fourth and most excruciating day on the witness stand finally ended. In the hallway outside, he attempted to qualify his troubling answers by explaining that he held "a secret place in [his] heart" that Morrow could have run and avoided death for him and the children. Asked if that brought him comfort, he said: "There's nothing easy about living with this. Nothing. It's one of the small, very small comforts, I live with that."

Nearby, D'Agostino called Wingo's answers "a classic example of the defense. Now they're blaming the dead man."

The next day D'Agostino continued with a period of cross-examination that was one of her strongest moments of the trial, and Wingo's answers sent the defense team into even greater distress.

"Were you told what a safe distance was going to be?" the prosecutor asked.

"Yes. A safe distance is what Paul Stewart decided is a safe distance. That is his responsibility. I do not know what a safe distance is. Across the river to me was a safe distance to be. To start with. Anything beyond that was an added safety barrier. If I knew there were explosions along the shoreline and they were going to go up as I turned we would all have looked terribly suicidal."

"Mr. Wingo, that is exactly the point, you didn't know about the explosions on the shoreline. Isn't that what you previously told everybody?"

"Yes."

Then Wingo surprised even Eugene Trope with his revelation that minutes before the fatal 2:20 A.M. flight, he had devised an alternative flight plan without informing anyone on the ground. He did not use it, but there was telling import to his comment. After stressing that safety required everyone to know ahead of time what was to happen, and that there must be no deviation once the flight began, he was now saying that he might have flown in a direction totally unexpected by those firing the mortars on the ground:

"And I've never expressed this to anyone, but it was my plan within a plan that the field of explosions would be my guide as when to begin, not flying away from the village but to parallel the shoreline. And if Roger was late in the shot he wanted, too bad. That was my plan. To play it by ear, I told Dan Allingham that."

When Wingo's testimony was over, and Klein was leaving the courtroom, he had a weary look on his face. "This was the most excruciating testimony I ever had to sit through," he said.

The next day Trope brought a forensic psychiatrist to the witness stand who confirmed the diagnosis that Wingo had suffered from posttraumatic stress syndrome. Dr. Mark J. Mills, a man with exceedingly impressive credentials—he had graduated from Harvard Law School and Stanford Medical School and held full professorships in both law and medicine at UCLA—succinctly supported Wingo's contentions about memory loss.

He was unflappable and a match for D'Agostino, who had been invigorated by her strong cross-examination of the pilot. "Which do you think is a stronger motive, Doctor, money or staying out of jail?"

"Well, I guess, Mrs. D'Agostino, it would depend on how much money, how long in jail."

Of Wingo's integrity, Mills, who had studied Wingo's psychological record and also interviewed him, said: "He values his self-respect more than anything else, and he believes the only way he can regain that self-respect coming away from this tragedy is by being scrupulous, and at times painfully honest in what he tells you or any of the attorneys in this trial."

The cross-examination of Mills spilled over to the following day. When D'Agostino asked Mills about the coincidence that he was not contacted until one day after Trope had learned that Wingo's NTSB testimony would come in, Trope yelled, "Objection, Your Honor! This is outrageous!"

Her question inappropriately suggested that Wingo, upon learning that the NTSB statements damaging to his defense would be introduced as evidence, had quickly sought to concoct an excuse based on psychological impairment. Boren sustained the objection, and Mills did not have to answer.

The issue was debated at the sidebar, and when Boren had ruled, the lawyers once again took their seats. Neal slammed his pen on the counsel table and said loudly enough for others to hear, "I'm getting sick of her. It's a disgrace."

Later, Neal approached D'Agostino in the courthouse corridor and said in reference to Mills, "You know what I wanted to do yesterday? But I thought he would charge too much. And that's to have him analyze you."

"I thought he could do you," the prosecutor replied, "I figure he could do you in about a half hour."

I was standing with Tom Budds watching the exchange. Neal walked over to us and said to the detective, "Do you think the jury is listening? I think they stopped listening two weeks ago. You should have stopped two months ago when you either had us beat or you couldn't win."

Budds, his arms folded across his chest, shuffled his feet and stared at the floor without answering.

SEVENTEEN

LEA D'AGOSTINO often displayed a bitterness toward the defendants and their lawyers, sometimes expressed in demeaning sarcasm and other times in anger. Her intense reactions, she told me, were a reflection of her commitment to a prosecutorial cause: "Whenever I get a case involving defendants who I believe have committed dastardly crimes, I become emotionally involved with the victims. In this case, you are not talking about people who are a danger to society being out in the street, although there is that element as far as Landis is concerned."

D'Agostino's outrage erupted in its most publicly acrid display at the end of the court day on April 7, a session that had already proved disappointing for her because of a successful attack by the defense on her expert witness, a Bell Helicopters engineer. There had been unusual tension and animosity exhibited by the adversaries in the courtroom this day, and the lawyers' tempers were obviously on edge.

Leaving the courtroom, D'Agostino chatted with Associated Press reporter Linda Deutsch. The Jewish observance of Passover was the following week, and in a joking reference to the defense attack on her witness, D'Agostino, who is Jewish, used a Hebrew phrase that is part of the traditional Passover service. "Ma nishtanah halailah hazeh?" the prosecutor said wearily, a sentence that in English means, "Why is this night different from any other night?"

There were several of us passing through the courtroom vestibule at the time, including Landis, who also is Jewish and was walking just in front of the two women. He covered his ears in mock horror and said, "Please don't use Yiddish in front of me." The director's voice seemed devoid of any particular rancor, his reaction typical of his sarcastic spontaneity. Landis continued talking, uttering in Yiddish, "A shanda on the goyim," roughly translating as, "It is a shame for a non-Jew to use the language." It was a peculiar remark to make to D'Agostino, whose ethnic background was well known, unless Landis had mistaken her ethnicity.

Landis said no more and, once in the corridor, quickly walked away from D'Agostino. The prosecutor, however, stopped to talk to several of us. She turned her gaze toward Landis, whose back was to her now. She glared at the director and at a voice level approximating a stage whisper, and with a venomous emphasis, said, "Murderer!"

D'Agostino noticed that *Los Angeles Herald Examiner* reporter Andy Furillo was taking notes. She looked at him and said, "Don't you dare print that. That's off the record."

Furillo and other journalists, however, were under no ethical constraints to keep the quote out of print or off the air. On the contrary, the context of the incident was a legitimately newsworthy event. Furillo, Deutsch, Paul Dandridge of KABC television, and others reported the incident, infuriating D'Agostino.

D'Agostino, in fact, had continued her comments about Landis as several reporters gathered around: "I don't know whether [Landis] thinks I'm not Jewish or wants to preserve the Jewish language only for him. It offends his hearing. It doesn't offend him to kill three people. I'm so angry, I don't even want to talk about it. What I'm more ashamed of is that someone of my faith is him—and don't you dare put that in print—I'm ashamed he's Jewish. I don't want someone like that tainting our religion."

Labeling Landis a murderer was unquestionably unprofessional and entirely inappropriate. In private she was rebuked by Garcetti. The incident, however, was one of many instances of D'Agostino's expressions of aggressive animosity toward the defendants and typical of her temperamental relationships with reporters. She frequently chastised those who she believed betrayed her by publishing articles she interpreted as critical of her and supportive of the defense (as she did with Furillo the next day). She was obviously not as experienced in dealing with the press as were Neal and Braun, who recognized that the daily journalists covering the trial were, on balance, providing fair coverage of the proceedings, even when the defense was not presented in a flattering manner.

D'Agostino's behavior became more questionable as the trial went on, and reporters treated her with increasing skepticism. She mistakenly viewed the coverage of her actions as a mean-spirited attack on her by reporters who had been duped by the defense attorneys. In fact, many reporters covering the trial privately agreed that a strong prosecution of the moviemakers was warranted, but they were not about to abandon their responsibility to be fair in the presentation of both sides of the case.

As the trial neared its end, D'Agostino said to a group of journalists, "You're listening to these [defense attorneys] trying to put nonsense in your heads. They can tell you there's no moon tonight. Are you going to believe that just because you can't see it? These guys are notorious for telling you press people anything they want."

When the defense attorneys completed their presentation of witnesses, D'Agostino was allowed to rebut with more witnesses of her own. The rebuttal, however, began disastrously with the engineer from Bell Helicopters, Larry Dooley, and concluded anticlimactically.

D'Agostino intended Dooley to counter the defense argument, which had been compellingly presented, that the crash was the result of heat delamination and not debris. Dooley had concluded that even if one tail rotor blade lost its metal skin through delamination, the helicopter could still be flown safely. Rules of evidence didn't allow D'Agostino to ask Dooley what did cause the crash (he had not done the appropriate testing to confirm a hypothesis). The implication of his testimony, however, was clear: He was saying that the cause must have been debris.

Dooley was quickly discredited in cross-examination by Jim Neal. The engineer had been requested only two weeks before to undertake the study, and he had only done mathematical calculations on paper. There had been no physical testing. He had studied only the effect of delamination on the aerodynamic balance of the tail rotor blades. He admitted that he wasn't qualified to determine, for example, whether the "structure stiffness" of the blade mass was a factor.

As an experiment, to demonstrate the point for the jury, Neal picked up the delaminated four-foot-long tail rotor blade and tried to bend it, causing the metal to flex with a crackling sound. When he did the same to the tail rotor blade that still had its metal skin covering, the blade was unmoving. Neal's point was that a blade weakened by the loss of the metal skin might bend enough to cause the necessary aerodynamic imbalance.

There were two tail rotor blades in question. One, undeniably, had been delaminated. The other had broken in half in flight and was marked by a gaping dent, but retained its metal skin. Defense experts said delamination of one blade caused an aerodynamic imbalance strong enough to rupture the other blade. D'Agostino argued that the dent was caused by debris and was the catalyst for the fracture of the dented blade. In fact, there were indications that the dented blade had fractured and been hurled from the aircraft before the remaining blade delaminated. One of the difficulties facing the experts trying to reconstruct the sequence of events at the tail rotor was that it all happened in time measured in fractions of seconds.

In the hallway after Dooley's testimony, Neal taunted D'Agostino. He called out the prosecutor's name, and when she turned to him, he said, using his thumb to point to Dooley over his shoulder, "This man has a plethora of ignorance." D'Agostino replied coolly, "You should only have his brains, my dear."

With the end of the trial nearing, D'Agostino remained convinced that if the jurors saw a demonstration helicopter flight, they would respond with the same kind of horror that she had experienced at Indian Dunes. She told Boren, "It is the single most important thing that could possibly be presented to the jury in the entirety of this trial, and I think it's even more important than the movie."

The prosecutor suggested that the demonstration would frighten jurors, a proposition Boren viewed as intellectually intriguing because, if so, "Should it not have scared somebody else that night?" Boren, however, denied her request once again. He said that the jurors saw helicopters daily and that the size of the UH-1B could be described verbally in argument. Boren told me later that California case law clearly discourages such jury views if the actual circumstances of the incident cannot be reasonably recreated.

D'Agostino called two rebuttal witnesses to counter directly testimony of John Landis. Steve Larner, the director of photography, testified that at Indian Dunes he had never heard any discussion that the helicopter would be a camera platform stopping on the opposite side of the river as Morrow and the children crossed. He also said that he never attended a meeting on the set at which safety was specifically discussed.

Casting agent Michael Fenton was called to corroborate the testimony of his then-associate, Marci Liroff. Landis, of course, had testified adamantly that he had not asked the casting agents to hire Vietnamese children.

Referring to the June 18, 1982, casting session with the director, D'Agostino asked, "At that meeting, did John Landis ask you to hire two Vietnamese children for the Vietnamese segment of *Twilight Zone*?"

"Yes," Fenton answered without hesitation.

D'Agostino had no further questions, and surprisingly there was no defense cross-examination of Fenton. Neither side wanted to risk a damaging answer by asking Fenton if he had heard Liroff tell John Landis she thought the scene sounded dangerous. Previously, Fenton had been hazy in interviews with Budds on whether he recalled such a conversation.

After Kesselman's testimony, Boren had said that he didn't believe the evidence thus far proved that anyone had committed perjury and told the lawyers that he didn't want the dispute, which he considered ancillary, to continue in front of the jury. However, at D'Agostino's request, he did allow Budds to return to the witness stand for limited questioning.

The issue was thus revived a final time, but now with curious testimony from Budds. The detective was obviously under a great deal of pressure —he believed he had been dragged into the middle of a controversy of which he wanted no part. But in contrast to his clandestine stairwell talk with Levine the previous September, he now contradicted Kesselman. Budds testified that in the Spring of 1983 he had gone to interview Cynthia Nigh because Donna Schuman had told Kesselman about Folsey's "going-to-jail" statement: "I went to interview Cynthia Nigh [in 1983] for the express purpose of confirming the George Folsey statement."

Braun, who cross-examined Budds on the issue, was angered by the testimony and said outside the courtroom afterward, "Budds is confused. I don't know if he's made up a story, but he's reconstructing to help his criminal prosecution. Budds is making up a story to try and impeach Kesselman. I don't think he's lying. I just think he's completely confused. He's trying to remember things to help his case." Levine was harsher in his assessment and told reporters that Budds was "absolutely" lying now.

Braun was right about Budds's confusion. Budds later told me that, indeed, he had not testified from memory, but only just prior to his appearance on the stand had instead deducted from a review of his 1983 notes that he already knew about the Folsey quote when he went to see Nigh. The detective's notes, however, are ambiguous at best and easily allow for two interpretations.

Braun and Kesselman had become allies, at least on the question of whether Donna Schuman was telling the truth. As the *Twilight Zone* trial progressed, Kesselman watched himself being ostracized in the district attorney's office, and he now believed he was fighting not only for his reputation but his career. He and Braun communicated through the use of code names. When one wanted to contact the other, a secretary would leave a message with the code name. Kesselman was "Mr. Warner," and Braun was "Mr. Fox."

Braun believed that the real reason Budds had been sent to interview

Cynthia Nigh was because Schuman had suggested Nigh knew before the crash that Landis and others recognized they were courting danger, not because Schuman had told Kesselman that Nigh could confirm the "going-to-jail" statements.

(One bizarre clue which had sparked Budds's interest before the 1983 grand jury was a studio artist's drawing, done before the crash but depicting the Vietnamese village and a crashed helicopter in the river. Budds wondered whether the sketch was evidence that the moviemakers had actually considered crashing a helicopter. It was only an odd coincidence, though. When the Indian Dunes set design was being planned, the artist had thought a helicopter carcass owned by Paramount Studios would add a touch of authenticity to the war scene, so he made a drawing of what the set might look like with a downed helicopter in the river.)

Budds was obviously uncomfortable testifying against Kesselman. Prior to his appearance, Budds had been asked by D'Agostino and deputy district attorney Peter Bozanich to write a memorandum, which they could introduce as evidence, recounting negative experiences with Kesselman. Budds refused, and D'Agostino wrote her own memorandum based on her interview of him—a report the detective later told me had "her gloss on it" and was misleading in its interpretations of Kesselman's motives.

The questioning of Budds took place on April 15, and afterward D'Agostino told Boren that "the people rest." The defense had no rebuttal witnesses. On the one-hundredth day of testimony before the jury, the presentation of evidence was ended.

During this period of time the lawyers in the parents' civil suits secretly agreed to settle the case, and payments of approximately $2 million were made to each family by Warner Brothers and insurance companies representing the defendants. The amount is considered to be an unusually high-priced resolution under California law.

The terms of the settlement prohibited any party involved from disclosing details, other than to confirm that the matter had been settled. The wording of the settlement, I was told by lawyers familiar with the matter, left unanswered the question of whether any of the defendants had been negligently responsible for the deaths. Such concessions are routine elements of out-of-court settlements.

The defense settled when it did out of fear that a guilty verdict in the criminal trial, at least for Landis, now seemed quite possible, and there was concern that a conviction on the criminal charges could have resulted in a much higher civil settlement later.

But even without a criminal conviction, there was little doubt that the families would be awarded some relatively large payment for the deaths, since the standards for civil liability are much less stringent than what the law requires in a criminal case. In the civil case, the mere act of hiring the children illegally was sufficient for a decision against the defendants, James Sanders told me. "The decision to settle was a business decision," he said.

Unusually, for a case under as much press scrutiny as was this one, there were no leaks to the local press of the settlement, and it was not made public until after the criminal trial verdicts, as the defense attorneys had hoped.

On Tuesday, April 21, D'Agostino made her way through a larger than usual crowd in the hallway. She was smiling confidently and carried an armful of folders containing her notes for her final argument to the jury. Budds followed with a collection of large charts.

All the lawyers considered the closing arguments in this case important because so much complicated testimony had been presented. Even with their well-honed trial instincts, the lawyers could not discern the impact the testimony had had on jurors.

D'Agostino's closing argument was predictably long, close to sixteen hours over a four-day period. The presentation was a sometimes rambling, detailed repetition of the salient points made by each of her witnesses. She had refused several recommendations from colleagues that she be concise.

She began, however, by labeling the defendant's actions in the starkest of terms: "Maybe there are endeavors in this world that might be worth risking a human life for. Making a movie, no matter how much we might love to go to the movies, is certainly not one of them. You know, in ancient Rome, when Caesars were the emperors, they used to send gladiators into the arena, and these gladiators would be sacrificed for the entertainment of the masses. But fortunately we do not live in those days. Maybe it's because of the utterly senseless, needless loss of three lives for a motion picture that is what makes what these defendants did so barbaric."

She referred to what she believed were the three categories of defense that had been offered in the trial: "The 'SODDI' defense—'Some other dude did it.' He's James Camomile." (Use of the acronym is common among deputy district attorneys, but has a racist tinge to it, for which D'Agostino was criticized by defense attorneys.) "Defense number two was what I'll call the red herring defense, the technical defense, confused with technicalities that obscure the facts. Really sort of razzle-dazzle and a lot of brilliance and stuff a lot of people don't understand very well. And the third one was the 'B' defense, and ladies and gentlemen, I assure you it was not in honor of my broach. This one was 'Blame everyone else.' Or another way, 'Everyone else is lying.' "

She presented James Camomile as an innocent victim of circumstance and suggested that Paul Stewart, standing behind Camomile during the two-twenty shot, should have noticed that something was wrong with the helicopter and stopped him from firing any more mortars.

She made important points, such as the fact that none of the special-effects technicians working the firing boards during the two-twenty shot had been told about the problems encountered by the helicopter at eleven-thirty. She also pointed out that when Camomile received his cue to fire, he looked up and concluded that the helicopter was in a safe position. Thereafter, he concentrated on watching the position of Morrow and the children.

"Let's assume that James Camomile was negligent," she posed. "That he should have looked at the [firing] board, the helicopter, and [the actors] before each shot, no matter how impossible it was for him to do that. Under the law, negligence of a third person does not relieve these defendants from liability."

Over time, though, significant arguments by the prosecutor appeared to get lost and underemphasized in the mass of material she was presenting.

Her theme throughout was that the basic elements of the scene were inherently dangerous, and that should have been recognized by Landis and the others: "When you are dealing with dangerous things, such as helicopters and special-effects explosions that close to human beings, you simply do not call it that close to the vest. Human error is always a factor that must be anticipated and must be guarded against."

She warned jurors not to be fooled by the defense's delamination issue. "They have got to blow smoke in your eyes and confuse you with technical details as to the cause of the crash."

Her primary device to attack the credibility of Landis was a "liar's chart," which, when she finished, contained the names of twenty-four witnesses, all of whom, she said, were lying if John Landis was to be believed. Among those she listed on large sheets of paper tacked to a bulletin board near the jury box were all of the parents, casting agents Marci Liroff and Mike Fenton, cameramen Steve Lydecker and Randy Robinson, photographer Morgan Renard, special-effects technician Kevin Quibell, fire safety officers George Hull, Jack Rimmer and Jack Tice, Anderson House, and James Camomile.

The prosecutor spent relatively little time talking about Donna Schuman, although the defense undoubtedly would attack that witness with great intensity during their final presentations. D'Agostino was at a disadvantage—of her own making, the defense contended—because Boren had ruled that she, in effect, could not argue her own credibility in the Kesselman dispute.

(Deputy district attorney Peter Bozanich, technically representing the state and not D'Agostino, did that later. He told jurors that it would "appear to be so" that the controversial "going-to-jail" statements had been made. "I submit to you that this entire issue of Kesselman-Shuman-D'Agostino is a directed illusion to confuse you, to get you away from the facts of the case," he said.)

D'Agostino focused on Landis: "The major star of the 'blame-every-one-else' defense, or 'Everyone else is lying,' was none other than the defendant, John Landis himself. What can I say about his testimony? The man is an actor. He's told you that. That was quite obvious when he took the witness stand in almost-but-not-quite tears. The little catch in the throat now and then. He is also an admitted good, or great, storyteller. And he outdid himself in that particular category when he was on the witness stand. And he's a director, able to direct his answers to say what he wanted to say, whether or not it responded to questions I was asking him.

"How can Landis on the one hand tell you he did not know anything about the bomb under that hut, and on the other tell you how very organized and coordinated the whole set was, and how everybody knew everything. Those two things are totally inconsistent.

"He told you with a perfectly straight face that in 1982 he believed he could get a waiver to put children in the scene under a helicopter. If you believe that, there are a lot of things a lot of salesmen can sell you, and you all know what they are. That is prepostrous beyond all belief."

D'Agostino was now ready to "get down to what I call the real bloopers, the real whoppers, the real out-and-out lies and inconsistencies between what he told you up here and what he said on previous occasions." She referred to on-set meetings to which Landis had testified only at this trial and not previously, discussions with Stewart about blowing up huts, and the discrepancies about whether the helicopter was to have been a camera platform away from the village at two-twenty.

"Everything you heard on that witness stand from John Landis, if you take that in conjunction with what the other witnesses have said and in conjunction with what he has personally said on previous occasions, makes what he told you in this courtroom nothing more than one blatant lie."

There were certainly effective moments in the prosecutor's presentation. When she talked about the dimensions of the UH-1B, using the
courtroom length for perspective, there was drama and emotion in her
voice, but the presentation was controlled and striking.

As the stakes were rising in the courtroom, so was the intensity of the
hallway interchanges. At the end of the second day of her argument an
interaction with Neal outside the courtroom was true theater.

Neal had preceded her into the hallway and was speaking to reporters
as she approached the gathering: "Her explanations of inconsistencies is
somewhat Byzantine. The Byzantines are somewhere closer to the Middle
East than the barbarians, but we'll have something to say about the
barbarians. I want Mrs. D'Agostino to get in here. This is her hour."
Laughing, Neal added, "Her week, I guess. Come in, Mrs. D'Agostino."

With a sugary emphasis, the prosecutor replied, "Your courtesy over-
whelms me, Mr. Neal."

"I want you to take some time to talk, after all," the Nashville lawyer
said.

With a derisive imitation of Neal's Southern accent, D'Agostino replied, "I can say twice as much as you in the same amount of time 'cause
I'm not using your accent."

"You don't have as much to say as I do," Neal said.

"I don't know about that, Mr. Neal. But it is a pleasure having you in
California," she said, still using the affected accent.

"You ought to read a little Shakespeare—" Neal replied, but was cut
off by the prosecutor, who said, "Oh, I do." Neal continued, ". . . about
the virtue of brevity. It says something about you."

"No," D'Agostino said. "It's 'The quality of mercy is not strain'd. It
droppeth as the gentle rain from heaven upon the place beneath.' "

"You remind me very much of Portia," Neal said.

"Well, would you believe me if I tell you I did Portia in school?" the
prosecutor asked.

As Neal walked away, he said, "The only thing is, you aren't going to
get your pound of flesh."

"Oh, I don't know about that," D'Agostino replied confidently.

(Neal had his own acting accomplishments. Through a Nashville
friend, country singer Johnny Cash, Neal was cast, not surprisingly, as a
country lawyer in a 1983 television movie, *Murder in Coweta County.* Neal's
movie client, portrayed by Andy Griffith, effectively convicts himself by
taking the witness stand against his lawyer's advice and blundering under
strong cross-examination. Coincidentally, the movie had aired on a local
television station just a few weeks before. The next morning one juror

jokingly said to Neal in the elevator, "Can I have your autograph?" In another apparent coincidence of scheduling, another Los Angeles television station aired a "John Belushi Week," including showings of *Animal House* and *The Blues Brothers*, during the period when defense attorneys were making their closing arguments to the jury.)

On Thursday, the prosecutor's third day of argument, D'Agostino continued her critical analysis of John Landis's character: "It isn't that John Landis decided wrongly to violate the law. It's that he thought he was above the law. He didn't think the law applied to him. He wanted to get those kids, and he was going to have them."

She summarized why the defendants faced criminal charges. Regarding the involuntary manslaughter counts based on the fact that the children had been hired illegally, D'Agostino said that Landis, Folsey, and Allingham "knew from day one that the children were going to be placed in a scene involving special-effects explosions and a helicopter and that Landis intended on doing it at night. Common sense tells you that is a dangerous scene. No one has accused these defendants of being stupid. How could they not know that?"

But she also pointed out that the law did not require for conviction that the moviemakers had to have recognized that the scene was dangerous. She cited an instruction that would be read later to the jurors by Boren: "The fundamental requirement for criminal negligence is that the defendant either knew, or reasonably should have known, that his act tended to endanger life."

The second set of charges were for the allegedly reckless acts of Landis, Wingo, and Stewart on the set, committed, she said, with "wanton disregard of these three human beings."

The reactions of the defendants to D'Agostino's presentation varied. Wingo sat stiffly, staring at the back of Trope's chair. On occasions he wrote letters to his family, using a yellow legal pad. Paul Stewart, unflappable throughout the trial, sat with his hands folded on the table in front of him and stared without emotion at his accuser. During one recess he said to me jubilantly, "I've caught her in four different lies." During another break, Landis and others, including some of the lawyers, stood in the men's room giddily criticizing D'Agostino's "muddled" argument.

D'Agostino, who was spirited and forceful in the final moments of argument before she relinquished the floor to the defense, did not believe her points were hazily made: "What you had on this set, basically, ladies and gentlemen, was a tyrannical dictator. You had a man who various witnesses have described as demanding, loud, a yeller and a screamer. Do you get the feeling that here is a man possessed and obsessed with his quest for realism? Who's willing to go to just about any extent necessary in order to achieve this big spectacle that all the people are waiting there to see? He took a calculated risk. He took a gamble with other people's lives, and he lost. He lost."

By court procedure, D'Agostino, as the prosecutor carrying the burden of proving guilt beyond a reasonable doubt, would have the final word to the jurors when the defense had finished.

Defense attorneys in their closing arguments dwelled on their basic position, that the defendants did not know the scene was dangerous, that it had been planned properly, and that unforeseen events, including mistimed explosions by Camomile and delamination of one of the helicopter tail rotor blades, had caused an accident.

Jim Sanders was the first of six defense lawyers to speak to the jury. He began with John Landis's confession that the case involved "the regrettable and inexcusable fact that John Landis intentionally violated the child labor law." Sanders accused the district attorney's office, though, of "stretch[ing] beyond the truth by arguing that the reason for the violation was not to shoot after hours, to shoot at night, but because of safety."

Sanders began with a nervous edge to his voice, but his delivery quickly became smoother and more confident. He appeared articulate and committed, devoid of the excesses which had marked D'Agostino's sometimes rambling effort: "There is one main issue and one main truth in this case, and that is whether Mr. John Landis believed that the scene was dangerous and acted in a reckless, wanton, or grossly negligent manner."

Sanders contended that the prosecution witnesses who formed the cornerstone of the state's theory were liars. As anticipated, Donna Schuman was the focus of such remarks. Sanders, after all, had been instrumental the previous fall in damaging Schuman's credibility with his strong cross-examination of her. "You will never see or hear a more striking and obvious development and evolution of a fabricated story as long as you live, a more clearly marked trail of patent lies," he said.

He spoke for only an hour and ten minutes and turned the podium over to Neal, whose national reputation stemmed, in part, from his dazzling closing argument at the Watergate trial in Washington more than a decade before. His performance here would not receive such accolades, but he would be effective.

Neal's bass voice took on a preachy boom as he remarked, "Not one of these defendants intended to hurt anyone; not one of these defendants thought the accident scene, as planned and rehearsed, was dangerous."

Assuming that jurors would conclude that some mishandling had taken place during the movie's production, he emphasized the distinction between civil and criminal liability: "Negligence is acting unreasonably, and when you act unreasonably, you get sued for money damages. Criminal negligence is acts which are aggravated, wanton, amounting to an indifference or disregard of human life."

As did others, Neal pointed to the trust he said the defendants had reasonably placed in Camomile: "How could anyone foresee that a man holding the highest powder card issued by the state of California would not follow instructions, would not follow the first principle of his profession, and would prematurely set off a special effect with the helicopter right there?"

Neal dealt with D'Agostino's "liar's list" with a succinct response, "Mr. Landis didn't say anybody was lying."

The defense focused on the state of mind of each defendant, arguing that each believed no one on the set was ever in any danger. Neal said, "That John Landis and George Folsey thought the scene was safe is eloquently described, not here from the stand, but the fact that on Wednesday night when they thought this scene would be shot [according to the original schedule], Mr. Folsey had his wife and children there, and Mr. Landis had his wife there."

The Nashville lawyer closed with a personal, sentimental touch, saying that the director's "scars are deep and everlasting. He was determined before he took the stand not to break down—"

He was interrupted by D'Agostino, who said disgustedly, "Oh, objection, Your Honor." The rules governing argument to juries are quite liberal, allowing for a wide breadth of comment, but the prosecutor thought Neal's comments were all beginning to sound too syrupy. Boren agreed that Neal was getting off track and sustained the objection. D'Agostino, however, was not supported in her next objection, and Neal was allowed to say to jurors, "I suspect that when [Landis] looks at [his children] Rachael and Max, he will remember Renee Chen and My-Ca Le."

Neal finished: "Members of the jury, we submit that the proof justifies, even requires, you to say to Mr. Landis: 'Mr. Landis, you were wrong, but we know you do not use barbarian tactics. We know you are not a tyrannical dictator. We know that you did not intend to hurt anyone. We know you are not guilty of the charges in this case.' "

Arnold Klein's rehearsal of his closing argument caused consternation among new neighbors who did not know that he was a lawyer. The father of a baby born just a few months before, Klein did not smoke inside the house. So, in the early morning hours, well after midnight, he paced in front of a flower bed, honing his delivery and causing the neighbors to ask his wife the next morning if he was troubled. Just before the session during which he would speak, Klein joked nervously, "The daffodil was a holdout." Klein recognized that Paul Stewart could be viewed by jurors as the defendant most directly responsible at Indian Dunes, because he controlled the special effects and had the authority to override any director's plan if he thought it posed a danger.

The lawyer chose a literary analogy to make his point by alluding to Lewis Carroll's famous children's book, "This was a prosecution that was based on lack of understanding, misconception, rumor, and innuendo, a real *Alice in Wonderland* type of prosecution where safety meant danger."

Klein argued that truth had taken "a wrong turn" when Camomile answered questions of the NTSB and Tom Budds in 1982—based on Camomile's recollection, the detective had developed the theory, proven untrue after the indictments, that Stewart had switched mortars under hut four in an attempt to mislead investigators.

"The evidence shows that Paul Stewart approached the task with careful consideration of the safety of those around him, that he thoughtfully considered placing a mortar under [hut number four] because of the design, shape, the size of the bomb, and way it should be canted," Klein said. "I am not trying to blame Jim Camomile, but Paul Stewart cannot be held criminally responsible for the acts of Jim Camomile."

"Dorcey Wingo might be classified as a scapegoat," Eugene Trope told the jurors. "I must say one thing about all types of pilots. I never met one that wanted to commit suicide. They all wanted to make that trip home. His helicopter was blown out from under him. Let Dorcey Wingo rebuild his reputation. Let him resume his career. Let him resume his life. Do not punish him for having done nothing wrong, unless his wrong was to have survived and assisted in the saving of five other lives."

By widespread agreement, Leonard Levine's closing statement was the most articulate and compelling of the defense attorneys' final arguments. He began by criticizing D'Agostino for a presentation having more style than substance: "Argument without facts is no argument at all. Passion in the pursuit of justice is no vice, and passion in the pursuit of injustice is no virtue."

Levine reminded the jurors that Allingham was not accused of recklessness on the set but for his involvement in the illegal hiring of the children weeks before, when he allegedly knew that they would be at risk at Indian Dunes. "[Allingham] took the risk that [the production team] would be charged, convicted, and punished [for illegally hiring the children], but he never would have taken the risk [had he thought] that these children were in any danger of losing their lives, that they were likely to be killed or injured greatly."

The lawyer pointed to what he believed was dereliction on the part of the fire safety officers: "It's very interesting that the only man on that set who said he thought it was dangerous was Mr. Ebentheuer. And what did he do? Nothing."

Levine demeaned the notion that the case deserved to be in a criminal court at all: "It's time for the prosecution to go back to what they do best, or should be—prosecuting real criminals and real crimes. These five men were not perfect. The last perfect man was crucified two thousand years ago. They are not heroes. They are not martyrs. They are not saints. But they were not prophets, either. And they are not guilty."

Harland Braun took the chance of alienating jurors by criticizing the parents of the dead children. His client, George Folsey, had been accused of misleading them while recognizing the danger himself. Braun suggested that the parents' claims that they had not been fully informed was an attempt to assuage their own guilt: "I sympathize with the difficulty of dealing with them. If it is a psychological crutch that they need, then it is a psychological crutch I would not want to take away from them. It's another thing to take the crutch and smash it over my client's head and imply that he lied to them."

George Folsey was the defendant most affected by Donna Schuman's testimony, and Braun challenged not only the truth of the woman's words but her psychological state: "The statements come from a witness who looks like she's emotionally distraught, unbalanced, probably guilt-ridden. Not in the sense that she's guilty of anything, but psychologically, in the sense that she participated in the hiring of some children who died."

He challenged D'Agostino's motives as well: "Winning. It may mean more sometimes to a prosecutor in a high case like this, because you are publicly out on a limb. Maybe the prosecutor is a victim of this overemphasis on winning. It's in a moral pressure cooker of the big case that your true mettle comes out."

Judge Boren kept an account of the time each attorney used in argument. D'Agostino had used eight hours, the defense a total of sixteen hours and thirty-six minutes. D'Agostino was told she could use eight and a half more hours to conclude her argument.

One incident during the three days it took her to finish overshadowed much of her presentation. D'Agostino's lack of technical and scientific knowledge had been evident throughout the trial, but now it made her a laughing stock in the courthouse.

Even though she had presented no expert witnesses to support her conclusion that debris had damaged the helicopter, she still argued that point to the jury. Unknown to anyone else in the courtroom, she also had a demonstration ready.

She began by asking rhetorically how it could be that only one of the blades delaminated. She quickly answered, "Because [the other one] had already been struck by debris and was down on the ground."

FBI agent James Ronay had testified that his experiments showed that the explosive power of the mortars used at Indian Dunes and the known angles at two-twenty indicated that debris could not have caused the damage. When Kesselman had been confronted with that dilemma years before, he realized that he would have to have his own expensive studies done to counter the FBI report. Other scientific evidence, particularly from the NTSB, suggested that the FBI analysis was too limited.

D'Agostino had not commissioned scientific studies but had adopted an idea presented to her by NTSB investigator Abdon Llorente. "Don't, ladies and gentlemen, buy the defense argument that there wasn't sufficient force," she said to jurors. "You know why? I'll show you why."

As she spoke, she reached behind the wood panel that encircled the now empty witness stand and grabbed an item that was not immediately discernible to those watching.

She spun on her heels toward the jury, holding a large raw potato in her left hand. With a quick stab of her right hand she plunged a plastic straw through it and said with dramatic flair to the astonished jurors: "If a little ninety-pound woman can do this with a straw and a potato, think what a round piece of bamboo can do to a rotor blade."

Judge Boren, out of the presence of the jury, admonished D'Agostino, indicating that she should have been well aware that such a demonstration was inadmissible during final argument and that her action bordered on contempt of court. Later, he told the jurors to disregard the incident.

During a recess, *Los Angeles Times* reporter Paul Feldman asked the prosecutor a question that brought smiles to the faces of everyone nearby except D'Agostino. "Do you have any more vegetables up your sleeve, Lea?" he posed. She snapped in return, "I could do it for you with an onion, Mr. Feldman." Harvey Giss, a respected district attorney prosecutor, told me, "That's one of those things that goes around the office in two minutes flat. The phones start ringing, and it's an inside joke." Laughing, he added, "As tragic as the case was, what if the straw didn't work? Jesus!"

D'Agostino, however, remained proud of her surprise display. At lunch afterward she told me and others that she had successfully used dramatic demonstrations before. She won a conviction against a rapist after calling the defendant to stand behind her as she stood on a stool in front of the jury box, thus proving that a sodomy rape couldn't have been consensual because it was physically impossible as the defendant had described the incident.

On Monday, with about two hours of argument time left, defense attorneys angrily questioned why D'Agostino had placed a grocery store shopping bag, out of which a large, green-leafed celery stalk emerged, on the witness chair. She assured Boren and others that the produce would not be used during her argument. To avoid calling more attention to the bag and its contents, now that the jury was already seated, the judge rejected her offer to move it. He said to the prosecutor, "That's not very good. I don't care for that."

D'Agostino's final hour of argument may have been her best showing in the trial. Her presentation was concise, balanced, and logical. Undaunted, D'Agostino finished with a notable, well-spoken conclusion.

" 'The Plan' [that the helicopter would be safely away before the shoreline mortars were detonated] was obviously such a well-kept secret from so many people that maybe Mr. Landis could give some helpful hints to the FBI or CIA on how to prevent leaks. I submit to you that the only plan was for Jerry Williams and James Camomile to set off their explosions a second to a second and a half apart. The helicopter was going to be right there by that sampan when the bombs went off. I submit to you that there's not a director worth his salt in Hollywood who would come in here and tell you that what [the defendants] did was okay."

She continued: "What is no illusion is that three people are very dead. You have to be completely oblivious to reality not to know or reasonably perceive that that was a life-threatening scene.

"You have the power now by your verdicts to make sure that never again will an overzealous director or other person producing a picture, in their eagerness for box office success, in their quest for realism, risk a human life for that picture. You've got the power to set the standard. The victims in this case were unable to be here and speak for themselves, but their memories are eloquent in their condemnation of these defendants and their recklessness, and they cry out to you: John Landis—guilty; George Folsey—guilty; Dan Allingham—guilty; Paul Stewart—guilty; Dorcey Wingo—guilty. The guilty verdicts in this case will finally end a most sordid chapter in the history of motion picture making and will justly condemn the excesses of these filmmakers brought about by their reckless arrogance. Let Vic and My-Ca and Renee rest in peace, knowing that justice has been done."

Out of superstition, D'Agostino wore the same outfit she had worn on the first day of the trial, a tan skirt and silk blouse. When she had completed her argument, she remarked to several of us that, as light as she was, she had lost even more weight in the past months and was now under ninety pounds, and the once-tight skirt now fit loosely. In her office, I watched her take some celery from the shopping bag that had been in the courtroom and two hard-boiled eggs from her purse, and gobble them hungrily. The *Twilight Zone* case was completely out of her hands now.

One more procedure remained before the jurors would be sent to their deliberations. Final instructions from the judge, including definitions of legal terms and the charges the defendants faced, took an hour to read and forty-nine transcript pages.

Boren pointed out that "[admissions of illegal hiring] do not in themselves prove criminal negligence." The jurors could not convict if they had reasonable doubt, which he explained was "that state of the case which, after the entire comparison and consideration of all the evidence, leaves the minds of jurors in that condition that they cannot say they feel an abiding conviction to a moral certainty of the truth of the charge."

Acts of criminal negligence, Boren explained, "are such a departure from what would be the conduct of an ordinarily prudent or careful person under the same circumstances as to be contrary or incompatible with a proper regard for human life or, in other words, a disregard for human life or an indifference to consequences."

The charges against the defendants were complex and required the jurors to make certain judgments that were not easily quantifiable—the most important one being their determination of what any reasonable person would have done under the same circumstances the defendants had faced at Indian Dunes. In effect, the jurors had the opportunity to set a community standard. The most important sentence in Boren's instructions gave the jurors discretion in making that decision: "The fundamental requirement for criminal negligence is that the defendant either knew or reasonably should have known that his act tended to endanger life."

The twelve jurors began their deliberations on Monday, May 18, at 3:17 P.M., by electing Lois Rogers as their foreman. The housewife and grandmother had been taking meticulous shorthand notes throughout the trial. In the view of others on the panel, she combined an admirable sense of organization, efficiency, and equanimity.

EIGHTEEN

THE CAMARADERIE of the jurors was evident throughout the nine-month trial. But the depth of the friendship and strength of the bond that had grown among all of them was unknown to the other trial participants as the twelve men and woman retired to the jury room to begin their deliberations.

They were "family," and out of that special relationship came a study of the issues that would be without strong divisiveness and would be completed in a temperate atmosphere.

As a group they displayed friendship and a sense of humor. In the early days of the trial they had played word games on the jury room blackboard or put together board puzzles. Just before they entered deliberations, they completed a puzzle that produced a portrait of the late actor, James Dean. As any group of people would over a period of time, they encountered personality frictions, but these soon passed and were ultimately inconsequential.

The jurors consoled each other over the deaths of relatives, celebrated the births of grandchildren, and developed a mutual respect. They brought homemade food, and each time someone celebrated a birthday (seven times during the trial), a cake was shared in the jury room.

Boren chose not to sequester the panel. On the first full day of deliberations, he ordered the media to stay a hundred feet from the panelists when they were outside the building and not to attempt to photograph or document them in any way. During deliberations, the jurors were escorted in a group by deputy sheriffs to nearby restaurants for lunch.

In the jury room, Rogers quickly established decorum. On her home computer she devised work sheets to be used during discussions: one for each of the defendants, including the counts against him as well as the legal requirements, as stated in the judge's instructions, for proving the count.

Clearly, the jurors who led the discussion were imbued with a sense of responsibility. Crispen Bernardo, the one-time college chemistry professor from the Philippines, was proud to be performing what he termed his "civic duty." He told me, "I had an idea they were millionaires. I was awed by the fact that these rich people, these 'Beverly Hills crowd' people, in a way, [their] fate[s], [are] in my hands." Early in the proceedings, Bernardo asked to be appointed, in an unofficial sense, the jury's "devil's advocate." He wanted to make sure opposing viewpoints were aired. Paul Gonzales was also particularly vocal about airing all viewpoints.

One juror requested a vote be taken as the first order of business. While many jurors were no doubt already leaning toward a particular verdict when deliberations began, Rogers and a few others insisted that no expression of a position on the verdicts be made until after the evidence had been discussed.

Initially, the jurors made two requests to the judge for materials that they wanted to review. First, they asked that all the testimony by Donna Schuman and Gary Kesselman be read back to them. That took almost three days. They also asked for a videotape machine so they could play the evidence film of the crash, which they did a number of times using the freeze-frame function.

As the defense attorneys had hoped, the Schuman-Kesselman controversy had raised doubt about D'Agostino's case. A number of jurors believed that Schuman lied. Schuman had been D'Agostino's first witness and had taken the stand on Thursday, September 4, 1986. As Lois Rogers listened, she wrote in her notebook that day, "Donna Schuman is a liar. I don't like her. She seems well coached." Gary Kesselman was believed.

The credibility issue, however, was more a distraction than a foundation of the jury's decision. (After the trial several key jurors recreated their deliberations for me.) Rogers later told me that the "going-to-jail" statements were no doubt uttered by the defendants but were not an indication that the men thought what they were doing was dangerous: "It sounded like they actually were joking about the whole thing. They were not actually serious. I can imagine in the motion picture business they can make all kinds of remarks and not mean a thing that they say."

Indeed, the jurors had questioned the truthfulness of some defense witnesses as well, including both defendants who took the stand. "I think

John Landis said what he had to say in order to make us, or try to make us, sympathetic to his cause," Rogers said. James Ross and others thought that Dorcey Wingo had exaggerated his testimony about safety meetings on the set.

Important to the jurors' perspective of the defendants, however, was their view that these five men were, at the core, generally decent men who did not harbor evil. This issue is vital because in the view of the jury, D'Agostino had lost credibility by her harsh portrayal of the defendants.

According to Wilbert Fisher, the retired army colonel who had been the second choice for jury foreman, "We didn't think they were hardened criminals at all. [That] just weakened her presentation." Also distasteful to the panel was the prosecutor's attack on Wingo's testimony about his psychological suffering after the accident, trauma which jurors believed he had truly endured.

Jim Neal's theory—that in a long trial the jurors carry with them broad perceptions of the presentation rather than the minutiae—proved accurate. Lois Rogers conceded that the task of assimilating the material, primarily in the prosecution's side of the case, had been overwhelming: "We were so bogged down with information from so many people that I'm sure somewhere along the line that all of us, at one point or another, turned off what somebody was saying."

While the lawyers debated detail, sometimes for days on a single, limited element, the jurors seemed to have viewed the matter with a broad perspective that did not always incorporate the fine points or contradictions within a given issue.

Sometimes the contradictory and voluminous testimony presented to the jury clouded their ability to determine whether certain things had really happened at Indian Dunes, even some events to which defense attorneys readily conceded. For example, Bernardo said he doubted whether Landis really had given the order for the helicopter to lower just before the two-twenty shot.

In another instance, some jurors accepted that the plan of the moviemakers at Indian Dunes had been that the helicopter would be on the opposite shore filming before the last explosions were detonated at two-twenty. Neal, who had presented "The Plan," recognized that this notion rested primarily on the testimony of cameraman Randall Robinson and was challenged by other testimony. John Landis himself had finally testified that the helicopter would only be an unspecified "safe distance away." In their questions to witnesses, however, defense attorneys had continually reinforced the notion that "The Plan" was proven fact.

Crucial to the deliberations was the testimony of James Camomile, the man who operated the firing board controlling the fatal explosions. The jurors were bewildered by his appearance as an immunized witness for the prosecution rather than as a defendant himself. They accepted the defense position that he had erred in not looking up at the helicopter before firing each mortar. "That's the man that should be up for trial, knowing good and well what could happen when he didn't do what he was supposed to be doing," Fisher told me. That Camomile had not been informed of the problems encountered during the eleven-thirty shot was "not an issue" with jurors.

While the granting of immunity to Camomile had logic to it—according to the prosecution's theory—the jurors hadn't been offered its justification. Rogers said, "Consequently, these things hang big question marks with us. And if you don't tell us why, then we can't assume anything else. We thought he was really going to have some significant evidence that would be key to convictions."

Unquestionably, the prosecutor's personality negatively affected the jury during the trial, sometimes diverting their attention. In time, panelists became annoyed with what they believed was an unseemly attempt to communicate with them through facial gestures. Lois Rogers told me, "Her eyes would roll up to the heavens. It went on constantly, a little mincing smile [as if to say], 'They're liars.' I can honestly say I don't think I got one idea like that from any defense attorney."

While most jurors seemed diligent about avoiding the newspapers and television news reports about the trial, in accordance with the judge's order, it was impossible to block out all outside comment. For example, early on, the jurors learned that D'Agostino was called "Dragon Lady," a nickname that they assumed had been given her by the *Twilight Zone* defense attorneys. Although much of the lawyers' debate over personality was conducted out of their presence, the jurors, nonetheless, observed the residue of extreme rancor between the opposing lawyers in the courtroom.

Such matters, though, ultimately seemed to have little real impact on their study of the facts of the case.

The jurors did conclude that the defendants had not always acted properly. The dilemma, as they viewed it, was to match the conduct with their definition of criminal negligence. "There might have been some aspects of [recklessness], we agree with that, but the total criminal negligence, we don't think that was really proved," Fisher said.

I discovered that the jurors who led discussions had misinterpreted the judge's instructions regarding the definition of criminal negligence. The standard, according to the law, is either that the defendants knew they were courting danger and ignored it, or—and this is the element the panelists confused—should have known. The jury had the authority to determine what any reasonable person would have done and judge the defendants by that standard.

Instrumental in ensuring that the jurors discuss the relationship between the charges and the conduct of the five defendants was Bernardo. Unlike some other jurors, he had listened to D'Agostino's case with admiration for the prosecutor.

Bernardo told me, "My understanding was that criminal negligence meant that they knew, they're aware. [For example], if it is true Liroff made those statements and Landis did not believe her, [then] he did not have foreknowledge. He may be wrong in his judgment, but the way I interpret it is whether he knew or not, not whether he should have known. So [we had to place ourselves] inside the person's mental state and find out. Did he think that way? So, really, they were not totally clean. So that it's not that they were pronounced not guilty because they didn't do anything wrong. They did something wrong. But by definition they did not do enough, or the case did not prove enough, that all those elements that we had to look out for were present."

Rogers said, "I don't believe that I ever thought that they believed there was any danger. You have to know in the back of your mind that this is going to be inherently dangerous and you shouldn't do it, in the very beginning. I don't think any of them did that. I really don't."

In the end, though, the incorrect definition used by the jury appears not to have been a deciding factor. Whether the jurors' discussions would have been significantly different otherwise appears unlikely, based on their view of the evidence.

"That was an accident. I don't think there was anything that anybody could have foreseen that this would have happened to this helicopter. That's just black and white to me," Rogers said.

Rogers did say, though, that one circumstance might have made a difference: "I think if D'Agostino could have proven to me and the rest of us that it was debris from the explosion that brought the helicopter down, things might have gone differently."

The uncertainty about the cause, however, was coupled with many other doubts in the minds of jurors.

As sympathetic as they were, they thought that the parents bore some, although minimal, responsibility for allowing their children to work late at night illegally. The jurors believed that the parents had been given sufficient information about the scene.

The jurors also concluded that government employees had not performed according to the rules. They questioned why the state would even publish a book of regulations governing child workers, when a top state official testified that she routinely granted waivers. The fire safety officers were not impressive to the jurors, who believed that Jack Tice, who was also a teacher-welfare worker, had seen the children prior to the crash and had done nothing.

The jurors did not debate guilt or innocence so much as they concluded that they had reviewed the material thoroughly enough to justify a vote. Their tally was unanimous, and their work was finished in mid-morning on Friday, May 29, 1987. They sent a message to Boren, who quickly assembled them in the courtroom.

"I will not ask for any verdict right now until counsel gets here," Boren said. Rogers gave the judge the verdict forms, sealed in a large manila envelope.

"Have a good lunch," the judge said, and called for court to reconvene at 1:30 P.M., giving the lawyers and their clients time to come downtown from Century City, the San Fernando Valley, and Hollywood.

The defendants and their lawyers were tense. Allingham at first didn't believe Levine when the lawyer called and said there was a verdict. He was so nervous he could hardly shave as he prepared to head downtown. He told me: "I always felt confident that we did nothing wrong, but whether or not twelve people were going to convict us emotionally—I was hoping not, but I wasn't sure."

Budds watched Landis walk into the courtroom: "He looked worse than probably anybody I've ever seen. So did his defense attorneys."

There was no confidence to be seen in any member of the defense team. Two of the lawyers had told Budds as they walked in that they were sure the jury was coming back with guilty verdicts.

At 1:47 P.M. Boren began the session. The procedure was routine but excruciatingly long for those waiting to find out what was written on the verdict forms. "Good afternoon, everyone," Boren said. "The record will reflect the presence of all counsel in the *Twilight Zone* case. All defendants are present, all the jurors and alternate jurors are present. And my understanding is, Mrs. Rogers, you are the foreperson?"

"Yes, I am," she said.

"Has the jury reached a verdict in the case? Yes or no?"

"Yes, we have, Your Honor."

Several people in the courtroom noticed Judge Boren's face redden and his knuckles whiten as he grasped the verdict forms and, in silence, methodically checked each one, as is procedure, before passing them on to the court clerk to be read aloud.

Clerk Sylvia Felien read the first verdict: "Title of court and cause: We the jury in the above entitled action find the defendant John Landis not guilty of involuntary manslaughter, as charged in count one of the amended information, signed this twenty-ninth day of May 1987, Lois M. Rogers, foreman."

Stewart and Wingo had also been named in count one, for the involuntary manslaughter death of Vic Morrow, based on their actions on the set. Felien read their "not guilty" verdicts in the same format.

There was still some tension, though. Count two named Landis, Folsey, and Allingham in the death of Renee Chen, and was based on the illegal hiring. Of the three men named in count two, John Landis was the first to hear that he had been found not guilty.

As one "not guilty" after another was read, Lea D'Agostino turned to the jurors and looked each in the eye. Her murderous glances chilled those panelists who happened to look back at her.

When the fifteen verdicts had been read, Boren said, "The defendants are discharged." The gallery, filled mostly with family and friends of the moviemaker, broke into applause.

The last statement by a defense attorney recorded by the court reporter was uttered by Braun in reference to his caustic comments to the judge over the months. With a smile to Boren, Braun said, "I take back everything I said."

Boren returned to his chambers. Even before the verdicts, he had some sense of his plans had the defendants been found guilty. For one, John Landis would have been taken into custody immediately and released only after payment of a high bail, perhaps a million dollars or more, imposed to insure that he did not leave the country. Upon conviction, Landis would have faced a maximum sentence of six years in state prison, and the other defendants five years. Sentencing regulations would not have required imprisonment in this matter. Simple probation could have been issued. Boren's initial thought, though, was that the director would be levied a two-year prison term.

Shunning the bustling around her, D'Agostino slowly stood, faced forward, and gathered her papers.

The crowd began pushing forward on one side of the bar, and the former defendants moved to receive handshakes, hugs, and kisses.

Only one person still had an official function to perform in the *Twilight Zone* trial. The court reporter wrote the last words in the transcript, on page 26,138:

At 2:07 P.M. an adjournment was taken.

In the hallway, surrounded by a bank of television cameras and dozens of reporters, a smiling Landis said: "Almost five years ago an accident happened on the set of one of my films that killed three people, and none of this changes that. It's a terrible moment in my life, in our lives [turning to his wife, Deborah], in many people's lives. I'm repeating myself. I'm very grateful to the jury, and I really appreciate their patience in what has been . . . a trial, and I'm very grateful to my attorneys, and obviously I'm relieved. But it's been five years; it's very difficult right now to sort of have an instantaneous response."

D'Agostino had a dazed look on her face when she walked out of the courtroom a few minutes later: "I believe that the evidence was overwhelming in proving that the defendants acted recklessly. Fortunately, we live in a country where twelve jurors make that decision. I respect their right to come to a contrary opinion. I don't agree with it, but I do believe, if nothing else, this prosecution has served as a deterrent to any director who might possibly think or conceive of doing a dangerous scene and endangering human beings, especially little children. And if we've succeeded in saving even one life and deterring even one director from doing this in the future, then I think the prosecution has been very well founded."

"It's a wonderful time," Wingo said. "I wish we could get the jurors close for a minute. I want to kiss at least half of them and hug the rest."

George Folsey, Jr., who among all the defendants had expressed publicly feelings of loss for the victims, said, "We feel vindicated, but we'll never be the same after what happened on that set. I mean, three people got killed on our set, and we'll always think of them; we'll always feel sorry about that."

When the jurors and defendants were able to greet each other, they did so with joyous exuberance, both sides relieved that a long ordeal was over. Deborah Landis climbed up on the jury box railing to lean over and hug Rogers.

"They were a pretty smart jury, weren't they?" Folsey said to reporter Paul Dandridge.

Publicly, D'Agostino was composed, but as soon as she was in the privacy of her office, she plunged into despondency. Her close friend, Miriam Leavitt, whom D'Agostino refers to as her "sister," convinced D'Agostino that she must not immediately become reclusive. That evening the two women and their husbands went to dinner at the Bistro Gardens in Beverly Hills, an expensive, popular restaurant.

During the final weeks of the trial, D'Agostino had complained to Leavitt of being tired. At the restaurant, D'Agostiono was somber, sometimes just staring down at her plate. She was approached by an elderly woman in a wheelchair, who commiserated with the loss and expressed her upset over the verdict. That encounter sent D'Agostino further into upset. Both D'Agostino and her mother told me that the prosecutor cried for days after the verdict. Berta Purwin recalled, "She was sobbing her heart out. It was a nightmare. She was saying, 'What am I going to tell the parents of the children? Where is the justice?' "

There were two defense parties Friday night. One was at the home of John Landis, hastily put together by his wife, Deborah. The Los Angeles-based defense attorneys met at a restaurant, unaware of the Landis party and that, of the defense team, only Neal, Sanders, and Levine had been invited.

In the days following the verdicts, John Landis talked to a few selected newspaper reporters, expressing his "outrage" at this "terribly and completely dishonest prosecution." He told the *Los Angeles Times* that the jury's response to the defendants was "thrilling. It was like a Frank Capra movie. These people were remarkable, forthright, and intelligent, and that was very, very moving to me."

Of the prosecutor, he said: "Candidly, Mrs. D'Agostino is a grotesque, an aberration. And she is very unimportant. What is important is the Los Angeles district attorney's office spending this kind of money pursuing something that they know damn well is bogus."

Following the trial, D'Agostino was unwavering in her opinion that she neither could nor should have handled the case any differently than she had. I asked her if she viewed any aspect of the case as having gone wrong for her. "I don't think it went wrong for me personally," she answered. "If I live to be a thousand, I will not know the answer to that. The evidence we presented was overwhelming. [The jury] obviously chose to ignore it all." D'Agostino maintained that the overriding influence on the jurors was their veneration of Hollywood.

D'Agostino's pique at the jurors, demonstrated in her piercing looks at them during the reading of the verdicts on Friday, was verbalized directly to foreman Lois Rogers the following Monday morning. D'Agostino was a guest on the KABC radio talk show hosted by Michael Jackson, an affable and influential commentator whose daily program has a large audience.

D'Agostino, who had remained mostly isolated and despondent through the weekend, emerged again Monday morning in a publicly feisty mood.

"I don't think it's so much a personal loss as a loss for the justice system," D'Agostino told Jackson. "When five people who are responsible for killing three individuals are acquitted, I believe that's a loss for the justice system." She continued to accuse Landis: "What more could that man have done and not be held responsible?"

When Jackson opened the show to callers, one man said, "I do feel Mr. Landis and others got away with blatant murder," to which D'Agostino replied, "I totally agree with you." The prosecutor promoted her Hollywood thesis: "I think the high visibility here, and maybe subliminally, maybe the jury did not do it consciously. You've got to remember one thing: This [trial defense] was a very choreographed, orchestrated scenario. You saw the defendant on a daily basis with his wife, hand-holding, looking into each other's eyes, kissing each other. They ate in the cafeteria where many of the jurors did on a daily basis, stood in line with the peons, carried their own trays. They were just one of the guys. I'm not saying what they did was wrong. It was very carefully orchestrated to make the jury believe he was just a regular guy despite his wealth, and it was very clever. Because of high visibility, and because of the celebrities he caused to be in the courtroom, you have the end result."

Listening to the show while doing housework in her San Fernando Valley home was Lois Rogers. Disturbed by the prosecutor's characterizations, the jury foreman called KABC and was put on the air: "I just wanted to tell whoever was listening that as far as the jury was concerned, we were none of us awed by the fact that these were Hollywood people. In fact, I think the majority of us had never heard of John Landis before we ever went to trial. I think we all, to a man and woman, decided this case strictly on the facts and evidence that was given to us, and primarily with the judge's instructions in front of us, and that's the way we settled the case."

Other jurors later told me that they also resented the prosecutor's remarks about their susceptibility to fame. Wilbert Fisher laughed off the implication, telling me, "Seeing a celebrity doesn't amount to a hill of beans."

D'Agostino was anything but content to let the jury verdict stand and continued to challenge Rogers in a breathy tone of voice she sometimes employs, one which sounds arrogant and condescending. Pressed by D'Agostino about the Landises' public show of affection, Rogers said, "I, frankly, just saw a couple who were very, I mean, after all, they hadn't been married that long, who were great hand-holders. But it didn't affect me."

Although Rogers had not been impressed with D'Agostino's courtroom presentation, she was diplomatic in this debate: "We all believed that Mrs. D'Agostino did a marvelous job. We just didn't believe she had as much to work with as she needed."

D'Agostino, although she couched her critical remarks in appreciation for the jurors' diligence, was unforgiving: "I have to tell you, based on the mail I have received about the trial from all over the world, England, Australia, it appears as though everybody in the country, if not in the world, totally agrees that these people are guilty, except the twelve jurors. That's what I find so amazing."

The response, of course, ignored the fundamental precept that the American system of justice offers adversarial trial by jury, not popular polling. Rogers quickly made that point by asking, "Well, isn't that what the system is for?" D'Agostino was forced to admit that the jury foreman was correct. But the prosecutor still wasn't going to accept the result: "I feel almost like Pamela Ewing on *Dallas*. I'm going to wake up, and the whole thing has been a dream. I'm going to wake up, and the truth is going to come out."

Lois Rogers had not been the only *Twilight Zone* trial participant listening to the show. Among several defense attorneys was Eugene Trope, who was listening on his car radio as he drove to his office. Trope had been incensed by what he had heard and used the opportunity to turn the tables on the woman who, eleven months before, had questioned his abilities during the secret session with Judge Roger Boren.

Trope also called the radio station and was put on the air: "Mrs. D'Agostino was shocking to me. As a deputy district attorney of Los Angeles County, she's taken an oath to defend the Constitution. And at all times, during this Bicentennial year [of the U.S. Constitution], to attack the jury system is virtually what she's doing. The fact she lost is due to her incompetence. You can't prevent the truth from coming out."

According to the jurors, one of the elements missing from D'Agostino's case was evidence that Landis had a penchant for reckless behavior.

After the verdict I visited the archives of the American Film Institute in Los Angeles to continue research for this book. One of the items available for review was a tape recording of a lecture Landis had given to a group of students on January 27, 1982, six months before the *Twilight Zone* tragedy and even before Spielberg had approached Landis to work on the project.

The collection of buildings now belonging to the American Film Institute perches on a pretty piece of land just below Griffith Park, at the eastern end of the Hollywood Hills. Here, film and its creators are studied with academic respect.

I sat in AFI's Louis B. Mayer Library and listened to the tape. Landis's voice, of course, was now quite familiar. Unlike what had been seen and heard in the courtroom, though, it was filled with a more carefree exuberance, a presentation bubbling with energy and enthusiasm. The tape revealed a Landis remarkably different from the man seen and described in the courtroom. He was variously erudite and charmingly humorous. Sometimes he was testy in his answers. Throughout, though, there was passion for making movies.

And there were some comments unlike any that had been attributed to him by D'Agostino or her witnesses during the trial.

The American Film Institute speech appeared to provide compelling insight into Landis as a moviemaker. Later, when I talked to some *Twilight Zone* defense lawyers about the comments, I was told that the remarks also could have been greatly influential if they had been presented at the trial.

"I don't make films for *moi*," Landis said early in the talk to the students in the winter of 1982. "I don't make films for critics. I make films for audiences. Money is a direct corollary to how successful [I am].

"I'd much rather make a film like *The Blues Brothers* and be attacked viciously and have it make a lot of money than make a movie that is acclaimed as a masterpiece of work and have it not be seen. I'm not interested in making movies that aren't seen."

Landis was thirty-one years old as he spoke, and he recognized that he commanded the power of Hollywood independence: "My deal is structured in such a way that [studio executives] leave me alone. That's the only way I'll make a movie now."

He also displayed the pride of authorship.

"Of course I conceived the car crash scene," he said testily to one student, who had asked about the demolition of dozens of cars in *The Blues Brothers*.

"I determined very early on, everything is real. Up until then people hadn't really done it with real cars. It's probably virtuosity for its own sake and means nothing and didn't help the movie any. We used those ramps they started using in Australian thrill shows, and I've got cars entering frame three feet off the ground at fifty miles an hour."

He emphasized his point and punctuated his exposition by mouthing sound effects: car crash and explosion noises.

"It makes *no* sense whatsoever!"

He did give credit to stunt coordinator Gary McLarty for his role in the planning. "We figured it out," Landis said of the precision driving in the movie. (McLarty, later stunt coordinator for *Twilight Zone: The Movie*, had not been involved in the planning for the village-rescue scenes.)

Stunt drivers are one legitimate element of filming, but Landis also talked about achieving such realism with his actors.

"I was wrong, probably, but I decided we're not going to speed up the camera [so the vehicle, on film, appears to be going faster than it actually had]. We're going to go one hundred twenty-five miles an hour with the *principals* in the car!"

The principals were the Blues Brothers themselves, portrayed by comedy stars Dan Aykroyd and John Belushi. Aykroyd, whom Landis described affectionately as "a complete motorhead in terms of cars," was the driver.

"How fast is this?" Landis quoted Belushi's asking anxiously.

"We're going sixty, John," Landis, in storytelling fashion, indicated he had replied to the actor.

"It was probably unnecessary. It's obviously very real," Landis told the students.

I had anticipated that the Landis lecture would be technically and academically oriented, since AFI offers graduate-level study. With my experience of observing the trial for nine months, the comments that followed the discussion of the cars were startling, especially when put in the perspective that Landis had made them six months before he filmed *Twilight Zone.*

"The big coup was landing helicopters next to the Picasso [outdoor sculpture in downtown Chicago] because the FAA [Federal Aviation Administration] was shitting bricks," Landis told the students as he talked more about making *The Blues Brothers.*

"You can't do that!" Landis attributed to some unidentified FAA authority in his narrative manner.

"We're not! Don't look behind us!" he said in deep-toned voice of a 1940s radio drama.

(There had been a brief reference in some trial documents, not made public at the time, to Landis and the FAA. In a memorandum D'Agostino gave to defense attorneys as part of discovery, she recounted her interview with a potential trial witness named Ross Reynolds: "He was to do Blues Bros. Movie. Went to Chicago about a month ahead of time to discuss various things with the FAA etc. When Landis came out he started to tell him what the FAA said and Landis stated to the effect 'F--- the FAA, they're not going to tell me how to make my movie.' " Reynolds was not called by the prosecution to testify.)

Later in the talk with the students Landis related his feelings about spontaneity by others on his sets, and his method of relating to actors.

"Someone improvises in front of my camera, I'll [stop filming] and kill them. I'm real strict. Every single actor is different, so every actor is treated differently. I can be a lover or a father or a best friend or a sister or daughter or Hitler. I'll be whatever I have to be to get the performance."

For an example, he referred to Stephen Furst, who plays the role of Flounder, one of the *National Lampoon's Animal House* college fraternity ensemble.

"[Furst] is genuinely one of the most natural film actors I have ever seen and I was *mean* to him. I mean, I brutalized the hell out of him. He didn't know what was happening. I was constantly screaming at him in front of the camera—using the pressure of the camera. It was wonderful for the part."

In *Animal House*, objects, usually containers of beer, are periodically hurled into the scene from off-camera.

"Almost ninety percent of the actors didn't know I was going to throw a bottle at them. It's like goosing the action. I sometimes do that. It's not very legitimate or nice to trick actors."

Furst is pummeled with grocery items in a store scene. One sharp-cornered box strikes him hard on the chin.

"He didn't know that was gonna happen! He knew that Tim [Matheson] was gonna throw the Mazola bottle, but he didn't know there were four of us going to go *wham! wham! wham!* and he would never have caught them if he knew. It's ridiculous."

Landis's presentation was fast-paced and exuberant, displaying a remarkable breadth of film history and insight into its social impact.

With a figurative example, he emphasized the hypocrisy of modern movie standards that allow excessive violence on the screen but rail against sex. As he spoke, Landis, of course, could not have known how poignantly inappropriate his illustration would become: "The [movie industry] ratings board reflect[s] the morals of the times. So now, with Reagan as president, it's all right to shred children, but bare breasts are pretty disgusting. The morality of the times is deeply sick."

On this January day the *Twilight Zone* troubles were in the future, and Landis left no doubt with the film students that he found joy in his work.

"I'm so lucky. Because I am one of the few people who can make movies," he said, explaining that "like 'em or hate 'em, the bottom line is, I've had total control of everything I've done, everything except *Kentucky Fried Movie.*"

I talked with several defense attorneys and Boren about the director's comments. Boren said that the statements would likely have been allowed into evidence. The defense attorneys, Harland Braun among them, said that had D'Agostino skillfully used the transcript of the speech in her cross-examination of Landis, the director might have been found guilty. "I would have been scared shitless," Braun told me.

In the months following the trial, analysis of the case inevitably brought up the question of whether D'Agostino had, by her skills and manner, "lost" the case. She responded with vitriol to an article in *The American Lawyer* that concluded as much. The answer to the question of whether proof positive was mishandled by the prosecutor is elusive. As Tom Budds had recognized years before, when he first brought his case to the district attorney's office, there was no "smoking gun" evident. Any review of the case involves debatable judgments about levels of responsibility and culpability.

But like the strength of the evidence, the quality of the prosecution can be measured in degrees. Every defense attorney concluded that D'Agostino's presence in the case ultimately aided their cause. Leonard Levine told me, "I think another [prosecutor] could have come closer [to a guilty verdict]. She worked hard, and she was diligent and tenacious. I think she made a lot of tactital mistakes. Had it been tried by a more low-key, better-skilled prosecutor, I think they would have come closer perhaps." Arnold Klein, who was just satisfied that Paul Stewart was acquitted, said, "John Landis's vision blew up, and so did hers."

District attorney supervisors regretted their acquiescence to her adamant stance that she would try the case alone, without accepting co-counsel. Gil Garcetti told me he expected that the district attorney's office would never again allow a major case to be prosecuted by one lawyer.

After the trial I asked D'Agostino if she allowed room for the notion that she had become overly entangled in the emotion of this case. Quickly, she replied: "No. To the degree that people think I became overly emotional, I categorize that as sour grapes. I really do, because what you're dealing with here is two tiny babies. And every time I thought of those babies and Vic Morrow, twenty-four feet under that gigantic helicopter, I saw red. I just saw red. I'm sorry. And when I actually physically saw that helicopter at Indian Dunes, no amount of viewing that movie, no amount of realizing, 'Oh, my God, only twenty-four feet' could possibly prepare me for what I felt when I saw that helicopter. I was scared. I was scared."

Translating that strong emotion into a courtroom style seemed to have been D'Agostino's most significant weakness. George Folsey, for one, recognized that the public perception of him was negative, and he hadn't been sure that a trial could change that. He told me, "You read about yourself in newspaper and magazine articles about what a terrible, callous person you are. She did the one thing I never thought she'd be able to do, nor would I think she would attempt it. She made us appear sympathetic. I don't think she realized what she was doing by going so far and being so vitriolic. That's an odd thing, to make us look like halfway-nice guys."

Throughout the trial, D'Agostino's ambition was questioned. The two investigators who worked with her, Budds and Loeb, observed that well before the conclusion of the trial, D'Agostino expressed confidence that the jury would return guilty verdicts and she would be propelled to greater accomplishment, including writing a book. In December 1986, well before she had even completed presenting her side of the case to the jury, she told *Los Angeles Herald Examiner* reporter Andy Furillo and me that she had been offered a book contract.

She also eyed politics, telling Loeb that she planned to run for district attorney. With her friend, Miriam Leavitt, she joked about running for governor of California.

There is precedent of deputy district attorneys in Los Angeles going on to greater fame and fortune because of the publicity of one big case. The most successful to do so is Vincent Bugliosi, who prosecuted cult leader Charles Manson, wrote a top-selling book about it, and has continued with an accomplished writing career.

Turning the *Twilight Zone* case into a triumph for herself seemed an unlikely prospect for D'Agostino. One top-ranking district attorney official told me afterward that her career in the office was at a standstill. Indeed, her request for appointment to the special prosecutions unit was denied. In the months following the *Twilight Zone* case, she prosecuted routine cases, including the robbery of a taxi driver.

That D'Agostino would persevere, however, was not doubted by those who know her. She sought a book publisher, which she had pursued actively after the verdicts by submitting a formal proposal to publishers. That effort was later abandoned.

On March 1, 1988, she took a bold step: She announced that she would oppose Ira Reiner in the primary for Los Angeles County district attorney. At a press conference she told reporters that she blamed Reiner for the bloodshed and violence caused by gangs and drugs in the county.

She had no campaign war chest but one of her first contributors gladly wrote out a check: Harland Braun gave D'Agostino $250 and noted on the document that the money was "for the good fight." (In June 1988 she lost by a wide margin.)

D'Agostino had other fights as well. She had been named in a multimillion-dollar federal lawsuit filed by Kesselman, who accused her, Garcetti, Hecht, and Reiner of a conspiracy to publicly impugn his integrity in an effort to save the *Twilight Zone* case.

Kesselman's fortunes in the district attorney's office had plummeted as the case went on, until he was finally an isolated and dejected man. Fellow prosecutor Harvey Giss told me: "It was the demise of a fine trial lawyer for the purposes of this office." In October of 1987, Kesselman was arrested by Los Angeles police after being caught in his car with a prostitute who was performing a sex act. The lawyer later told me that he could only relate the incident to the unusual stress he had undergone. Not surprisingly, he was fired from the district attorney's office.

Kesselman seemed headed for some vindication, however. In the summer after the trial, Donna Schuman's husband, Harold, made a formal complaint against Kesselman to the district attorney's office. Citing a conflict of interest, authorities there turned the matter over to the California attorney general's office. The move by the district attorney's office to pass on Schuman's letter was seen as a backhand attempt to discredit Kesselman who, by this time, had put the county on notice that he was preparing a lawsuit. The attorney general's office, however, was forced to begin a criminal investigation to determine whether Kesselman had committed perjury.

The state investigation did not go as the district attorney supervisors had planned. I was told by high-ranking lawyers in the attorney general's office that the probe had concluded that Kesselman apparently had been honest. In addition, the evidence made the investigators suspicious of the truthfulness of D'Agostino and Donna Schuman.

By the spring of 1988, though, investigators were reaching a conclusion that there was not sufficient evidence to file criminal charges against anyone involved in the dispute over the *Twilight Zone* testimony.

In the meantime, Landis and Folsey had gone back to moviemaking, working on a film with comedian Eddie Murphy. Among those friends of Landis's shown in the background of one scene were Ralph Bellamy and lawyers Neal, Sanders, and Levine. Allingham had left the Landis production team after the trial, to produce a movie based on the book about alien visitors to earth, *Communion.* Paul Stewart worked on special effects for the television show *Moonlighting,* and Dorcey Wingo performed commercial flying, although no movie work, for Western Helicopters.

Tom Budds returned to full-time investigating as supervisor of an organized crime squad in the sheriff's department. Boren was appointed an associate justice of the California Court of Appeal.

There were two official actions involving the moviemakers after the verdicts. The state Occupational Safety and Health Administration dismissed all but $1,350 of the more than $62,000 in fines in 1982. The Directors' Guild of America voted to reprimand Landis, Allingham, and Elie Cohn for conduct "unprofessional, inconsistent with their responsibilities, and extremely prejudicial to the welfare of the DGA." Joel Behr told the board that the reprimand, which involved no disciplinary action, was "unfair."

John Landis, with emotion, had told the jurors during his trial testimony that he had not filmed a movie with a helicopter since July 23, 1982. One had to wonder what lessons others in Hollywood had taken from the *Twilight Zone* matter.

Hollywood as an industry had not been on trial, but the *Twilight Zone* case was very much of Hollywood, particularly its institutional ambitions and ethics. Many film professionals undoubtedly reacted to the results of the moviemaking at Indian Dunes with a cautious review of their own manner of work. But it is beyond cliché to state that film production of this era is too often the intellectually unchallenging execution of money-making formula. And spectacular action is a central element of the concoction.

An important question was the effect the deaths and the trial had on Hollywood sensibilities. After the trial, there had been various pronouncements throughout the movie industry that since the *Twilight Zone* crash, safety had been improved. In the fall of 1987, five months after the verdicts, an investigative report by Michael Szymanski of the *Daily News*, a Los Angeles newspaper, concluded that accidents and injuries had actually increased. Szymanski wrote: "In the quest for realistic movie and television thrills, 10 people have been killed and 4,998 injured in California productions since 1982, and complaints of unsafe conditions have more than doubled."

The reporter went on to say that government monitoring of movie industry safety had dimished greatly with the disbanding, earlier in the year, of the California Occupational Safety and Health Administration, whose work was assumed by a federal agency that had not investigated a single movie-related incident.

A companion news article by another *Daily News* reporter suggested that elected state officials, many of whom are the recipients of large campaign donations from producers and studio executives, are reluctant to tighten industry standards for fear that more production will be moved out of state, threatening a $6-billion-a-year industry.

One of the more disturbing concessions in the aftermath of the *Twilight Zone* crash was the relaxation of state child labor laws, which were changed to allow younger children to work later hours, including permission for preschool-age children to work after midnight.

An article in the *Los Angeles Times* of November 2, 1987, reproduced here in its entirety, left only a feeling of disbelief in me and seemed a chilling epitaph to the entire episode, an indication that Hollywood continued business as usual:

Sylvester Stallone had a close call on the set in Israel of "Rambo III" on Sunday when a helicopter buzzed him during a stunt and missed his head by a few inches. "I suppose if it had gotten any lower I could have saved the cost of a haircut," production spokesman Tom Gray quoted the actor as saying. Stallone ducked just in time and escaped unharmed, he added. Gray said the scene called for a French-made Puma helicopter to buzz Stallone as explosives went off and fired around the actor. The helicopter was supposed to fly about six feet above Stallone's head, but Gray said the pilot misjudged the distance because dust and flames shrouded the set. The scene was filmed in Elat, a Red Sea resort 190 miles south of Jerusalem.

INDEX